The Contemporary New Communities Movement in the United States

The
Contemporary
New Communities Movement
in the
United States

Edited by **Gideon Golany** *and* **Daniel Walden**

University of Illinois Press

Urbana   Chicago   London

Library of Congress Cataloging in Publication Data

Golany, Gideon.
    The contemporary new communities movement in the
United States.

    Includes bibliographies.
    1. New towns—United States. 2. Cities and
towns—Planning—United States. I. Walden, Daniel,
Aug. 1, 1922–   joint author. II. Title.
HT167.G65   301.36′3′0973   74-13861
ISBN 0-252-00434-5

For Lewis Mumford, who,
through his vision and work,
has illuminated
the past and the future

Contents

Contributors
and Editors

Benjamin H. Cunningham is presently the senior vice-president/planning and design for New Community Enterprises, the developers of Park Forest South. He was previously vice-president and director of design of Jonathan Development Corporation, Chaska, Minnesota. He directed the first feasibility study for Jonathan, and he participated in the community's planning and management for approximately seven years. This work led to honor awards in design excellence for Jonathan in the fourth and fifth biennial HUD awards program. In addition, he has served as a general consultant to the Harbison Title VII project in South Carolina and the Shenandoah Title VII project in Atlanta.

Edward Echeverria is president of Planners Incorporated in Washington, D.C.; his firm combines the services of planners, architects,

engineers, and social scientists. As chief advisor with the Ford Foundation from 1957 to 1960, he directed an interdisciplinary team of consultants in the preparation of a projected twenty-five-year master plan for Delhi, India. He has also directed the planning of the new communities of Germantown, Maryland, and Maumelle, Arkansas, and in 1973 he consulted on a comparative social and economic analysis for alternative types and sizes of new communities as part of a feasibility study for the New England Regional Commission.

Gideon Golany is professor of urban and regional planning and chairman of the graduate program in the department of architecture at Pennsylvania State University. He has taught at Virginia Polytechnic Institute and State University, at Cornell University, and at the Technion–Israel Institute of Technology. He has also been a consultant in new towns planning, in urban and regional planning, and in the planning of traditional villages. His most recent publication is entitled *New Towns Planning and Development: A World-Wide Bibliography.*

Royce Hanson, former director of the New Communities Study Center of Virginia Polytechnic Institute and State University at Reston, Virginia, is currently chairman of the Montgomery County Planning Board of the Maryland National Capital Park and Planning Commission. From 1966 to 1971 he was president of the Washington Center for Metropolitan Studies; he was also professor of government and public administration at American University, Washington, D.C., until December 1972. His two most recent publications are *New Towns: Laboratories for Democracy* and *Managing Services for New Communities.*

Robert W. Marans is senior study director at the Institute for Social Research of the University of Michigan at Ann Arbor. He has been active as a regional planner in the Detroit area; as a consultant architect-planner in Tel-Aviv, Israel; and as a consultant planner in Providence, Rhode Island. In addition, he has taught at several schools, including the Technion–Israel Institute of Technology, Michigan State University, Florida State University, and the University of Michigan at Ann Arbor, where he is currently associate professor of architecture. He is author of several publications and co-author of *Planned Residential Environments.*

Hugh Mields, Jr., is a Washington-based consultant specializing in community development and intergovernmental relations. He has served as the associate director of the United States Conference of Mayors, assistant administrator for congressional liaison with the Housing and Home Finance Agency, and assistant director for federal activities of the American Municipal Association (now the National League of Cities). *Federally Assisted New Communities: New Dimensions in Urban Development* is his latest book.

John W. Reps is professor and former chairman of the department of urban planning and development at Cornell University. He was a member of the board of directors of the American Society of Planning Officials from 1966 to 1969, and an observer at the United Nations Conference on the Planning of New Towns, held in the Soviet Union in 1964. Among his published works are *Tidewater Towns: City Planning in Colonial Virginia and Maryland; Town Planning in Frontier America;* and *The Making of Urban America: A History of City Planning in the United States.*

Charles E. Stuart is currently president of the Interstate Land Development Company, Inc., in St. Charles, Maryland. He also serves as vice-president of United States operations for the Interstate General Corporation of San Juan, Puerto Rico, and St. Charles, Maryland. In November 1968 he was employed by President Nixon, first as part of the "transition" staff and then as part of the White House staff until 1971.

Jack A. Underhill is senior program officer in the Office of New Communities Development of the Department of Housing and Urban Development (HUD). He began his government career in 1959 in the Office of Emergency Planning in the Executive Office of the President. In 1964 he was transferred to the Open Space Division of HUD, and in 1968 he joined HUD's new communities offices. Presently he is working on policy development and research for the New Communities Administration.

Daniel Walden is associate professor of American Studies in the department of English at Pennsylvania State University. He has taught at Michigan State University, Queen's College, and the New School for Social Research. Some of his recent publications are *American Reform: The Ambiguous Legacy* (editor); *Readings in American Nationalism* (co-editor); *On Being Black: Black Writers from Douglass to the Present* (editor); and *W. E. B. Du Bois: The Crisis Years* (editor); and *On Being Jewish: American Jewish Writers from Cahan to Bellow* (editor).

Robert B. Zehner is senior research associate at the Center for Urban and Regional Studies of the University of North Carolina. He has taught at the University of Michigan, where he served as research fellow with the Detroit area study and as assistant study director at the Survey Research Center. He is also a co-author of *Planned Residential Environments* and *Across the City Line: A White Community in Transition*.

Preface

This volume was motivated by a series of lectures on new communities given during the spring of 1972 at Pennsylvania State University. The new communities seminar, under the instruction of Gideon Golany, is part of the new towns curriculum within the graduate program of the department of architecture. Initiated in 1970, this curriculum includes six sequence courses and is open to interested graduate students from various programs within the university. Although teaching is the focus of this curriculum, research, publication, and bibliographical work on new towns is continually in progress.

The contributors, all leading experts in the field of new community planning and development in the United States, represent a full range of involvement in the new towns effort. The volume has been designed as a unit which encompasses the offerings of university research faculty; new town planners, developers, and consultants; and government officials. John Reps's essay presents a review, with analysis and conclusions, of the American tradition of public initiative in new communities, and thus provides historical background for this study. Hugh Mields describes the development of legislation for new communities at the federal level, while Jack Underhill treats the process of new community planning and development, and the closely related issue of national growth policy. Royce Hanson offers ideas about various forms of governance and the civic experience, and he urges experimentation in new community governance so that other communities may also benefit from large-scale citizen participation; Robert Marans and Robert Zehner discuss the social issues of new communities. The three selected planner-developers, Benjamin Cunningham, Charles Stuart, and Edward Echeverria, retell the beginning days of the actual development of their new community projects. Each case is unique yet representative, and together they offer the reader opportunities for comparison. Gideon Golany's opening essay introduces an analysis of this century's new communities phenomenon. He reviews the potential for new urban patterns, as well as the role of the public contribution in their development.

Alice Gannon, from the department of English, was the first copyeditor of this volume. She has been involved with nearly all phases of this project. Sharman Stanic Mullen, also from the department of English, was the copyeditor in subsequent preparation.

The editors are most grateful to all who have helped in preparing this volume, and especially to Margaret Shultz, Cindy MacNab, Jeanne King, Louise Jones, Judy Stine, Elaine Foresman, Michael Rudden, Thomas Berry, and William Steigerwald. Special appreciation is extended to the assistant dean for research, E. Lynn Miller, and to Raniero Corbelletti, head of the department of architecture, for their support and encouragement of this project.

In the belief that this collection fills a gap in the contemporary literature of new communities in the United States, Pennsylvania State University is pleased to introduce this American experience to readers both in the United States and abroad.

The Editors

Pennsylvania State University
University Park, Pennsylvania

New Communities in the United States: Assessment and Potential

Gideon Golany

NEW COMMUNITIES: INITIATIVE OR MOVEMENT?

If we define a movement as a series of organized and synchronized activities working harmoniously toward definite objectives, then the twentieth-century new communities phenomenon in the United States does not yet merit the label of a movement. A movement is a phenomenon which has its own uniquely identifiable character within the mainstream of events, exerts a continuous and powerful influence, generates its own required energy, and leaves a marked imprint upon the times. Also characteristic of a movement are quantity, in this case, the development of a significant number of new communities; magnitude, combining a variety and quality of new communities; and duration, or a historical dimension. Individual twentieth-century new communities in the United States have developed sporadically and without reference to a common goal. Furthermore, the brief period since the late sixties is not sufficient to provide the historical dimension necessary for verification of an actual movement.

A review of the settlements since the Country Club planned communities in Kansas (1906) shows that this phenomenon of sporadic single development has not had strong continuity, a powerfully radiated influence beyond its own locale, or the clearly defined goal characteristic of a movement. However, since the late sixties, recognition of the need for a common goal has become stronger. These recent years have been more promising because of the encouraging public financial and legislative contribution, which has been motivated by the strong increase in the popular demand for a better physical environment. These factors are the seeds for the beginning of an actual movement toward new community development. There are signs of a burgeoning movement. The United States is now at the crossroads, faced with a choice between supporting the continuity of this new goal-directed movement, or electing to continue the individual large-scale developments which until now have lacked a common goal. Only time will tell if this burgeoning new community development will emerge as an identifiable, goal-oriented, influential phenomenon meriting the designation of a movement.

Throughout this century in the United States, three stages of development related to new communities may be generally identified.[1] The first, up until the forties, was marked by sporadic, noncontinuous development beginning with the Country Club planned communities in Kansas and Sunnyside Gardens in New York City, and continuing through Radburn, New Jersey; Chatham Village, Pittsburgh; Phipps Garden Apartments, New York City; the Valley Stream Project outside New York City; the Greenbelt settlements of Greenbelt, Maryland; Greenhills, Ohio; Greenbrook, New Jersey; Greendale, Wisconsin; and, finally, Baldwin Hills Village in Los Angeles.[2] The second stage, during the fifties and sixties, was a period of large-scale development concentrated mainly close to the urban centers. At this time the main goals were the provision of housing and a profitable financial return. Most existing large-scale developments of the twentieth century which have contributed to the design theory (Radburn and Chatham Village) were no larger than the neighborhood unit.[3] The first application of the new town idea was in Greenbelt, Maryland. Even though the Greenbelt settlements were implemented by the federal government and provided job opportunities, both the first and second stages of the development of these new communities lacked national policy which would have func-

tioned both as a force and as a goal. In both stages the support of public contribution (except in the case of the Greenbelt settlements) was also lacking. The third and present period began in the late sixties and has been marked by a reasonable desire to define a goal in the form of national and state policy supported by legislative power, as well as a recognition of the need for public contribution to implement such a policy. In this period there has been effective public financial contribution in support of specific types of new community development. Nevertheless, private enterprise will still continue with its previous and primary goal, the provision of profitable housing. The vast majority of the housing developments in the United States, since the very early ones in the twenties, have not fully implemented the original concept of Ebenezer Howard, although some of them were initially designed according to this concept.

Even though a new communities movement in the United States has been needed since the early twentieth century, no such movement actually began because of the lack of a motivating new communities ideology. Normally, new urban patterns, in the form of suburbs, have been generated by dynamic forces active within the central cities. On the other hand, except in rare cases, regional planning and development combining country and urban areas has not been implemented on a very large scale.[4] Exceptions are those projects related to water resources, such as the Tennessee Valley, Columbia River Basin, and other flood control projects, which were developed by the public sector to cope with the urgency of flood problems. Reexamination of the large-scale regional development concept would not only suggest rational redistribution of population and a more effective use of national natural resources, but it would also, in turn, encourage a more coherent distribution of transportation intensity. Integrated regional planning could promote development of the country's cultural and historical heritage, and thereby promote local pride and identity. The significance of regionalism is its carefully considered goal of reestablishing some equilibrium within an area.[5] Integral relationships based on a hierarchical settlement pattern are one way of obtaining such equilibrium, although it is difficult to achieve this in an economically dynamic country such as the United States.[6] The lack of such ideologically motivated large-scale regional planning and development is a product of America's unique socioeconomic and political system, one which has its own strong historical roots. Isolation, the identity of local government, and the strong alienation of individuals and groups from the regional, state, and especially the federal governmental power structure have always led in the direction of self-reliance, as opposed to mutual cooperation between the government and the people. This attitude is most identifiable and unique in the United States, and it weakens the effectiveness of the central government.

The second reason for insufficient consideration of the role of regional planning in the United States has been the existence of vast natural resources within the country. Wealth and poverty influence attitudes toward the necessity for planning: the smaller the country and the fewer the natural resources, the higher the concern for planning and development. Good examples of small countries with limited natural resources are England, Israel, and The Netherlands. English new towns were created to solve urban and regional problems, Dutch new towns were established to introduce a regional pattern, and the Israeli regional development towns were designed to challenge social issues.[7] As a consequence of the vast natural resources in the United States, however, an attitude of rugged individualism has resulted in a situation in which there is no common agreement regarding the development of resources for the benefit of all. The lack of strong regional planning in this coun-

try has led to the lack of a new communities philosophy and a new communities movement. The types of towns acceptable to Americans since the sixties have been those directly related to the existing urban centers, rather than to the less developed regional areas; developments such as satellite towns and dormitory subdivisions have been wholeheartedly welcomed. There is no assurance that such new settlement types will continue to dominate the scene. There are a few signs, such as recent new communities legislation, which anticipate that other types of settlements related more to regional development will be widely accepted, since it is being realized that some urban problems may be solved through regional planning. Therefore, long-range development policy should be formulated jointly on the regional and urban scales. Only wide acceptance of this correlative regional aspect will accelerate the new communities movement. It is the responsibility of the regional, state, or federal bodies to bring about this shifting in the emphasis from urban-related new communities to region-related new communities.

Clearly, then, the significance and effectiveness of most settlement projects in the United States have been on a small, local scale. Their development has not been integrally related to their hinterlands. Exceptions may be found when a unique quality of planning has been introduced, as in Radburn, New Jersey; the four Greenbelt towns; and Columbia, Maryland. All brought their influence to bear far beyond their immediate environs. The strength and the weakness of many of those sporadic large-scale developments exist because their sponsorship and implementation have been carried on solely by private enterprise; only the Greenbelt settlements were an exception. Private developers have been justifiably concerned with financial return, and in most cases have lacked national vision (which is, of course, not their responsibility). Nevertheless, the contribution of the private developer to such national needs as housing and job opportunities has been beyond expectation, and has surpassed similar contributions in many other nations. The contribution of the public sector could have tied these various endeavors together and thereby improved their effectiveness on the state and national levels. But development of new settlements has lacked not only adequate public contribution in this country, but also the strong backing by professionals in planning and architecture similar, for example, to that given Ebenezer Howard's concept by the Town and Country Planning Association of England. Lack of a new communities ideology has been a basic reason for the absence of a new communities movement in this country, and it is also one reason for the absence of an urban growth policy. There is an urgent need for active involvement in the formulation of a policy for future urban growth, in large-scale regional planning and development, and in the introduction of a rationale for the various potential types of new urban patterns. This has recently become a national issue of primary concern because of the current acceleration of urbanization.[8]

In some developing countries, urbanization has contributed to both the rise of the middle class and the organization of workers;[9] it has also resulted in economic improvement and cultural enhancement in such highly developed countries as the United States. On the other hand, this recent acceleration of urbanization has created an imbalance between the nation's needs and its natural resources, disproportionate development in various regions of the country, threats to the physical environment, increased urban congestion, and intensified rural poverty. The increased intensity of urbanization has also tended to promote social tensions and negative social climates; for example, statistics show a continuing increase in the crime rate over the past decades. Because of the ever-growing disproportion between urban complexity on the one hand, and lack of management capability on the other, urbanization has encouraged such negative consequences as social, economic, and physical environmental deterioration.[10]

In spite of the fact that the trend of urbanization in the United States will probably continue, accelerate, and have a far-reaching impact on all aspects of environmental conditions, the issue of changes in the social climate is the most crucial.[11] Among the many negative consequences of urbanization, the social quality of life is one that is not instantly reparable. The predictable impact of future urban growth before the end of this century will be enormous, especially in terms of the needs for infrastructure and resources.[12] Improvement in social quality should become our main concern. The historical lesson of the metropolis is that its agglomeration neither promotes nor improves a social climate.

Too little recognition has been given to the advantages which still exist outside the megalopolis. If we reexamine our urban existence, a variety of issues must be questioned and reevaluated. If the megalopolis will not be avoidable in the future,[13] will American people still prefer urban agglomeration in spite of an expected increase in social alienation? On the other hand, if we succeed in restraining urban development, what promising alternatives can absorb urban growth? Could these alternatives continue to retain the advantages of the megalopolis? Does restraint of megalopolis growth require strong centralized controls on migration, land use, and economic activities? Has the totalitarian system of centralized control succeeded in avoiding this megalopolis development? Whatever the issue, our major concern should be with quality, rather than growth. Our quality of life will determine our urban management capability. Of the many possibilities, there are three significant alternatives which could improve this quality and help to reestablish a man-environment equilibrium: stabilization of population,[14] population redistribution,[15] or some combination of the two.[16] Cultural and religious determinants have made limitation of population growth difficult; furthermore, it requires generations to accomplish. Population redistribution is more acceptable to individuals and groups and, therefore, more feasible than control of population growth.

POLICY FOR POPULATION REDISTRIBUTION

Population redistribution is defined as the establishment of a fairly uniform dispersion of settlements within a country in order to reduce polarization of population aggregates. This does not mean that the pattern should be even. The fact that an even distribution pattern has rarely been accomplished throughout the history of human settlements shows that such a pattern is virtually unachievable.

Population redistribution involves reattracting a population to areas outside existing metropolitan regions. Redistribution can create an equilibrium among the aggregates of the population within the overall national or state land use; it can also ease an overconcentration of urban human settlements which increases congestion, and minimize the gap between the extreme size ranges of urban settlements. Redistribution is needed for solving both the causes and the consequences of overconcentrated urbanization.

If the phenomenon of the present urban situation continues, the nation will face more social problems than ever before. Furthermore, the situation will become even more crucial as long as there is no long-range national policy.[17] Although every country is unique, one lesson the United States may learn from countries which have already experienced population redistribution is that such a policy should be an integral part of national planning and development. To be effectively implemented, any population redistribution policy must provide a wide variety of alternatives to the existing urban pattern, so that many new socioeconomic opportunities would provide an incentive for a desired migration pattern.[18] In discussing the related problem of future urban growth, we tend to forget that the primary issue is not necessarily the growth itself as much as the pattern of distribution. This has been and will continue to be a major determinant in the formulation and the discussion of any American urban growth policy.

Whether we admit it or not, the question of a policy either for redistribution or for "no distribution" is a key issue (see figure, "Alternatives for Future Urban Patterns"). If many urban problems are by-products of overconcentration in urban areas, then obviously the distribution of this concentration would ease those problems. Although the economic price of either policy is difficult to estimate, the social consequences of each are incalculable. On the other hand, solutions to social problems become unconventional when they ignore the cost involved, and, unfortunately, they are often rejected.

If we accept "no distribution" as a policy, however, the federal and state governments of the United States will be implementing a policy of overconcentration in urban centers and will continue to neglect the possibility of redistributing population. When we examine the consequences of many financial practices of public investment in the past, we see that these practices have encouraged migration to large urban centers. Examples of such incentives are the benefits of welfare, housing, transportation, and lower taxation in some areas of the cities. The significance of the issue of population redistribution is that its acceptance could have far-reaching effects, not only of relieving physical congestion, but, more important, of alleviating the serious social tension of the cities, creating a new social climate, providing different opportunities for racial integration, and, above all, establishing many new job opportunities.

ALTERNATIVES FOR FUTURE URBAN PATTERNS
AS RELATED TO THE ISSUE OF POPULATION REDISTRIBUTION

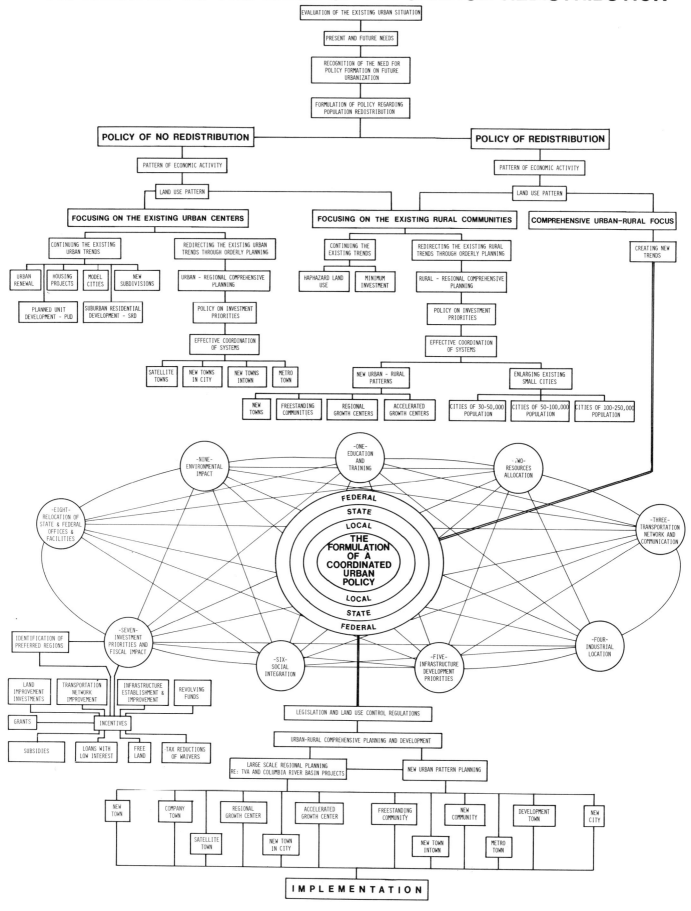

In considering a population redistribution policy and its possible implementation, the contributing forces and resources, which should be directed by some prospective public agency, must also be considered. These include present patterns of migration, existing transportation networks, and availability of job opportunities. Acceptable means must be found to effectively change current patterns of urban migration within the free market economy so that significant social and economic results may be achieved. However, planners recognize that in a democratic society it is more feasible to direct and influence the migration trends than to control them totally. Even though migration is clearly the result of countless other forces, most of those forces are conditioned by various governmental policies and programs which are executed by federal, state, and local governmental bodies. In the long run, this is felt by private enterprise and influences decisions on business location.[19] Population redistribution might be more achievable in a mobile society than in a traditional nonmobile society, if a policy of economic incentives is combined with it. This is obvious since, of the many forces operating, the economic factor is the strongest catalyst for migratory movement.

Second, because of their distribution and their impact on development, sophisticated federal and state transportation networks in a less developed and less urbanized region could increase that region's potential to absorb population and new economic activities. The development of such a network would be a major supporting factor for population redistribution, especially if it could also be related to export and import.

Third, the scale, variety, frequency, and availability of job opportunities form an issue directly related to both the policies and the potentials for attracting industry and related infrastructure, and to the distribution pattern of the national, state, and regional natural resources. After all, the population distribution pattern has historically been a by-product of resource distribution, especially in the case of agricultural land, water, and minerals.

As has been mentioned, among the socioeconomic and political forces, the economic factor has the greatest effect on migratory patterns. A major goal of a national policy for population redistribution in a democratic country should be creation of those economic forces which would steadily direct migration patterns toward the desired redistribution. Economic planning combined with orderly spatial planning could affect most migration patterns—urban to rural, interurban, rural to urban, central city to suburb, suburb to outskirts, and interregional. But any national policy for redistribution would not be effective without mechanism for implementation; moreover, results of such a policy would not be immediately evident. Its success would depend much more upon its comprehensiveness and its coordination with related development policies.

The critical dilemma of this planning approach is that, even though the negative aspects of urban growth in the last three decades may be recognized, some planners often continue to think, evaluate, and introduce solutions in the traditional manner, without comprehending that drastic changes are needed in methods of problem-solving. Neither professionals nor political leaders can continue in this manner unless they want to be left outside the mainstream of events. Long-range solutions for overurbanized regions are not necessarily found within them or on their immediate fringes. One solution might well be large-scale regional development.

A forthcoming bill entitled "The Balanced National Growth and Development Act of 1973," which will be introduced in the Ninety-third Congress, seeks, among other things, a redistribution of population through appropriate policies based on the findings and recommendations of organizations established by this act and the requirements of balanced economic growth.[20] This bill also calls for the implementation of a national growth and development policy through a national system of regional development commissions, and through the development of planned communities of optimum size.

The existence or adoption of a policy is an issue in the United States today, but more important is the orientation and content of such a policy. Existing governmental programs are already affecting urbanization and migration trends in the country. An overall national urban growth policy would serve to coordinate these programs and could create the comprehensive linkages necessary to make results consistent with a directed national urban goal. Needed are long-range objectives to guide future urban growth as an integral part of national urbanization policy. One such objective could be the creation of new urban patterns.

NEW URBAN PATTERNS

Any future urban growth policy should create a condition which would favor the acceptance of new urban patterns, especially if a policy for population redistribution is adopted. In terms of location, this policy should focus on three major areas: existing large urban centers, new urban alternatives, and existing medium and small towns.

Solutions should examine existing urban patterns and consider introducing innovative and unconventional patterns, rather than directing energy only into new urban centers.[21] Many people probably will continue to prefer the existing large urban centers to the new ones; thus new urban patterns should also be promoted within existing urban centers (such as new towns intown and *new towns in-city*[22]) or close to those centers (such as satellite towns and metro towns). This focus on the existing urban centers would be very im-

portant if a policy for "no distribution" of population is accepted, and if a policy for population redistribution is accepted or encouraged.[23]

A pattern of new urban alternatives should be introduced and implemented in sparsely populated yet developable regions. They should be able to absorb large-scale regional development and act as integral parts of new urban patterns. Such new urban alternatives should include new towns, new communities, company towns, freestanding communities, regional growth centers, accelerated growth centers, and development towns. The vast scale of this country, the existence of many undeveloped regions, and the existing sophisticated transportation networks combine to make such development highly feasible. The present low land value of such regions is important, too; semi-arid regions, for example, could profitably be developed along with water transference or water desalinization facilities.

Attempts to develop future urban patterns should also focus on regions in which medium and small towns could be expanded, especially if a policy for population redistribution is adopted.[24] With their many physical and political limitations, cities with small populations would then have the advantage of an alternative established community to accommodate their economic expansion and population growth.[25] To make the enlargement of those settlements more effective, it would be necessary to combine them with large-scale regional planning so that the cities could maintain their functional centrality within the region.

Orientation for the planning and development of these future urban patterns must focus upon several fundamental elements, regardless of the acceptance or nonacceptance of a policy for population redistribution. Such planning orientation should incorporate innovation, comprehensiveness, and variation.

The planning and development of future urban patterns should provide a significant opportunity for innovative systems in all aspects of development—building and construction technology, communication and transportation, social arrangements, economic settings, governance and power structure, public health services, and the delivery of public utilities. Moreover, new urban patterns could be viewed as multi-purpose laboratories, and their findings could be used to improve the existing urban patterns.

Any specific type or section within the new urban patterns should be planned and developed as an integral part of a comprehensive regional plan which, in turn, should be related to an overall national policy. All levels of comprehensiveness should tie the new settlement with its hinterlands economically and strengthen its role within its region.

These new urban patterns should introduce a wide variety of settlements, differing not only in location and type, but also in size, function, and cultural and economic opportunities. The cultural and geographical heterogeneity of the United States requires a variety of settlement types. Variation would certainly increase the heterogeneity of the human resources attracted to those new urban patterns.

Various kinds of settlements could be considered for existing urban patterns or for new patterns. They include such distinctive types as company towns, accelerated growth centers, regional growth centers, freestanding communities, new communities, new towns, development towns, new cities, satellite towns, metro towns, new towns intown, and *new towns incity*. Of these twelve types, the first eight have relatively sound and independent economic bases, and they provide a variety of land uses, housing, and job opportunities. The last four are integrally related to major urban centers and have less independence and variety.

The company town is a pioneering economically motivated settlement in an underdeveloped and often unexplored region, cre-

ated to utilize natural resources. It can act as an agent for required growth if, after its establishment, its economic base is successfully diversified.

The accelerated growth center, an alternative to urban sprawl, is a self-sustaining urban setting which stimulates economic growth and radiates this growth throughout and beyond its own peripheries. It is intended to combine public initiative with private enterprise.[26]

The regional growth center may be defined as a concentration of newly developed facilities and amenities on a relatively large scale, in order to revivify an economically depressed and sparsely populated region of rural or small urban communities. It provides job opportunities for its surroundings and, along with its region, forms a self-sustaining and self-contained unit.

The freestanding community is defined as a "rural-urban" community located in a non-urban region with some basic economic identity, providing services both for itself and for its own region. Its scale is small enough so that it may be readily implemented.

"The "new community," a term coined in the United States due to its unique conditions, describes a new type of settlement meant to be similiar to, but not the same as, the new town.[27] New communities are defined as pre-planned large-scale developments built as expansions of existing urban centers, or in newly developed areas on privately owned land. They are usually initiated and constructed by a private developer or corporation, occasionally with public support. New communities are planned to provide a range of housing, basic social and cultural services, public utilities, shopping centers, educational facilities, and other daily amenities. As such, they also include a diversity of land uses. They are intended to be self-contained, self-sustaining, and well-balanced communities with sound economic bases and adequate employment opportunities. They have usually been located adjacent to urban centers, and sometimes incorporated with them. New communities can provide opportunities for experimentation and innovation for existing urban developments.[28]

The term "new town" was originally meant to describe a new settlement intended to combine urban and country atmospheres. Surrounded by a green belt of open space, the town is built on publicly or semi-publicly owned land in order to insure land use control. It is meant to be self-sustaining and self-contained, with a population which includes a diversity of socioeconomic and age groups.[29] The new town is also planned to include a variety of land uses, and to be self-governed.

The development town was introduced in Israel to serve the economically and socially diversified immigrant population. It includes varied land uses and is occasionally designed to function integrally with agricultural hinterlands. The development town is initiated by the government on publicly leased and untransferable land; later, the involvement of private enterprise, supported by public money, is encouraged.[30] Development towns are implemented according to a coordinated national urban growth policy.

The new city is a large-scale urban development, planned either as a newly developed area or as a significant expansion of an existing community in order to meet population growth needs.[31] The new city should include diversified social classes, races, and age groups, as well as a variety of job opportunities for a population of 100,000 or more. It is meant to provide opportunities for joint endeavors of private and public agencies in a high standard of planning and design, and therefore to be coordinated by state, county, and local governments.

The satellite town is a new large-scale settlement built within commuting distance on the metropolitan orbit in order to provide for urban population growth. Primarily a dormi-

tory development, it has limited types of land use and is economically, and sometimes administratively, dependent on its adjacent urban center. It may provide minimal required services and educational facilities.

The metro town is a new settlement built as a satellite to a major urban center and linked to it by a public transportation system. It exists in a symbiotic relationship with the central city and with other metrotowns, which form a regional cluster. Although each metro town will not have a diversity of land uses, the complex as a whole will provide not only that diversity, but also a variety of jobs and cultural or social opportunities.

The new town intown is an attempt to revitalize one section of a large city; it offers a wide range of new dormitories and new commercial and cultural opportunities.[32] This newly developed unit is designed to provide a new physical environment better than that of the major city, and to create a new economic focus. It should "encourage and support the proper growth and development of metropolitan areas and inner cities."[33]

The *new town in-city,* this author's original concept, is based on the application of the original new town idea within sections of a central city in order to bring about a drastic positive social change. The social issue is of prime concern in this concept. A cleared deteriorated section of a city should be planned, designed, and developed physically, socially, economically, and governmentally as an independent unit, and should include the traditional neighborhood patterns, bound and interspersed with green areas and open space. The population should have socioeconomic, age, ethnic, religious, and racial diversification and so develop its own identity. The population and town size should be limited enough to be manageable, yet large enough to provide its own services and infrastructure and to sustain its own sound economic base. It should provide a maximum variety of job opportunities, in order to minimize the job-commuting pattern. It should also have its own local independent government that could be federated with the central city government.

If we consider the feasibility of implementing some or all of the above-mentioned twelve types of new urban patterns, it becomes clear that the public has a responsibility to initiate and generate such involvement, as has traditionally been the case in this country.

PUBLIC CONTRIBUTION

If the quantity and variety of new settlement development throughout the world in the last five centuries is reviewed, the United States may be seen as a leader in this field. Within its brief history both the public and the private sectors have made many achievements. It is mainly in the twentieth century, however, that the public role in the establishment of new communities or large-scale developments has been declining, leaving the private developer to struggle with this endeavor. Nevertheless, legislation in the sixties and early seventies has shown a notable revival of the American tradition of public contribution to new urban development. An examination of the past and present roles of the government in the development of new urban patterns raises two important questions: Is public contribution needed? If so, what is the most desirable and effective type of contribution?

The dominant role of private enterprise in the development of existing and future urban patterns should not be eliminated or reduced. Rather, it must be realized that a significant portion of this effort could be far more successful, and indeed could not be completed without the involvement of the public. The combination of the public power structure in coordinated support of the imaginatively creative initiative of private enterprise could consistently improve the quality of urban development. The role of the public should not be one

of competition with private enterprise; rather, it should be complementary. On the other hand, stimulation of new national or state urban patterns, or of a new communities movement, is beyond the capacity of private enterprise. Considering the large scale of the projects and the investments required for such development, the private developer cannot afford the risk of losing. The failure of many private developers would certainly diminish the chance of developing new urban patterns. Traditionally, the private developer comes along after public agencies have been pioneering. New urban developments with high standards, and especially new communities, are risky ventures. They become more risky when the developer is requested to insure the provision of low-cost housing. Public involvement would insure quality standards of planning and development in the physical, social, economic, health, education, and utilities efforts.

Public contribution to the development of future urban patterns should focus on five major areas. This involvement is conditional to the formulation of a national policy for urban growth, whether it be a policy of population "no distribution" or redistribution. The five major areas of contribution are: site selection, provision of financial incentives, land assemblage, provision of standard utilities, and the creation of a mechanism for implementation. Coordination in each area should facilitate satisfactory results.

The site selection of new urban centers should become the concern of the federal or state government. This phase precedes any planning or development initiative and will naturally reflect public policy on regions designated for future growth. These regions will have major government support for private or public developers. Government preferences should not and would not prevent private developers from selecting and receiving support for development in other areas not designated by national or state growth policy. In designating for development, the policy would not necessarily indicate the definite site for growth; rather, the selection of location would be on a regional level. If policies for population redistribution were formulated and accepted, site selection preference would be given to sparsely populated areas.

Provision of financial incentives is a second area in which public contribution could be a powerful instrument for achieving effective redirection of growth, or, more specifically, population redistribution. The economic factor has been a strong catalyst in the process of urban growth throughout the history of human settlements. As it has been experienced in some countries, there is an endless variety of possible incentives which might be provided in order to attract job opportunities to a region.[34] These could include tax exemption or relief for industries, income tax loans to individuals with little or no interest, revolving funds, grants, loan insurance, land grants or land adjustment for development, subsidies for industries and businesses, subsidies for houses, and provisions for regional investment projects to stimulate growth (see figure, p. 6).[35] These types of support could be oriented toward attracting basic and non-basic industries and infrastructure which would, in turn, establish the foundation for job opportunities.[36] In addition, they would support the developer, especially in his early investment initiative, in order to overcome the massive financial burden related specifically to the land purchasing process. Without this public contribution it may be anticipated that, in spite of positive environmental or social achievements, many projects would remain economically infeasible and would therefore jeopardize the initial investment of private developers. Financial incentives to encourage development of new urban patterns should become a part of national and state policy for investment priorities, and should be related to and coordinated with the site selection preferences

policy. Without such coordination, the incentives would lose their effectiveness.

Land assemblage, the third area in which public contribution is most desired, is the most crucial phase in the development of new urban centers, and especially of new communities in the United States. The level of success of this process could dictate life or death for the project. Three major factors to be considered throughout this process are the efficiency, intensity, and tactics required in speculation; the process that requires a very large portion of the total project expenses; and the power and excellent administrative ability needed to handle the process most quickly. To expedite these requirements, the public sector should formulate legislation for land acquisition and compensation. Once land becomes available through public support, the developer can devote his time and energy to the total project implementation process. Without such an arrangement, success for the private developer would be doubtful, as would his involvement with nationally desirable projects. The initial investment for land assemblage is usually more than 20 percent of the total new community project investment. This "front end" money is paid in the early phases of development, yet without any immediate return; for the developer, however, there is payment in addition to the county or local taxes which are due until the marketing of the houses.

Public contribution to the land assemblage process could be channeled through land acquisition, combined land purchase, state land purchase, or any possible combination of these. Legislation should be enacted on the state level and supported by the federal government, so that country and city land can be acquired at its market value for the needs of large-scale development and new urban centers. Such power could be delegated to a publicly established corporation, which would be in charge of the creation of a "land bank" for that state's planned urban patterns. Land would then be given to the developer under long-term lease or purchased for the designated development. The terms should coincide with the state urban policy. Land owners adjacent to the acquired land should contribute to the corporation a portion of all the benefits gained in their own future development which are consequences of the corporation-initiated development.

Combined land purchase should be made through the establishment of a state-private corporation which would insure at least the primary land for public use, such as public buildings, open spaces, green belts, and parks. This land, if purchased with federal and state money, should be absolutely nontransferable to private control, and its originally designated use should not be changed. Such an arrangement, if it is to remain consistent, should include the power to guarantee at least the minimum required elements for a sound community land use pattern. This would also significantly reduce the financial burden of the private developer. Such a state-private corporation could be established with the developer, or jointly with the landowners themselves, in a land development profit-sharing plan. However, the "land bank" of the landowners should also contribute a percentage of land for public use as compensation for the benefits to be gained from the forthcoming public-private large-scale development. Land purchase might be achieved by compensation, exchange, or joint sharing with the original owners.

Land could be purchased or acquired by the state for new urban development. It could then be developed by the state land development corporation, or it could be given to private enterprise to be developed for sound land use as regulated by public policy. However, land purchased or assembled by the public, but designated for development solely by private developers, should be conditional to land use control regulations constituted by the public, in order to avoid future misuse or over-

use of the land. In the final analysis, public contribution will also benefit the private developer. In any case, legislation would be necessary for the success of the process, although in most cases the law might not have to be used in the actual land acquisition.

Within the last decade there has been relatively notable federal and state legislation facilitating the development of new urban centers and new communities. Although the frequency of such legislation is increasing steadily, it may still be anticipated that power of eminent domain or land assemblage capability will not soon become a nationwide phenomenon. Public opinion in this country does not now favor public land assemblage. Legislation is only one way of preparing public opinion; the traditional feeling of alienation toward government, the motivation of profit-making, and the absence of continuous education in public needs have all succeeded in developing a lack of faith in the public role. Public interference has been looked upon as a hindrance to private enterprise. This issue of changing the public image requires education and time, as has been demonstrated in Europe. Unless such preparation takes place, new urban patterns and the new communities "movement" will remain sporadic.

Section 704 of the Housing and Development Act of 1965,[37] Title X of the National Housing Act,[38] and Title VII of the Urban Growth Policy and New Communities Act of 1970 provide mortgage or financial guarantee for private and public developers in land purchasing. However, none of this legislation provides the powerful tools necessary for land acquisition.[39] The absence of this phase of legislated cooperation detracts from the effectiveness of federal and state financial support. Advance acquisition supported by legislation would not only preclude land speculation in the early stages and save much money, time, and effort; it would also encourage more medium and small-scale private developers to enter the new communities development business. The experience gained through new community development in Columbia, Maryland; Reston, Virginia; and other places has shown the vast amounts of energy, effort, administrative capacity, and innovative techniques which are required to overcome the immense obstacles encountered in the existing land assemblage and land speculation system.

Provision of the minimum standard utilities is the fourth major area for public contribution in the development of new urban patterns. Utilities here include sewage and water systems, internal and access roads, health and education buildings and equipment, basic recreational facilities, and public land such as open space, green areas, and parks. The provision of these public utilities should be granted by the federal or state governments in order to insure the minimum high standards, and also to relieve a major investment burden from the private or public developer.

The legislative creation of a federal or state agency which would be advisory and action-oriented is the fifth area for public contribution to the development of new urban patterns. This agency should be commissioned to select the site, provide financial incentives, assemble land through a land development corporation, and provide standard utilities. It should also be required to insure high quality in the actual development; to review and evaluate the developer's plans and the quality of his implementation; to carry on applied research activities, especially those oriented toward innovation; to examine environmental impact; and to provide advice and instructions to the developer.

Although the above-mentioned five areas for public contribution would substantially aid the efforts of the developer, the actual development process and the main investment of the project would still be carried on by the private developer himself. Public contribution is to support private enterprise, not to replace it.

On the other hand, there still could be some projects developed solely by public enterprise. The public developer, in the form of local, regional, or state governments, should always be eligible for the same rights as the private developer.

Common to most of the sporadically developed "new communities" initiated in America before World War II was the attempt to implement the original philosophy of the Garden City of Ebenezer Howard. In reality, the absence of an established philosophy or a national vision and goal, the dominance of the profit motive, and uncoordinated and undirected growth could only lead to small and scattered accomplishments. Clarence Stein has accurately described this: "That is how it started. We intended to create a Garden City in America. But time and place and the so-called economic cycle mold the ultimate reality of our dreams. So we built Sunnyside, a community within the rigid framework of New York's gridiron. Then Radburn, realistically planned for the Motor Age, but not a Garden City as Howard saw it."[40] On the other hand, the new urban centers developed after World War II possessed a socioeconomic homogeneity of population; they became representatives of the middle class. They have solved some housing needs but have not adequately coped with the social issues of rapid urbanization. If the pace of the new communities program of the Department of Housing and Urban Development continues at its present slow rate and remains underfunded and understaffed, newly developed communities will not bring about effective changes in the social climate or significant modifications in American urbanization patterns. A national urban growth policy can be effective only if an efficient executive mechanism is combined with it. Without such an apparatus, policy is meaningless. If the creation of new urban patterns as a foundation for population redistribution is adopted as a goal to meet the urban growth crisis, new communities will become an integral part of this new national urban pattern.

NOTES

1 These stages of development are reflected in the following projects: the Country Club planned communities, Kans. (1906); Kohler, Wis. (1913); Kingsport, Tenn. (1916); Longview, Wash. (1923); Sunnyside Gardens, N.Y. (1924); Radburn, N.J. (1928); Chatham Village, Pittsburgh, Pa. (1930); Phipps Garden Apartments (I), New York City (1931); Hillside Homes, New York City (1932); Columbia Basin (small hydroelectric towns), Wash. (1933); Phipps Gardens Apartments (II), New York City (1935); Valley Stream Project, N.Y. (1935); Greenbrook, N.J. (1935); Greenbelt, Md. (1937); Greenhills, Ohio (1938); Greendale, Wis. (1938); Baldwin Hills Village, Los Angeles (1941); Fontana, Tennessee Valley (1942); Levittown in Long Island (1947), Pennsylvania (1951), and New Jersey (1958); Irvine Ranch, Calif. (1960); Columbia, Md. (1963); Reston, Va. (1965); Jonathan, Minn. (1965); Cedar-Riverside (new town intown), Minneapolis, Minn. (1968). These should be considered as landmarks and as the seeds for the burgeoning of a national new communities movement. The planning concept behind some of these projects has been partly or fully associated with the original philosophy of new towns.

2 In speaking of the new communities in America built in the thirties and forties, Clarence Stein stated that "none of them was comprehensive enough in scale or functions to fully deserve the title of New Town" (*Toward New Towns for America* [Cambridge, Mass.: MIT Press, 1957], p. 9).

3 As expressed by Clarence Stein, the planner of the Radburn project in New Jersey, the planning concept was aimed at combining urban life with a country atmosphere, adopting a green belt pattern, limiting size, providing dormitories and industry, adjusting the design to the needs of the automobile, having superblocks surrounding a backbone green area, designing hierarchy in roads, and effecting a complete separation of pedestrians and vehicles (ibid., pp. 37–74).

4 Lewis Mumford stated that Stein himself "advocated a public policy working for decentralization, industrial dispersal, new towns, and regional reconstruction." (See Mumford's introduction to Stein's book, ibid., p. 14). Thus these elements have been considered as interrelated components.

5 Stein himself stated that a group of leading professionals "formed the Regional Planning Association of America, to discuss regional development, geotechnics and New Communities" (ibid., p. 19).

6 The Regional Planning Association of America, formed in the thirties by Stein and others, envisioned policies for new communities and for regional planning as integrated and inseparable parts (ibid., p. 14).

7 "We have seen some interesting examples in recent years of modern urbanization patterns developed as an extension of the physical and historic texture of older communities of small to medium size in Europe, in England, and in the Middle East. I am encouraged to see so many signs that we are not about to abandon such centuries of investment, so much that is sound and good, in order to achieve the planner's or architect's dream of a perfect new town—perfect for whom? We in the United States have much to learn from the older cities and communities in other parts of the world. We have much to gain in watching closely the philosophy and techniques being employed in creating new communities in the underdeveloped areas of the world. Perhaps we have something to contribute to them if it is only the fact that we ourselves are a comparatively new country born of revolution and developed in a comparatively short time through all the adversities of a pioneering people in the raw wilderness of a new and strange world" (Oliver C. Winston, "An Urbanization Pattern for the United States: Some Considerations for the Decentralization of Excellence," *Land Economics* 53 [February 1967] :8).

8 "Natural increase is the primary factor affecting the growth of metropolitan population as a whole. To measure its effect, we asked the Census Bureau to project growth within fixed (1960) metropolitan boundaries, supposing there were no additions to metropolitan population through territorial additions or migration from within the United States or from abroad. Even assuming growth at the two-child rate, we found that the metropolitan population would grow by nearly 40 million people between 1970 and the year 2000, through natural increase alone.[*] If to this we add migration, territorial expansion of existing areas, and the growth of other centers to metropolitan size, it is clear that a metropolitan future is assured" (Commission on Population Growth and the American Future, *Population and the American Future* [New York: New American Library, Signet Books, 1972], p. 37). [*]U.S. Bureau of the Census, "Regional Metropolitan Projections" (special tabulations prepared for the Commission).

9 John Friedman, "The Strategy of Deliberate Urbanization," *American Institute of Planners Journal* 34 (November 1968):364.

10 "Even if the population of our country were to stop growing today, we would still have problems associated with rural depopulation and metropolitan growth. Our large metropolitan areas would still have problems of congestion, pollution, and severe racial separation" (Commission on Population Growth, *Population and the American Future*, pp. 43–44).

11 "If the national population should grow at the two-child rate, projections based on recent trends indicate that there will be 225 million people living in metropolitan areas by the end of the century. This would represent the addition of 81 million people to the 144 million persons who comprised our metropolitan population in 1970. An average of three children per family would cause our metropolitan population to swell to a total of 273 million by the year 2000, an increase of 129 million over the 1970 figure. Thus, our metropolitan population at the end of the century will be nearly 50 million greater if American families average three rather than two children.

"Where will these people live? In 1970, more than four out of every 10 Americans were living in a metropolitan area comprised of one million or more people. By the year 2000, the projections indicate that more than six of every 10 persons are likely to be living in these large areas. Not all of the additional people will be added to the 29 metropolitan areas of one million or more that existed in 1970. In the year 2000, there will be a total of 44 to 50 such places, depending on how fast the total population grows. If present trends continue, the locus of continued increases in our total population will be large metropolitan areas. This is to be expected so long as the total number of people in metropolitan areas keeps on growing" (ibid., pp. 37–40).

12 "Urban regions appear to be a prominent feature of the demographic future of this country. In 1920, there were 10 urban regions with over one-third of the total population. By 1970, about three-fourths of the population of the United States lived in the urban regions which already exist or are expected to develop by 2000.

"The total land area encompassed by urban regions is estimated to double in the period 1960 to 1980, while the number of such areas is expected to increase from 16 to at least 23. By 2000, urban regions will occupy one-sixth of the continental United States land area, and contain five-sixths of our nation's people.

"If our national population distributes itself according to these projections, 54 percent of all Americans will be living in the two largest urban regions. The metropolitan belt stretching along the Atlantic seaboard and westward past Chicago would contain 41 percent of our total population. Another 13 percent would be in the California region lying between San Francisco and San Diego" (ibid., pp. 41–42).

13 "In 1970, about 71 percent of our population was metropolitan; it is expected to be 85 percent by the year 2000. (The census figure for 1970 was 69 percent. Our projections were based on a modified definition of metropolitan areas; hence the difference)" (ibid., p. 37).

14 "Perhaps the most significant effect of population stabilization on the distribution of population is the most obvious: Zero growth for the nation will mean an average of zero growth for local areas. It may be that the most effective long-term strategy for stabilizing local growth is through national stabilization, not redistribution" (ibid., p. 43).

15 "According to the Commission's survey, 54 percent of Americans think that the distribution of population is a 'serious problem'; half believe that, over the next 30 years, it will be at least as great a problem as population growth.[*] This is in accordance with our belief that to reduce problems of population growth in no way absolves us of the responsibility to address the problems posed by the distribution of population" (ibid., p. 44). [*]National Public Opinion Survey conducted for the Commission by Opinion Research Corporation, 1971.

16 "How would stabilization of the national population affect migration and local growth? First, shifts in population composition—chiefly age and family structure—would alter the tempo of migration. Second, changes in the balance between natural increase and migration would influence local growth. Because of the momentum of past growth and the time it will take to achieve a stabilized population in the United States, the full effects will be long range" (ibid., p. 43).

17 "Migrations from backward to prosperous areas, and from country to town, are frequent both in Europe and in the United States; however, they mostly result from spontaneous demographic and economic trends rather than from a systematic planning policy. Even in the countries of the Eastern Block, whose economy is essentially guided by States Authorities, changes in the geographical distribution of population have been mostly 'by-products' of their industrial location policy" (Eliezer Brutzkus, "Planning of Spatial Distribution of Population in Israel," *Ekistics* 21 [May 1966]:350).

18 The English, Israeli, and Dutch national policies of redistribution of population combine economic and physical planning based on the selection of problematic areas as the preferable regions for development. These national policies are aimed at creating a balanced, but not necessarily even, distribution. In the case of England, the policy has been enforced by a series of acts; in the case of Israel, it has been accepted as an integral and essential part of an overall comprehensive national policy which has been popularly accepted since the resettlement movement at the turn of the century. In The Netherlands, the necessity for such a policy became an urgent issue because of the overconcentration of population in the western part of the country, called "Conurbation Holland." Therefore, a governmental policy of population redistribution was adopted to relieve the pressures from this conurbation.

19 The report of the Advisory Commission on Intergovernmental Relations (ACIR) has described the government's role as a new focus, stating, "The interplay of private and governmental policies and decisions has taken place in the context of governmental institutions which grew and developed in a nation primarily agricultural in character. . . . Governmental policies thus have just recently begun to assume an urban focus. Moreover, the focus has generally been sporadic, and while significant, it has been limited in scope. Regarding the location of urban growth, there has been no overall policy by which to guide public policies and programs affecting the geographic location of such development throughout the nation. Similarly there has been no overall policy to guide the character and nature of growth. Lacking a policy framework, specific program decisions concentrating on particular objectives have sometimes produced inadvertent results in terms of urbanization trends, altering or partially canceling out basic program goals" (U.S. Advisory Commission on Intergovernmental Relations, *Urban and Rural America: Policies for Future Growth.* Commission Report A–32 [Washington, D.C.: U.S. Government Printing Office, April 1968], p. 125).

20 A. L. Massoni, "Two Important New Bills Coming up on National Growth Policy and Evaluation of Priorities and Resources," *AIP Newsletter* 8 (February 1973):1.

21 John Friedmann, on the other hand, advocates only one solution: "The only viable alternative is to formulate national policies that will make existing major population concentrations—megalopolis—more livable. The job no doubt is difficult, but not impossible. We should take heart in the example of

West Germany, one of the world's most urbanized nations and a favorite of American tourists, which could be put down in the heart of Texas and still leave two-thirds of that State's territory to the citizens of Texas. There is plenty of room in America. Our true challenge is to learn to use it well" ("The Feasibility of a National Settlement Policy for the U.S.A.," *Ekistics* 32 [November 1971] :322).

22 The *new town in-city* is the author's original concept, based on the application of new town principles to major sections of a central city. It is briefly described in this paper, and is thoroughly discussed in his forthcoming book, *Principles and Practice of New Town Planning.*

23 "We tried to learn how much the growth of the large metropolitan areas might be reduced if the growth of smaller, less congested places were stimulated. Commission researchers picked 121 places ranging in size from 10,000 to 350,000 whose growth in the past decade indicated that they might be induced to grow more rapidly in the future. They listed all places of this size that had grown faster than the national average during the 1960's and were located more than 75 miles from any existing or projected metropolitan area of two million people or more.

"Such places had a total population of 14 million in 1970. If they were to grow by 30 percent each decade, their population in the year 2000 would be about 31 million. If this were to happen, our calculations suggest that these places might absorb about 10 million of the growth which is otherwise expected to occur in areas of one million or more, assuming the 2-child national projection. However, these large areas would still increase by 70 million under the 2-child projection, and by 115 million under the 3-child projection. If the smaller areas were to grow faster than 30 percent, they would, of course, divert more growth from the large areas. But to obtain substantial effects, these smaller places would have to grow 50 percent per decade.[*] At that point, one must ask if the cure is any better than the disease.

"Moreover, most of the smaller areas which are capable of attracting many people are in urban regions, or would be by the year 2000. Thus, stimulating their growth would have the useful effect of decongesting settlement in urban regions, but would do little to retard urban region growth" (Commission on Population Growth, *Population and the American Future*, p. 40). [*]Edward E. Murray and Ned Hedge, "Growth Center Population Redistribution 1980–2000" (prepared for the Commission, 1972).

24 "In applying my experiences and observations in this city [Binghamton, N.Y.] as a measure to the

opportunities in other communities of comparable size and character, I cannot help but feel more strongly than ever that the development of urban pattern based more on the sound smaller communities than on "new towns" and metropolitan "sprawl" is essential. Not that "new towns" should not be built—we shall need them too if they are conceived and planned with deeper understanding of the fundamental needs of their inhabitants and built with an appreciation of values other than pure economics and/or architecture. Developing and redeveloping metropolitan centers will go on too, to serve the changing social order. But the range of choice for our people can be considerably broadened by a very special consideration to the potential of the existing, older and smaller communities. They can be nuclei for clusters of well ordered, vigorous, attractive and soul-satisfying environments able to accommodate man's more intimate needs for a life of fulfillment and offering easy and continuous access to the recreational opportunities and the seclusion of the natural countryside around him" (Winston, "Urbanization Pattern," p. 6).

25 "Here, there seems to me to be an equal or even greater need for concern as to the potential offered for imaginative and intelligent planning. This brings me to the principal thesis which I would like to set forth in this paper—regional patterns of urban development based on existing smaller communities in congenial and harmonious settings with emphasis on the "civic" aspirations of man. There are at present in the United States some 312 communities in a population range of 50,000 to 500,000—a good number of which are so appropriately located and have such fundamental characteristics as to make them likely nuclei for developing into a kind of environment which could satisfy the broadest scope of human needs. People who would prefer this kind of environment are those who seek more intimate association and participation in cultural, political and economic life and who feel the need for close association with symbols of stability—heritages of the past. In addition, there are over 5,000 smaller communities of 2,500 to 50,000 people which offer additional considerations for imaginative and intelligent civic grouping" (ibid., p. 4).

26 The National Commission on Urban Growth Policy was formed in 1968 to study the idea of the new city and other urban alternatives. In *The New City* (ed. Donald Canty [New York: Frederick A. Praeger, 1969]), a report of its findings, the committee suggested that the development of the "accelerated growth center" be assigned to a special

agency: "In smaller communities designated as 'accelerated growth centers' these agencies should be empowered to stimulate growth through the acquisition of large quantities of land, the orderly installation of new public facilities, and the inducement of business and industry to locate in these areas.

"Thus, the Committee is recommending federal financing for development corporations, authorized under state law, which could stimulate needed large-scale development in and out of existing metropolitan areas and would have ample authority to bring about genuine balance in urban growth" (p. 174).

27 A.I.P. Task Force on New Communities, *New Communities: Challenge for Today,* ed. Muriel I. Allen, American Institute of Planners Background Paper no. 2 (Washington, D.C.: American Institute of Planners, October 1968), p. 6.

28 For another definition, see U.S. Advisory Commission on Intergovernmental Relations, *Urban and Rural America*, p. 64.

29 The elements of the new town concept have been separately expressed and developed throughout the history of human settlement either as utopian ideas or implemented projects. The ingenuity of Ebenezer Howard at the end of the nineteenth century was that he brought all those elements together to form one comprehensive and integrated concept.

30 Alexander Berler indicates that governmental aid should not be included as a criterion in the definition of the term "development towns" (*New Towns in Israel* [Jerusalem: Israel Universities Press, 1970], pp. 58–59).

31 The term "new city" was first coined by the National Committee on Urban Growth Policy in an attempt to suggest the development of 100 new communities each with a population of 100,000, and 10 new cities of one million each, all of which could accommodate 20 percent of what has been estimated by the committee as the total growth by the end of this century (Canty, ed., *The New City*, p. 172).

32 The concept of the new town intown was introduced by Harvey S. Perloff, "New Towns Intown: With Notes and Plans," *American Institute of Planners Journal* 32 (May 1966): 155–161.

33 U.S. Department of Housing and Urban Development, *Excerpts from Urban Growth and New Community Development Act of 1970* (Washington, D.C.: U.S. Government Printing Office, 1971).

34 For the example of Israel, see Brutzkus.

35 "A federal income tax credit might be a percentage of various bases: (1) investment in plant and equipment; (2) amount of payroll; and (3) value added to produce. Each method has its virtues. The first would

tend to encourage investment in the nonlabor factors of production, thus emphasizing automation and technological improvement. The second would emphasize the use of labor and thus would more immediately further the objectives of an urbanization policy seeking to attract people by jobs. But it might tend to discourage technological improvements. The value-added-base—relating the amount of the tax credit to the amount of value added by the business or industry's own activities—would steer a course between the other two. . . . Tax credits have greater appeal to business simply because they permit greater flexibility in managerial decisions" (U.S. Advisory Commission on Intergovernmental Relations, *Urban and Rural America,* p. 141).

36 "The Commission [Advisory Commission on Intergovernmental Relations] is of the opinion that national governmental policy has a role to play in influencing the location of people and industry and the resulting patterns of urban growth. Some of these ways are of proven capability; others are untried" (ibid., p. 137).

37 Section 704 of the Housing and Urban Development Act of 1965 (Public Law 89–117) is the federal program for advanced acquisition, designed to encourage communities to acquire, in a planned and orderly fashion, land needed for future construction of public works and facilities. It "authorizes grants equal to the interest payments for up to five years on money borrowed by State and local governments and agencies for advance acquisition of land for public facilities" (ibid., p. 152).

38 Title X of the National Housing Act (Public Law 73–479), as added by the Housing and Urban Development Act of 1965 (Public Law 89–117), is a land purchase and development loan guarantee program and is limited to loan guarantees for private developers. Other than the Urban Growth Policy and New Communities Act of 1970, this "is the only federal legislation dealing directly with new communities as such. It authorizes the insurance of mortgages to finance the purchase of raw land and its development as improved building sites by private developers" (ibid., p. 137).

39 None of the three acts related to the new communities development provides the power of eminent domain. This issue is left for the state government to take care of. Until now only New York has constituted such an act and has delegated this power to the UDC, the Urban Development Corporation (*Goals, Guidelines, Concerns of the New York State Urban Development Corporation* [New York: New York State Urban Development Corporation, 1971]). Be-

cause of political hesitation, the act has not yet been implemented. Pennsylvania has drafted a similar act, but it has not been approved by the legislature (Community Development Corporation Act, House Bill 2666, Harrisburg, 17 November 1970; and later Senate Bill 939: Pennsylvania Land Development Agency Act, Harrisburg, 19 July 1971). A few other states have expressed positive attitudes about the need for such an act, but none has yet brought it to final form. The situation still leaves public or private developers racing against a very powerful and discouraging land speculation system.

40 Stein, *Toward New Towns for America,* p. 19.

READING LIST

A.I.P. Task Force on New Communities. *New Communities: Challenge for Today.* Ed. Muriel I. Allen, American Institute of Planners Background Paper no. 2. Washington, D.C.: American Institute of Planners, October 1968.

Akzin, Benjamin, and Yehezkel Dror. *Israel: High Pressure Planning.* Syracuse, N.Y.: Syracuse University Press, 1966.

Alonso, William. "The Mirage of New Towns." *The Public Interest,* no. 19 (Spring 1970), pp. 3–17.

Apgar IV, Mahlon. "New Business from New Towns?" *Harvard Business Review,* January/February 1971, pp. 90–109.

Appalachian Regional Commission. *Developing a Strategy for Growth.* Washington, D.C.: Appalachian Regional Commission, November 1965.

Beckman, Norman. "Toward Development of a National Urban Growth Policy: Legislative Review 1971." *American Institute of Planners Journal* 38 (July 1972): 231–249.

Berler, Alexander. *New Towns in Israel.* Jerusalem: Israel Universities Press, 1970.

Brutzkus, Eliezer. "Planning of Spatial Distribution of Population in Israel." *Ekistics* 21 (May 1966): 350–355.

Carruth, Eleanore. "The Big Move to New Towns." *Fortune,* September 1971, pp. 95–98.

Clapp, James A. *New Towns and Urban Policy.* New York: Dunellen, 1971.

Commission on Population Growth and the American Future. *Population and the American Future.* New York: New American Library, Signet Books, 1972.

Commonwealth of Pennsylvania, General Assembly, House. Community Development Corporation Act. House Bill 2666, Harrisburg, 17 November 1970.

Commonwealth of Pennsylvania, General Assembly, Senate. Senate Bill 939: Pennsylvania Land Development Agency Act. Harrisburg, 19 July 1971.

Crane, David A. "Searching for 'New' Communities." Paper presented at the American Institute of Architects New Communities Conference, Washington, D.C., 3–6 November 1971.

Downie, Leonard, Jr. "The New Town Mirage." *Nation,* 15 May 1972, pp. 617–621.

Eckardt, Wolf Von. "The Case for Building 350 New Towns." *Harper's,* December 1965, pp. 85–98. Also in *Town and Country Planning* 34 (January 1966): 27–31.

————. "New Towns in America." *New Republic,* 26 October 1963, pp. 16–18.

Edwards, Gordon. "The Greenbelt Towns and the American New Towns." *American Institute of Planners Journal* 32 (July 1966): 225–228.

Eichler, Edward P., and Marshall Kaplan. *The Community Builders.* Berkeley and Los Angeles: University of California Press, 1967.

Evans, Hazel, ed. *New Towns: The British Experience.* New York: John Wiley & Sons, Halsted Press, 1972.

Feiss, Carl. "New Towns for America." *American Institute of Architects Journal* 33 (January 1960): 85–89.

————. "USA: New Communities—Or Their Simulacrum." *Town and Country Planning* 35 (January 1967): 34–36.

Friedmann, John. "The Feasibility of a National Settlement Policy for the U.S.A." *Ekistics* 32 (November 1971): 320–322.

————. "The Strategy of Deliberate Urbanization." *American Institute of Planners Journal* 34 (November 1968): 364–373.

Gans, Herbert J. *The Levittowners: Ways of Life and Politics in a New Suburban Community.* New York: Random House, Vintage Books, 1967.

————. *People and Plans: Essays on Urban Problems and Solutions.* New York: Basic Books, 1968.

Gladstone, Robert, and Harold F. Wise. "New Towns Solve Problems of Urban Growth." *Public Management* 48 (May 1966): 128–139.

Godschalk, David R., et al. "Creating New Communities: A Symposium on Process and Product." *American Institute of Planners Journal* 33 (November 1967): 370–411.

Golany, Gideon. "An Analytical Approach to Optimal Future Location and Distribution of Urban Areas of 'Conurbation Holland' into the Netherlands." Institute of Social Studies, The Hague, The Netherlands, December 1965. Mimeographed.

————. *New Towns Planning and Development: A World-Wide Bibliography.* Washington, D.C.: Urban Land Institute, 1973.

Great Britain, South East Economic Planning Council. *A Strategy for the South East.* London: Her Majesty's Stationery Office, 1967.

Harvey, Robert O., and W. A. V. Clark. "The Nature and Economics of Urban Sprawl." *Land Economics* 41 (February 1965): 1–9.

Holden, Constance. "Le Vaudreuil: French Experiment in Urbanism without Tears." *Science* 174 (October 1971): 39–42.

"The Housing Act of 1968." *Urban Land* 27 (October 1968): entire volume.

Hoyt, Homer. "The Growth of Cities from 1800 to 1960 and Forecasts to Year 2000." *Land Economics* 39 (May 1963): 167–173.

Israel, Ministry of the Interior, Planning Department. *National Planning for the Redistribution of Population and the Establishment of New Towns in Israel.* Jerusalem: International Federation for Housing and Planning, 27th World Congress for Housing and Planning, 1964.

Kimball, Charles N. "Time for Cities to Use Space Techniques." *Public Management* 47 (December 1965): 299–304.

Levine, Julius S. "New Communities American Style." Paper presented at the American Institute of Planners Conference, Boston, Mass., 11 October 1972.

Lowry, Ira S. *Population Policy, Welfare, and Regional Development.* No. P–3968. Santa Monica, Calif.: RAND Corporation, November 1968.

Mandelker, Daniel R. "Some Policy Considerations in the Drafting of New Town Legislation." In *New Towns and Planned Communities,* ed. James Lyons et al. New York: Practicing Law Institute, 1971.

Massoni, A. L. "Two Important New Bills Coming Up on National Growth Policy and Evaluation of Priorities and Resources." *AIP Newsletter* 8 (February 1973): 1–3.

Mayer, Albert. *Greenbelt Towns Revisited.* Washington, D.C.: Department of Housing and Urban Development, Urban Planning Research and Demonstration, October 1968.

McHale, John. *The Future of the Future.* New York: George Braziller, 1969.

Metropolitan Fund. *Regional New Towns.* Detroit: Metropolitan Fund, May 1970.

Miller, Brown, Neil J. Pinney, and William S. Saslow. *Innovation in New Communities.* Cambridge, Mass.: MIT Press, 1972.

Morrison, Peter A. *Chronic Movers and the Future*

Redistribution of Population: A Longitudinal Analysis. No. P–4440. Santa Monica, Calif.: RAND Corporation, October 1970.

—————. *The Rationale for a Policy on Population Distribution.* No. P–43474–1. Santa Monica, Calif.: RAND Corporation, July 1970.

—————. *Urban Growth, New Cities, and 'The Population Problem.'* No. P–4515–1. Santa Monica, Calif.: RAND Corporation, December 1970.

Moynihan, Daniel P., ed. *Toward a National Urban Policy.* New York: Basic Books, 1970.

National Committee on Urban Growth Policy. "Findings and Recommendations." In *The New City,* ed. Donald Canty. New York: Frederick A. Praeger, 1969.

New York State Urban Development Corporation. *Goals, Guidelines, Concerns of the New York State Urban Development Corporation.* New York: New York State Urban Development Corporation, 1971.

The Netherlands, Second Report on Physical Planning in The Netherlands. Condensed eds. Part 1: *Main Outline of National Physical Planning Policy.* Part 2: *Future Pattern of Development.* The Hague: Government Printing Office of The Netherlands, 1966.

"New Town: Philosophy and Reality." *Building Research* 3 (January/February 1966): 9–34.

"New Towns for America." *House and Home* 25 (February 1964): 123–131.

"New Towns: Are They Just Oversized Subdivisions —with Oversized Problems?" *House and Home* 29 (June 1966): 92–103.

Osborn, F. J. "New Towns for America?" *Town and Country Planning* 21 (January 1953): 44–49.

Perloff, Harvey S. "New Towns Intown: With Notes and Plans." *American Institute of Planners Journal* 32 (May 1966): 155–161.

Reilly, William K., and S. J. Schulman. "The State Urban Development Corporation: New York's Innovation." *Urban Lawyer* 1 (Summer 1969): 129–146.

Robson, William A. "New Towns in Britain." In *Planning of Metropolitan Areas and New Towns.* New York: United Nations Publications, 1967.

Rodwin, Lloyd. *Nations and Cities.* Boston: Houghton Mifflin, 1970.

—————, et al. *Planning Urban Growth and Regional Development.* Cambridge, Mass.: MIT Press, 1969.

Rouse, James W. "Cities That Work for Man— Victory Ahead." Speech given at the Lions International/University of Puerto Rico symposium on "The City of the Future," San Juan, Puerto Rico, 18 October 1967.

Schaffer, Frank. *The New Town Story.* London: MacGibbon & Kee, 1970.

Scott, Stanley. "The Large New Communities: Ultimate Self-Government and Other Problems." *Public Affairs Report,* Bulletin of the Institute of Governmental Studies, University of California, Berkeley, October 1965.

—————. "Urban Growth Challenges New Towns." *Public Management* 48 (September 1966): 253–260.

Smolski, Chester E. "European New Towns: Focus on London." *Focus* 22 (February 1972): 1–8.

Spiegal, Erika. *New Towns in Israel: Urban and Regional Planning and Development.* Trans. Annelie Rookwood. New York: Frederick A. Praeger, 1967.

Stein, Clarence S. *Toward New Towns for America.* Cambridge, Mass.: MIT Press, 1957.

Strong, Anna Louise. *Planned Urban Environments: Sweden, Finland, Israel, The Netherlands, France.* Baltimore: Johns Hopkins Press, 1971.

Sundquist, James L. "Where Shall They Live?" *The Public Interest* 18 (Winter 1970): 88–100.

Susskind, Lawrence, and Gary Hack. "New Communities in a National Urban Growth Strategy." *Technology Review* 74 (February 1972): 30–42.

Thomas, Ray. *London's New Towns: A Study of Self-Contained and Balanced Communities.* New York: Committee for Economic Development, 1969.

Thomas, Wyndham. "New Towns Development." In *New Towns and Planned Communities,* ed. James A. Lyons et al. New York: Practicing Law Institute, 1971.

Thompson, Wayne E. "Prototype City—Design for Tomorrow." *Public Management* 48 (August 1966): 212–217.

Thompson, Wilbur R. "Economic Aspects of Alternative National Urban Land Strategies." Paper presented at 1969 Biennial Congress International Fraternity of Lambda Alpha and the Land Economics Foundation, Washington, D.C., 16 October 1969.

Turner, Alan. "A Case for New Towns." *American Institute of Architects Journal* 54 (November 1970): 28–32.

Underhill, Jack A. "Proposal for Strengthening the Role of New Communities in Implementing National Urban Growth Strategy." Washington, D.C.: Department of Housing and Urban Development, 27 October 1971.

United Nations, Department of Economic and Social Affairs. *Planning of Metropolitan Areas and New Towns.* New York: United Nations Publication ST/SOA/65, 1967.

University of Minnesota. *Minnesota Experimental City (MXC).* Vol. I: *A Compendium of Publications Relating to Socio-Cultural Aspects.* Vol. II: *Economic and Physical Aspects.* Minneapolis: University of Minnesota/Experimental City Project, 1969.

United States, Advisory Commission on Intergovernmental Relations. *Urban and Rural America: Policies for Future Growth.* Commission Report A–32. Washington, D.C.: U.S. Government Printing Office, April 1968.

United States, Department of Housing and Urban Development. *Excerpts from Urban Growth and New Community Development Act of 1970.* Washington, D.C.: U.S. Government Printing Office, 31 December 1971.

United States, Department of Housing and Urban Development, Domestic Council Committee on National Growth. *Report on National Growth 1972.* Washington, D.C.: U.S. Government Printing Office, 1972.

Winston, Oliver C. "An Urbanization Pattern for the United States: Some Considerations for the Decentralization of Excellence." *Land Economics* 53 (February 1967): 1–10.

Public Enterprise and New Towns: An American Tradition Revisited

John W. Reps

Ian Menzies, urban affairs writer and associate editor of the *Boston Globe,* entitled one of his recent columns on the city: "Of New Towns and Hot Pants." It began, "New Towns have donned the fashion role of hot pants in the haute couture world of urbanology. It's the sexy thing to talk about." Menzies then continued, "once again we face the frightening faddism of America; that almost irresponsible desire for something new for the sake of newness; that fruitless search for an instant cure-all, an elixir for happiness without effort or sacrifices."[1]

His point is that as we gear ourselves up for an attempt to create a number of new cities, we should not forget the far more pressing problems of existing communities. While sharing that viewpoint, I add the further suggestion that we ought to look at our own past to see if there is something to learn from experience.

Our past is a relevant area for exploration, for this is a nation of new towns, towns deliberately founded and planned by men who understood that there could be no civilization without cities. Only the arrogance of a people ignorant of their own tradition could create the prevailing, and quite mistaken, belief that planning new towns as an instrument of public policy is an invention of our own era.

I intend to look at only one aspect of this tradition: the new towns founded in this country through public initiative. There are two reasons for this. First, while the full extent of new town founding on this continent is still not appreciated, scholars in recent years have begun to explore this subject. Most of their writing, my own included, deals with town planning by private, corporate, institutional, or religious organizations. The degree to which public initiative was involved in town planning has not yet received the recognition it deserves.

The second reason I concentrate on this aspect of our planning history stems from a belief that if a modern new towns movement is to play any significant social role now, public initiative, guidance, direction, and probably public ownership, at least of the land, must prevail. I think it is absolutely essential that state, regional, and metropolitan development corporations be established to initiate most of the new cities that will be needed.

Site selection, land acquisition, planning, and provision of site improvements should be responsibilities assigned to public agencies. Private enterprise should, in my opinion, play a subordinate role in the decision-making process involved in these aspects of community-building. Those who believe as I do will need all the ammunition they can muster in the political conflict that is inevitable before this policy can be established.

History is not usually thought of as a weapon, but it can be used as such, at least in the counterattack against the charge that publicly initiated new towns are somehow un-American and foreign to our tradition. Let me now show you how erroneous this position is. It suits my purpose to begin in the middle of the story, and then to roam back and forth to gather up its ends.

A decision was once made concerning a major project of urban development. To one man and his chief advisor fell the powers and responsibilities for carrying out this development. It was an undertaking of considerable size, embracing an area of well over 5,000 acres. All of this land was privately owned, most of it held in speculative anticipation of substantial profits to be made from the expected city development program.

The two men chiefly responsible for the project were themselves large landowners. One had actively speculated in land in his earlier years. Both were strong supporters of a private enterprise economy, and both were well known for their devotion to the cause of political democracy. Yet both saw clearly that only if the entire site for this project came into public ownership could the public interest prevail over the parochial views and narrow desires of the land proprietors.

While these two men possessed a wealth of both constitutional and statutory authority, they had little money. The senior official, following a suggestion made by his associate, was able to use his considerable personal prestige to obtain title to the land at minimum expense. The proprietors agreed to deed over all their land to him in trust, allow a plan for its development to be prepared, donate all land necessary for streets, receive compensation only for sites withheld for public buildings at an agreed rate, and then get back for their own use half of all the lots in the project. The public governing body would thus obtain exclusive planning powers and would have half of the lots available for sale to benefit the public treasury while paying only for the land to be occupied by public uses. It was an advantageous agreement of which any public official could be proud.

Following the transfer of land titles to the government, a city planner was assigned the task of preparing a design for development of the area. His work proved to be outstanding and resulted in the most notable city planning effort in the United States, and one ranking with the best in the world. With magnificent vision he provided numerous squares and plazas and a great central mall. The street system combined the efficient gridiron with a pattern of monumental radial boulevards, affording direct connections between the most important elements of the city and allowing major buildings to be seen to maximum advantage. Each year hundreds of thousands of visitors experience the unique character of this city. They, along with virtually all of its residents, remain ignorant of the fact that what made it all possible was the initial decision to acquire the entire site and to plan it in the public interest.

I have, of course, been describing the founding and planning of our national capital, Washington, D.C. The two men responsible for its founding and development as a planned new town created by public initiative were George Washington and Thomas Jefferson. Among the most active supporters of the legislation authorizing this project was James Madison. Un-American to create new cities through governmental action? Three presidents testify to the contrary.

While one might like to credit the founding fathers with inventing this enlightened urban land policy, they were in fact merely continuing and extending a practice with deep roots in the colonial period. The eighteenth-century statute books of Virginia contain literally dozens of laws directing county authorities to establish new towns, providing for public acquisition of the land by purchase if possible, but through eminent domain if necessary, and specifying the public sites which were to be set aside. When George Washington was a lad of seventeen and learning the land surveyor's trade, he helped Fairfax County surveyor John West, Jr., lay out the town of Alexandria under just such an act of the Virginia legislature in 1748.

Eighteenth-century Maryland was also the setting for many new towns planned through public initiative. Baltimore, dating from 1729, is a case in point. Tobacco-growers in the vicinity petitioned the legislature for the creation of a town and official port of entry in their vicinity. The Maryland Assembly authorized the appointment of county commissioners for this purpose; they purchased land for forty shillings an acre, planned the streets, blocks, and lots, and then put up building sites for sale at cost. No person could purchase more than one lot, and he had to agree to complete a dwelling of at least 400 square feet within eighteen months on penalty of forfeiting his title.

In the previous century both Virginia and Maryland created new towns in wholesale quantities. We may think that the British New Towns Act of 1946 was the first British legislation providing for the establishment of new towns as an instrument of national policy, but in fact the Virginia Act of 1680 preceded it by more than 250 years. Twenty sites were named in this legislation and in similar acts passed in 1691 and 1706.

Maryland followed Virginia's lead with half a dozen general town acts on the same pattern, designating some sixty locations for new communities. These laws also directed county officials to purchase the site or, if necessary, to acquire the land by eminent domain. The legislation specified that after certain parcels of land within the town were set aside for such public uses as a courthouse, a market, a customhouse, and landings, the remaining lots were to be sold either at fixed prices or by auction. The proceeds were to be used to reimburse the original landowners.

One major city—Norfolk, Virginia—owes its founding to this orgy of new town planning. Modern planners should not judge too harshly the qualities of its original design. It fit the restricted site and served adequately for many years.

Far more impressive, however, are the two superbly planned new towns founded at the very end of the eighteenth century in the Virginia and Maryland tidewater region. Public initiative and public landownership made possible their development as originally planned. Both owed their existence and designs to a remarkable man whose life we still know little about. Francis Nicholson had already served as lieutenant governor of New York when, in 1690, he was sent to Virginia in a similar capacity. There, with the governor residing in England, he secured the passage of the Virginia Town Planning Act of 1691. He also helped found the College of William and Mary at a place then called Middle Plantation.

After several months in England in 1693 and 1694, he received an appointment as governor of Maryland. One of his first accomplishments was to have the capital moved from St. Mary's in the south to a site at the mouth of the Severn River on the Chesapeake Bay. Here at Anne Arundel, renamed Annapolis, Nicholson planned the first of the two capital cities for which he is responsible.

Nothing like this plan had been seen in North America. The inspiration, of course, stems from European baroque city and landscape planning principles. Civil and ecclesiastical power were recognized and symbolized by the two circles, the smaller one for the church, the larger for the building to house the assembly, the governor, and the courts. A market square and a public landing were also incorporated into the plan. A great residential square, named Bloomsbury after its model in London, also appears in the plan but unfortunately was never developed.

Nicholson's plan for Annapolis is certainly not without flaws. He did not fully understand the baroque technique of using radial streets to focus on an important building or vertical feature. The street entering Church Circle from the northeast comes in almost as a tangent. His design is tight and cramped in places; one feels the need for greater space between the two circles, and for their connection by a wider thoroughfare. The street running from the public landing to the Church Circle creates one awkward intersection and several plots of almost unusable shapes and sizes.

Yet even with these faults, Annapolis has achieved a distinctive character and an urbane atmosphere possessed by few other American towns. Granting that part of this may be accidental, I would contend that much of its unique flavor comes from its original plan; and that its plan was made possible by public initiative, governmental direction, and control through the instrument of community land-ownership.

Nicholson used these same forces when he became governor of Virginia. In 1699 he moved the capital from Jamestown to Middle Plantation, renamed Williamsburg. The legislation which authorized acquisition of the site also specified the conditions of land disposition, required larger dwellings on the principal street, established a uniform setback line, and prescribed in considerable detail the architectural form of the chief public buildings. Nicholson's design was remarkably effective. The Duke of Gloucester Street forms the main axis, running from the Capitol to the College of William and Mary. Midway on that street the market square opens on either side. Beyond, at the site of Bruton Parish Church, a secondary axis leads at right angles to the Governor's Palace in the form of a long and narrow green.

The enlightened urban land policy of creating new capital cities, pursued in colonial Virginia and Maryland, was followed in many states after the Revolution. Two things stand out as significant. First, the plans of these cities were generally superior to those with more conventional origins. Public ownership of the entire site made possible a more imaginative plan, a more generous provision of open spaces, wider streets, and more numerous sites for public buildings and uses than those cities which started as private ventures in land speculation.

Second, these cities represented conscious efforts to create an urban environment of outstanding quality to symbolize the very best that could be achieved in community-building. Those who associate governmental enterprise with mediocre results should be aware that it was not always so in the past and that it need not be so in the future.

Columbia, South Carolina, was the earliest planned state capital, dating from 1786. In that year the legislature passed an act providing for the movement of the capital from Charleston to a more generally accessible site on the Congaree River near the center of the state. The act stipulated that a tract two miles square was to be acquired, the owners to be paid "a generous price for the land without reference to its future or increasing value." Lots were to be half an acre in size and "the streets . . . not less than sixty feet wide . . . with two principal streets, running through the centre of the town at right angles, of one hundred and fifty feet wide. . . ." A square or squares of eight acres were to be reserved "for the purpose of erecting such public buildings as may be necessary" and so located "as [to] be most convenient and ornamental." One-fifth of the lots were then to be put up for auction at an early date at a price of not less than twenty pounds for each lot.

The five commissioners appointed by the legislature were soon at work. Much of the site chosen was occupied by Colonel Thomas Taylor's plantation, and he and the other four commissioners fixed a spot on Taylor's Hill as a commanding site for the Statehouse Square. After the boundaries had been surveyed, the work of planning the city began.

Their plan was ambitious, if not very imaginative. The two 150-foot-wide streets, Assembly and Senate, intersected at one corner of Statehouse Square. All other streets were made 100 feet wide, exceeding the minimum specified in the act by a generous margin. In addition to the block set aside for the government buildings, two other squares were reserved in the original plan, but these locations are now unknown. One apparently was intended as a park, and the other as a public market.

Later, in 1802 and 1803, the commissioners reacquired some of the lots sold in several contiguous blocks southeast of the Capitol for conveyance to the newly founded South Carolina College, which opened in 1805. A bird's eye view of the capital city in 1872 shows the university, the statehouse, and the other buildings of the community only then beginning to fill the enormous grid that its optimistic founders had provided not quite a century earlier.

Colonel Taylor was said to have observed rather sourly that "they spoiled a damned fine plantation to make a damned poor town," but personal bias may well have colored his critical judgment. Columbia today is far from unattractive, and much of its spacious character can be attributed to the vision of the public commissioners responsible for its creation.

Georgia created not one planned capital, but two. In 1786 its legislature appointed three commissioners and directed them to purchase 1,000 acres of land and lay out a new city, named Louisville, for the seat of government. There were delays in putting this legislation into effect, and work did not begin until the constitution adopted in 1795 named Louisville as the capital. The first statehouse was completed a year later on grounds near the center of the gridiron town plan. Then, in 1805, this whole process was repeated, and the seat of government moved to Milledgeville, planned under state sponsorship for this purpose. Four twenty-acre reservations connected by streets 120 feet wide provided strong axial relationships and added variety to the otherwise regular gridiron of 100-foot-wide streets crossing at right angles. Ultimately, following the Civil War, the capital made its final move to Atlanta.

Raleigh, North Carolina, dates from 1791, when a commission appointed by the legislature was directed to select and acquire a site for a capital city and prepare its plan. The commission purchased 1,000 acres of land and, on a portion of that tract, laid out a town with main streets 99 feet wide, 66-foot-wide secondary streets, and 276 lots. They reserved five public squares, the central one being designated for the capitol. Lots were then sold at public auction, with the proceeds used for the construction of the state's public buildings.

Tallahassee, Florida, planned in 1824, had a similar plan with streets of generous width and an equally liberal pattern of five urban squares in the central section. Other sites were reserved elsewhere for the courts and for the governor's residence.

The commission, appointed for this purpose in Mississippi in 1821, adopted a theory of town planning proposed by Thomas Jefferson, calling for the permanent reservation as open spaces of every other block in the city. The commission added to that scheme three other sites for public buildings: the capitol, a college, and the courthouse. They connected these three sites with a gently curving street following the crest of land sloping upward from the river. Three of the four widest streets terminated at these buildings to provide impressive street vistas. Jackson, as it developed on this plan in the years before the Civil War, must have been a striking place.

A later generation was to subvert this achievement. The official map of the city in 1875 reveals that only one of the original open squares had survived. One was used for the state penitentiary; another was occupied by the possibly symbolic combination of the city hall and the Jackson gas works.

The year 1821 also saw the creation of Indianapolis, planned by Alexander Ralston on a site granted by Congress to the new state of Indiana. Ralston had assisted Pierre L'Enfant in his plan for Washington, and it was perhaps only natural that he utilized a combination of gridiron and radial streets in his own design for the new capital city. His plan focused on the governor's house, located in the very center of the city on a circular site. Three city blocks were set aside as open spaces toward the edges of town; the plan included two market places, and one block for the capitol building balanced by another for the court-

house in the central tier of blocks. Ralston had the good sense not to bring his diagonals all the way to the center, but to terminate them some distance apart. Nor was this a completely abstract plan disregarding topography. In the southeastern quadrant of the city, along the river, is an area intended as the site for mills and other industries requiring water power.

Five other states also resorted to public action to create new cities to serve as capitals: Ohio, Missouri, Iowa, Texas, and Nebraska. Columbus and Jefferson City still serve as seats of government. Iowa City was the territorial and first state capital before being displaced by the more centrally located and rapidly growing Des Moines.

Austin was planned in 1839 as the capital of the Republic of Texas. Here land had to be acquired by eminent domain. Edwin Waller designed the new city on a mile-square site. His plan—considering the date, the location, and the knowledge of town planning techniques then available—was excellent. Waller chose a commanding spot for the capitol building on the highest elevation. He also reserved land for a university, a prison, and other public and semipublic uses. Sales of town lots were brisk, and the money from this source helped meet construction costs of the public buildings. Austin is a handsome capital city, and much of its attractiveness stems from Waller's generous and orderly plan.

Equally impressive is the city of Lincoln, the last of the American state capitals planned through public initiative. In 1867 Augustus F. Harvey, working under the direction of a three-man commission, prepared its layout. Three major sites, each occupying an area of four normal 300-foot-square blocks, dominate the grid. These were for the capitol, the university, and a park. Many other squares or public sites were also reserved, each a city block in size; five elementary schools, one high school, a courthouse, a market, and the state historical and library association were thus to be accommodated. Three lots for each of ten churches, and one lot each for the Odd Fellows, the Masons, and the Templars were also reserved.

Lincoln grew on this plan with few modifications. The business district developed on O Street, where Harvey had plotted narrower lots intended for commercial use. The present capitol is the third building to be constructed on the original location. The state university, of course, has expanded well beyond the area first set aside for that purpose. But the plan has served the city well, and Lincoln is certainly one of the handsomest towns of the Great Plains.

Not only were the state capitals planned as new towns through public initiative; a good many other cities had their origins in this manner. The state of Pennsylvania was responsible for at least two.

An act of the legislature in 1783 had reserved certain lands for the benefit of veterans of the militia. One tract lay on the north bank of the Allegheny River across from the infant settlement of Pittsburgh. David Redick was directed by the Supreme Executive Council of Pennsylvania in 1784 to lay out a town there. Redick's design was an interesting one. At the center of the gridiron he set aside a great central square equal in size to four of the normal city blocks and amounting to one-ninth of the entire town. Surrounding the community he reserved a belt of common land, portions of which still serve as a city park. Then, beyond, he surveyed out-lots, or garden tracts, and each purchaser of a town lot at the first sale of land in 1788 received one of these outlying plots as well. The town of Allegheny has since incorporated with Pittsburgh, and is now the center of a large renewal effort.

The second tract of land reserved by Pennsylvania was farther down the Ohio River at the mouth of Beaver Creek. In 1791 this land, too, was planned as a state-sponsored new town. The survey was carried out by Daniel Leet. His plan resembled that of Philadelphia, with a large central square (actually consisting of four contiguous blocks) and four other public squares, one at each corner of the town.

Here also the state combined town lots with a system of out-lots for gardening and farm purposes. The founding fathers of Pennsylvania saw nothing wrong with using public powers to initiate urban development. Those who believe that similar steps are needed in the modern era may find this historical precedent of some value in overcoming political opposition to what might be considered a novel and untried venture.

Not all the cities created by public action were wisely and skillfully designed. The modern city of Chicago had its beginnings in 1830 on a tract of land granted by Congress to the canal commissioners of Illinois. They directed civil engineer James Thompson to lay out a town on the most favorable location so lots could be sold quickly to help finance the vast internal improvements contemplated by the state. Thompson's design was a gridiron virtually unrelieved by open space, with all streets and lots exactly the same size. It was a publicly initiated speculative real estate transaction similar to dozens of others sponsored by private individuals in the 1830's, that wild decade of land and town lot booming. The lesson is plain: public action alone is not sufficient if wisdom, taste, and skill are lacking.

I cannot resist including the story of an unimportant but completely enchanting early nineteenth-century town whose novel plan was made possible by public ownership of the site. The Ohio legislature in 1810 created Pickaway County halfway between Columbus and the Ohio River. Three commissioners appointed to select a site for the county seat were attracted to a location on the Scioto River. There they found one of those remarkable geometrical earthworks of the long-vanished mound builders. Low mounds flanked by moats formed a circle and a square. The land was already cleared and otherwise admirably suited for a new town. For less than $1000 Daniel Driesbach acquired the land from its owners and devised a plan which incorporated the alignment of the circular mound.

The name of the town, Circleville, was almost inevitable. In its center was a circular open space containing the octagonal courthouse, each face of which terminated the view down one of the eight radiating streets. The principal circular street followed the line of the original mound, and a second circle allowed the wedge-shaped blocks to be divided into more usable particles. What a relief from the almost ubiquitous grid of the other Ohio cities this little town must have provided!

The end of this story, like that of Jackson, Mississippi, is a sad but intriguing one. Certain citizens objected to the design as "a piece of childish sentimentalism." Others pointed out that a few more lots might have been obtained under a more conventional plan. Progress must be served, and a group of individuals bent on progress through urban redevelopment petitioned the legislature in 1837 for powers to reshape the city. Incorporating themselves as the Circleville Squaring Company, they succeeded the following year in convincing some of the landowners to cooperate in replotting their land. Others held out, no doubt believing that half a circle was better than none at all. Not until 1849 was the company able to take the next step. Three-fourths of the job had been accomplished. Finally negotiations with the last adherents of the old order proved successful; by 1856 the squaring of Circleville had been completed.

My own research in this area of public initiative in American new town planning is far from complete. I suspect that, when all the evidence is in, we shall find many more examples. Let me merely list a few of those others about which I have some knowledge. Brunswick, Macon, and Columbus, Georgia;

Greensboro, North Carolina; Perrysburg, Ohio; San Antonio, Texas; and San Jose and Los Angeles, California, are among the many towns with Spanish origins. Most of the towns in colonial Massachusetts and elsewhere in New England were founded as the result of public rather than private action. A number of the cities in Oklahoma were laid out by federal surveyors following the opening of the former Indian territory to settlement in 1889.

This heritage of public action in creating new towns was forgotten in the later years of the nineteenth century and the early decades of our own. Now we have a new and long overdue opportunity to revive this tradition.

The study of history can be a look back into the future. I submit that our own experience demonstrates the desirability of large-scale planning of publicly sponsored new towns as a means of guiding and controlling future urban growth. Contemporary European experience provides additional evidence to support this view. The task for the coming generation is to reestablish this early American tradition and recapture for the public the decision-making power over city development and the location and design of new communities.

NOTE
1 Ian Menzies, "Of New Towns and Hot Pants," *Boston Globe,* 11 March 1971, p. 24.

READING LIST
Akagi, Roy Hidemichi. *The Town Proprietors of the New England Colonies: A Study of Their Development, Organization, Activities and Controversies, 1620–1770.* Philadelphia: University of Pennsylvania Press, 1924.
Allen, James B. *The Company Town in the American West.* Norman: University of Oklahoma Press, 1966.
Andrews, Charles McLean. *The River Towns of Connecticut: A Study of Wethersfield, Hartford, and Windsor.* Baltimore: Johns Hopkins University, 1889.
Bestor, Arthur. *Backwoods Utopias: The Sectarian and Owenite Phases of Communitarian Socialism in*

America, 1663–1839. Philadelphia: University of Pennsylvania Press, 1950.

Bridenbaugh, Carl. *Cities in the Wilderness: The First Century of Urban Life in America, 1625–1742.* New York: Ronald Press, 1938.

Egleston, Melville. *The Land System of the New England Colonies.* Baltimore: Johns Hopkins University, 1886.

Feiss, Carl. "America's Neglected Tradition." In *The New City,* ed. Donald Canty. New York: Frederick A. Praeger, 1969.

Garvan, Anthony W. B. *Architecture and Town Planning in Colonial Connecticut.* New Haven, Conn.: Yale University Press, 1951.

Glabb, Charles N., and A. Theodore Brown. "Cities in the New Nation." In *A History of Urban America.* New York: Macmillan, 1967.

Menzies, Ian. "Of New Towns and Hot Pants." *Boston Globe,* 11 March 1971, p. 24.

Nuttall, Zelia. "Royal Ordinances Concerning the Laying Out of New Towns." *Hispanic American Historical Review* 5(1922): 249–254.

Reps, John W. *The Making of Urban America.* Princeton, N.J.: Princeton University Press, 1965.

———. *Monumental Washington: The Planning and Development of the Capital Center.* Princeton, N.J.: Princeton University Press, 1967.

———. "The Tidewater Colonies: Town Planning in the 17th Century." *The Town Planning Review* 34 (April 1963): 27–38.

———. *Tidewater Towns: City Planning in Colonial Virginia and Maryland.* Williamsburg, Va.: Colonial Williamsburg Foundation, 1972.

———. *Town Planning in Frontier America.* Princeton, N.J.: Princeton University Press, 1969.

———. "Urban Redevelopment in the Nineteenth Century: The Squaring of Circleville." *Journal of the Society of Architectural Historians* 14(December 1955): 23–26.

Riley, Edward M. "The Town Acts of Colonial Virginia." *Journal of Southern History* 16 (August 1950): 306–323.

Scofield, Edna. "The Origin of Settlement Patterns in Rural New England." *Geographical Review* 28 (October 1938): 652–663.

Scott, Mel. *American City Planning Since 1890.* Berkeley and Los Angeles: University of California Press, 1969.

Smith, Robert C. "Colonial Towns of Spanish and Portuguese America." *Journal of the Society of Architectural Historians* 11 (December 1955): 3–12.

Windels, Paul. *At the Crossroads.* New York: Regional Planning Association, 1948.

New Communities Planning Process and National Growth Policy

Jack A. Underhill

INTRODUCTION

There is no unified view of new communities, or new towns, in the United States. Many groups view new communities from different perspectives: private developers in existence before the federal government became involved in new communities through the Housing Acts of 1968 and 1970; private developers, represented by the League of New Community Developers, who have underway or are planning large developments meeting the criteria set forth in the 1968 and 1970 acts; public developers undertaking new communities for the first time; academic and community leaders advocating complete new approaches to new community development; Congress; the

* This paper represents the personal views of the author, and does not necessarily reflect those of the Department of Housing and Urban Development or of the developers whose new communities are described.
Edward M. Lamont, former Director, Office of New Communities Development, and Clifford W. Graves, former Acting Assistant Secretary for Community Planning and Management, U.S. Department of Housing and Urban Development, have made valuable suggestions and comments in the original manuscript. This article states a general view of the new communities program in mid-1973. However, since that time the New Communities Administration has been created, the staff has more than doubled, and Albert F. Trevino has been appointed Administrator. Currently the program is under basic review: future policy and program directions, processing procedures, basic policies, and management practices are being considered. Statistical information covers all but the last three communities for which commitments were offered. For current information on the program, write to Albert F. Trevino, Administrator, New Communities Administration, Washington, D.C. 20410.

federal administration; local governments; residents surrounding and within new communities; and students and writers who look to new communities as one way of meeting the pressing needs of urban and rural America.

This paper does not try to rationalize all of these views, but it does describe from a single viewpoint the detailed process of planning and implementing a new community and the closely related issues of a national growth policy. This is not a theoretical justification of this policy or a detailed description of each new community; enough has been written and said on that matter. The key problem now is making such a policy work effectively. This requires careful attention to troublesome details, any one of which may impede the translation of carefully laid conceptual work of the past several decades into the brick and mortar of new communities.

There is some justification for treating national urban growth policy and new communities at the same time. Congress intended the topics to be closely entwined. It placed growth policy requirements in Part A and new communities considerations in Part B of the Act, known as Title VII of the Housing and Urban Development Act of 1970, or the Urban Growth and New Communities Development Act of 1970.

A few salient points should be kept in mind when considering new communities in the United States as part of a worldwide movement. First, unlike new communities in most other countries, new communities in the United States are primarily developed by the private sector. Although federal guarantees and other supports have been used recently, the federal government in the postwar years had not engaged in large-scale development itself, and only a few localities and states have been involved as developers.

Second, they are not planned according to some "grand design" by federal, state, or regional governments; rather, they must meet detailed performance specifications by those government entities which must approve them.

Third, new communities planned or underway since the passage of federal new communities legislation differ sharply in composition and purpose from those large-scale developments before this legislation, although they may not vary considerably in appearance.

Fourth, new communities in the United States are probably more diverse than their European counterparts. By the same token, normal suburban development is probably more diverse than many writers have perceived.

Finally, new communities are rapidly becoming an accepted part of the urban development pattern, although there is still some institutional resistance to this idea.

The topics of national urban growth policy and new communities defy description, however, in that they each have a comprehensive scope. To plan a balanced new community, a developer must consider not only the traditional concerns of the land development industry, but also community facilities, the profound issues of race and class relations, conservation, governance of a city ranging in population from 20,000 to 250,000, efficient delivery of public services, recreation, culture, democratic participation, maintenance of good relations with the hodge-podge of existing governmental entities, public health, education, social services, and industrial and commercial development. At the same time, he must provide an acceptable rate of return to investors and meet the deadlines for the development's principal and interest payments. It is not unusual for the latest new community applications to cost around a million dollars, and still to be left with questions requiring later analysis. The total investment, then, may be from one to two billion dollars in a large new community.

The question of national growth policy is even more complex than the new community planning and development question, since new communities are presumed to be instruments of this national growth policy. The "policy," currently a series of interrelated governmental policies and actions, deals with patterns of national human settlement. It seeks to probe the dilemma of concern to all of us and to discover what actions government at all levels can take to help influence national patterns of growth. This policy seeks to respond to the fact that current unregulated growth is causing unwanted and chaotic expansion in many concentrated suburban areas and is simultaneously causing the tragic neglect and decline of both our center cities and our vast rural regions. The paradox of too much and too little growth occurring concurrently must be dealt with somewhere.

The problems related to national urban growth policy are complex because they are so intimately entangled among most other domestic urban and rural problems. Anthony Downs of Real Estate Research Corporation of Chicago summed up the problem in a recent meeting at the Department of Housing and Urban Development when he said that national urban growth policy is difficult to grasp because it is a code word for the future of the United States. I hope to touch on a few problems connected with growth policy, particularly as they relate to new communities implementation of this policy.

NEW COMMUNITIES PLANNING AND DEVELOPMENT PROCESS

In describing the new community development process, the following points are important: definition of a new community; the forms of federal assistance; progress in new communities development to date; an overview of the development process, broken down into the new community planning components and the time sequence; major problems and achievements in new community development.

Definition

An overly simplified concept of new communities is held by the public and by some academic and journalistic critics. This confusion is compounded by some large-scale subdivision developers who have wrapped their enterprises in the mantle of new communities. The general public often conceives of new communities only as satellite developments adjacent to large cities. Some academic critics conceive of them as part of a massive scheme to relocate population in nonmetropolitan areas. Their criticism is often aimed at existing suburbs purporting to be new communities, on the one hand, and grand schemes for creating free-standing developments on the other. Because of this confusion of definitions, there is virtually no agreement on the number of new communities existing in the United States today.

Perhaps the simplest way to approach the problem of definition is by using the federal new community regulations. The Act itself does not provide a definition, but only eligibility criteria for approval. According to the regulations, a new community is a development of significant size with a full range of urban functions. It must have most, if not all, of the functions, facilities, and services normally associated with a city or town, including jobs, housing, recreation, shopping, and schools. Large-scale developments without a significant job base are certainly not new communities and would not be eligible for federal assistance under Title VII. However, total self-sufficiency is not necessary. Most new communities, even in Europe, have a symbiotic relationship with nearby urban settlements, and particularly with large center cities.

The question of new community size is quite complicated. The average size and population of the new communities approved under the Act up to December 1972 was 57,209 at peak development on 5,611 acres. The peak populations range from 20,000 to 150,000, whereas the newest British and French new towns, which are actually "zones of urbanization," range anywhere from 250,000 to 700,000 in peak population since they embrace some old but mostly new development.

New towns intown under the Act may be as small as 12,000 people or cover 100 acres. Thus the size of new communities varies considerably. The general rule is that they should be significant in relationship to the surrounding cities or other developments. In a rural area, a new town may have a population of 10,000 or 15,000 at peak development, as long as this size is large enough to sustain a "critical mass."

Within this broad definition of functions and scale, there is room for many types of urban development. On one end of the spectrum are new towns intown within existing cities on land which is largely vacant or underutilized, such as Fort Lincoln in the District of Columbia, Cedar Riverside in Minneapolis, or Welfare Island in New York City. On the other end of the spectrum are the freestanding new towns in rural areas which are almost completely self-sufficient, such as Soul City in North Carolina, or Lake Havasu City in Arizona. Soul City was the first freestanding new community approved under the Act, while Lake Havasu was undertaken with private funds, making use of individual lot sale techniques with the provision of industry by the developer himself. In between are the small-town growth centers, such as the proposed Pattonsburg, Missouri, and the satellite new communities, which represent eleven of the fourteen new communities approved under the Act as of December 1972. Satellite communities are those within the market area of a metropolitan region.

Based on this definition and scale, there were probably about twenty non-Title VII communities in existence or in advanced planning stages when the new communities program was created in 1968. This is considerably fewer than the sixty-six large developments listed in 1969 by HUD, which were widely misunderstood as new communities. The list of eighteen new community developments (see Appendix 1) was culled from the broader 1969 list. The major criterion for selection was the presence of a substantial industrial component within the project.

Although these developments may be new communities, probably none would qualify without modification for federal assistance as new communities, since none has a substantial amount of low and moderate income housing and few have significant racial integration. Moreover, the quality of their planning varies considerably. Some other requirements they might have difficulty meeting, depending on the project, are the achievement of consistency with areawide planning, the preparation and filing of an environmental impact statement and the achievement of high environmental planning standards, the provision for adequate community services and facilities, citizen participation for renters as well as homeowners, compliance with an affirmative action program for equal opportunity in housing, employment, and minority entrepreneurship, and the demonstration of economic and financial feasibility. All these requirements are spelled out in the regulations which are based on broad criteria in the Act.

Forms of Federal Assistance

The major form of assistance provided by the federal government to new community developers is guarantee of long-term financial obligations which are sold by both public and private developers on the private market. Developers with projects approved under the Act sell bonds or debentures, typically with maturities of fifteen or twenty years, which bear the full faith and credit of the U.S. government. In case of financial default, the government would pay off bondholders. As security, typically the government would hold the first lien on the developer's property.

The importance of the guarantee to the private developer cannot be underestimated.

Private financial sources are simply not ready to make such long-term and, in their opinion, risky loans without asking for and receiving control of the project. The interest rates on guaranteed bonds, even including fees and charges of about 1 percent a year, would still be about 3 percent below comparable borrowings obtained without the federal guarantee for similar long-term projects.

Grants have been available which provide up to 20 percent of project cost to supplement the assistance provided under some thirteen federal programs, including HUD programs such as water and sewage systems and open space development.[1]

Assistance from other programs is also important. Without the interest subsidies from the FHA section 235 and 236 programs,[2] along with rent supplement payments (or some other form of housing or income supplement), it would be virtually impossible for developers to meet most of their full long-term obligations for low and moderate income housing. This federal support is quite significant for the fourteen new communities approved under the Act. The development plans and other documents show requirements for 67,502 units which, over the twenty-year life of all fourteen projects (approved as of December 1972), will assist persons and families within or below income limits for the federal 235 and 236 programs. This number represents 27 percent of the total 245,441 dwelling units for the life of all projects.

Another important source of help for the local governments impacted by new communities is the urban planning assistance program, which can assist public bodies in undertaking specific new community programs or in assessing the broader impact of the new community in other parts of the jurisdiction. This assistance has been made available to the state of North Carolina for planning the region around Soul City; to the Tri-County Planning Commission for planning around St. Charles, Mary-

land; and to the township of Flower Mound, in which the new community of Flower Mound is located in the Dallas-Fort Worth metropolitan area.

Progress to December 1972

Other assistance was authorized under the Act but has not been funded. The Act called for the creation of a Community Development Corporation within HUD governed by a five-man board of directors chaired by the secretary of HUD. The staff for the corporation is currently provided by the Office of New Communities Development.

As of December 1972 a total of fourteen projects had been approved under the Act. They cover 78,558 acres and will serve an estimated peak population of over 800,000. The total guarantee commitment was $253,-500,000. By then there were nineteen applications and twenty-five pre-application proposals. Given this "running start," in 1973 it was not unreasonable to project ten approvals each year for at least the next decade. At this rate of approval, if the new projects are of the same average size as the first fourteen, they would embrace 561,100 acres by the end of a decade and serve an eventual peak population of over 5.7 million. More recent estimates are much lower. Many pre-applications and applications have been rejected which were pending in early 1973.

Table 1 shows the acreage breakdown of these developments, Table 2 shows the low and moderate income housing, and Table 3, the guarantee dates of new communities.

By any reasonable estimate, new communities are becoming a significant part of the urban scene only a few years after the passage of the Act which established the initial program in 1968.

Development Process

The central task of this presentation is to

describe not the new communities program, but the planning application and review process. This process is shown graphically by the figure, "Illustrative New Community Process," which was prepared after the new community staff studied the development process for nine months and prepared the first draft of a 322-page handbook covering aspects of the new communities program. As of December 1972 the handbook was still being refined.

The diagram notes the components of the new community planning and application review process in the left margin from top to bottom and the sequence of steps (from right to left) required by a developer to plan a new community, as well as the series of federal actions required in reviewing these plans. The diagram summarizes over 100 steps of the process, from the idea in the developer's mind to the reality of the new community. It is improbable that any one new community developer would follow each of these steps; more likely, each one will follow a somewhat different pattern.

The diagram does illustrate a central point, however. Many goals and objectives (or components) must be considered at every step of planning the new community in increasing levels of detail. At each point, choices must be made in an attempt to optimize goals. If a logical, complete, and systematic process is not followed, basic problems may be discovered after the needless expense of hundreds of thousands of dollars. The more funds committed, the more difficult it becomes for a developer to turn back, regardless of whether or not federal assistance is provided (see figure).

Planning Components. The components of new community planning process are social, environmental, physical, economic, financial, governmental, and managerial. These components have formed the basis for reorganizing new community regulations and instructions to applicants. Conflict and compromise in the achievement of the underlying goals or com-

ponents occurs at every stage of the planning process. A far greater range of goals or components is considered in new community planning than in any other HUD program, with the possible exception of urban renewal or the model cities programs. Typically, the land development industry has been concerned with only several components, primarily the economic and financial matters, and has given minimal attention to governmental and environmental matters. A particularly poor job traditionally has been done by this industry in the social and environmental areas. Hence the need for HUD's more comprehensive approach.

Although there are considerable parallels with the general approach of the comprehensive planning process in the United States and the process shown here, there is one major difference. In the case of new communities, the developer owns the land and has the financial backing to carry out the plan which he has prepared. By comparison, a planning agency must rely on a whole host of public and private entities over which it exercises varying degrees of control. It cannot, itself, create a great commercial center. It can only influence someone who wants to build one. This ability to execute the plan on a fairly large scale severely tests the developer; his company's fortunes and those of his financial backers are literally "on the line." Furthermore, if he has received assistance from the federal government, he risks default at any stage in the process if he fails to carry out the plan to which he is committed. These risks have been reduced by permitting minor changes in the plan without governmental approval and allowing for annual revisions of the plan when conditions have changed, subject to the same criteria for approval as the original plan. The execution and completion of all these diverse elements calls for much more managerial ability than is normally required by builders and developers.

Time Sequence. Noted from left to right,

MAJOR STAGES:
PLANNING/APPLICATION PROCESS

BASIC FEASIBILITY	REQUIREMENTS ANALYSI
SITE SELECTION-ACQUISITION	BACKGROUND ANALYSIS - CONCEPT PLANS

FEDERAL SUBMISSION
REQUIREMENTS

INQUIRY   A-95 NOTICE   PRE-APPLICATION

SOCIAL COMPONENT

(10) REVISE AS NECESSARY   (10) REVISE AS NECESSARY   (10) REVISE AS NECESSARY   (10) REVISE AS NECESSARY

(02) DEFINE GOALS
(03) SITE SELECTION CRITERIA

(15) OVERALL SITE SUITABILITY ANALYSIS
(17) IDENTIFY MAJOR DEV CONSTRAINTS / OPPORT

(20) REFINE GOALS OBJECTIVES
(21) PRELIM REG & SITE ANAL (EXIST G DATA)
(22) PRELIM INVENTORY STATE -OF- ART
(26) PRELIM ALTERNATIVE CONCEPT PLANS

(30) REG & SITE ANAL (NEW DATA)
(31) REFINE STATE -OF- ART ANALYSIS
(39) REFINE CONCEPT PLANS

ENVIRONMENTAL COMPONENT

(02) DEFINE GOALS
(03) SITE SELECTION CRITERIA

(15) OVERALL SITE SUITABILITY ANALYSIS
(17) IDENTIFY MAJOR DEV CONSTRAINTS / OPPORT

(20) REFINE GOALS OBJECTIVES
(21) PRELIM REG & SITE ANAL (EXIST G DATA)
(22) PRELIM INVENTORY STATE -OF- ART
(26) PRELIM ALTERNATIVE CONCEPT PLANS

(30) REG & SITE ANAL (NEW DATA)
(31) REFINE STATE -OF- ART ANALYSIS
(39) REFINE CONCEPT PLANS

PHYSICAL COMPONENT

(02) DEFINE GOALS
(03) SITE SELECTION CRITERIA

(15) OVERALL SITE SUITABILITY ANALYSIS
(17) IDENTIFY MAJOR DEV CONSTRAINTS / OPPORT

(20) REFINE GOALS OBJECTIVES
(21) PRELIM REG & SITE ANAL (EXIST G DATA)
(22) PRELIM INVENTORY STATE -OF- ART
(26) PRELIM ALTERNATIVE CONCEPT PLANS

(30) REG & SITE ANAL (NEW DATA)
(31) REFINE STATE -OF- ART ANALYSIS
(39) REFINE CONCEPT PLANS

PROGRAMMING

(25) ROUGH NT POPULATION PROJECTIONS

(32) MATH MODEL DEV OR ACQUISITION/REFINEMENT

ECONOMIC COMPONENT

(02) DEFINE GOALS
(03) SITE SELECTION CRITERIA

(16) PRELIM ECONOMIC BASE STUDIES
(17) IDENTIFY MAJOR DEV CONSTRAINTS / OPPORT

(20) REFINE GOALS OBJECTIVES
(23) PRELIM DEMOGRAPHIC ANALYSIS

(32) MATH MODEL DEV OR ACQUISITION REFINEMENT
(33) REFINE ECONOMIC BASE ANALYSIS
(34) REFINE MARKET ANALYSIS
(35) REFINE & RECONCILE DEMOGRAPHIC ANALYSIS

FINANCIAL COMPONENT

(05) PRELIM FINANCIAL ANALYSIS / PLANNING

(17) IDENTIFY MAJOR DEV CONSTRAINTS / OPPORT
(18) OBTAIN FINANCING LAND ACQUISITION

(05) PRELIM FINANCIAL ANALYSIS / PLANNING

(32) MATH MODEL DEV OR ACQUISITION / REFINEMENT
(36) IDENTIFY SOURCES OBT FED PLANNING ASS'T

GOVERNMENTAL COMPONENT

(02) DEFINE GOALS
(03) SITE SELECTION CRITERIA

(12) IDENTIFY KEY GOV'T AGENCIES
(13) ESTABLISH GOV'T LIASON/REVIEW
(14) REVIEW AREAWIDE PLANS
(17) IDENTIFY MAJOR DEV CONSTRAINTS / OPPORT

(29) MAINTAIN GOV'T LIASON/REVIEW
(20) REFINE GOALS / OBJECTIVES

(29) MAINTAIN GOV'T LIASON / REVIEW

MANAGEMENT COMPONENT

(01) ON GOING MANAGEMENT

(01) ON GOING MANAGEMENT
(10) IDENTIFY/ASSEMBLE PLAN/MANAGE TEAM

(01) ON GOING MANAGEMENT
(27) LOCAL INVOLVEMENT PLAN (GOV'T & C P)
(28) PLANNING WORK PROGRAM

(01) ON GOING MANAGEMENT
(27) DEV / IMPLEMENT INTERIM LAND MANAGEMENT PLAN

IMPLEMENTATION

(38) PRELIM DISCUSSIONS INDUSTRIAL SALES

(38) PRELIM DISCUSSIONS INDUSTRIAL SALES

(04) IDENTIFY CANDIDATE REGIONS

(11) IDENTIFY CANDIDATE SITES

(100) LAND AQUISITION

COMMUNITY PROCESS

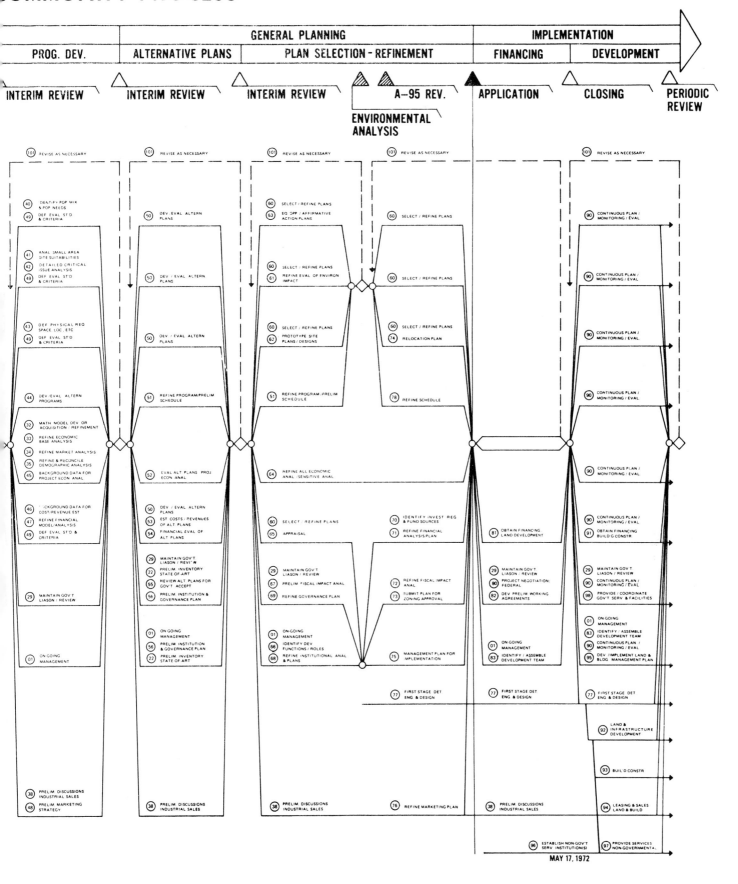

the diagram (see figure) details the time sequence of the developer's actions in preparing the new community plan, in applying for federal assistance, and the parallel federal action in reviewing plans and taking action at each stage of processing. The major benchmarks are the initial goal-setting, choices of site selection criteria based upon these goals, the "preliminary inquiry" with the federal government, the submission of a "pre-application proposal," the preparation of initial background studies as part of the formal application, initial programming decisions, the evaluation of alternative plans, the preparation of an environmental analysis and an environmental impact statement, the "A-95 clearance," the offer and acceptance of commitment, the project agreement, and finally the sale of bonds and project execution. This entire process may typically take several years.

Whether developers formally recognize it or not, the first step in the process is that of goal-setting. Where the goals are relatively simple, such as the maximization of profit, this process is not too complex. The site is chosen with the best access to markets and purchased at the cost and capability of producing expected revenues which will yield an acceptable rate of return. However, with the complex social, environmental, and other goals of a balanced new community, the process is much more complicated. Unless goals are made clear from the beginning and site selection criteria are specifically laid out to achieve these goals, the wrong site could easily be chosen. For example, there are certain areas which are unsuitable for development from an environmental viewpoint. Unless the developer considers environmental goals critical, he is not likely to weigh them very highly in his site selection process. Once a poor site is built upon, little can be done to correct the situation.

Often site selection is, in fact, based on "targets of opportunity." A developer or his partners may have a large parcel of land in prior ownership. From their viewpoint, it may be the only practical option. The developer will either develop this site as a new community or sell it for conventional residential or commercial uses. In other cases, sites are consciously chosen to optimize stated developer objectives. Soul City is a good case in point. Floyd McKissick wanted to develop a new community in an area which was politically feasible for strong minority involvement. He chose a rural county in North Carolina with a large, poor, minority population. Had he chosen a site closer to existing suburban development, it might not have been feasible to achieve this particular set of objectives.

Needless to say, in the absence of eminent domain authority, the private developer does not have unlimited options for locating a new community site. He is limited by a whole range of factors, including land availability at reasonable prices. Although public developers should have many options with eminent domain authority, our experience indicates that they, too, have difficulty with site selection. They are faced with a limited number of political "targets of opportunity."

The second step encouraged by HUD is the informal discussion of the project in the central office even before a "pre-application proposal" is prepared. This discussion reduces the possibilities of a developer's coming to HUD with a proposal containing obvious deficiencies. Literally hundreds of inquiries have been received in the central and regional offices over the past several years. This informal process of screening permits the department to exercise priorities and to encourage projects, by category and location, which are consistent with national goals.

Although these projects are encouraged or discouraged at this very early stage, this action is not a formal part of a "grand national design." Among the types of projects encouraged are: those which are in regions or sections where few applications have been approved; new town intown and small town growth centers, which represent types for which HUD has offered few commitments; and very innovative projects. Special attention is also given to projects which appear to be outstanding in terms of their ability to serve HUD's social goals.

Developers not seeking federal assistance would probably follow a parallel path with state and local governments when planning a new community. Informal checks would be made with political leaders to assess the climate of opinion before securing options, purchasing land, or making any other commitments of resources.

The first formal material sent into the HUD office is the "pre-application proposal." This constitutes a general treatment of the broad requirements of the law and the capability of the new community to meet them. Maximum use is made of existing inventories and analyses. A proposal typically includes a sketched physical plan, a discussion of threshold environmental issues, an indication of the political climate for the project, a rough economic feasibility study indicating the anticipated marketability of the new community, and an analysis of social goals and the means to their achievement. The critical purpose of this early analysis is the identification of threshold problems which would present insurmountable obstacles to approval at a later date. Pre-applications are examined not only for their capacity to meet the technical requirements of the law, but also for their attentiveness to the HUD priorities discussed above.

The parallel step in the private sector, where federal assistance is not involved, is a presentation to a bank or insurance company in order to secure initial land acquisition capital. The investor would, of course, want to know enough about the project to determine whether or not it appears to be a good investment.

The first significant federal action is the review of this pre-application proposal, and the expression of either a favorable or an unfavorable response. If a project is deemed desirable, a formal letter is sent to the developer indicating HUD's willingness to accept a full application. This letter implies no federal commitment to eventual approval of any kind.

Once work on the full application begins, the serious business of planning a new community is initiated. Ideally, first in this series of steps leading to the complete application are background studies and initial programming to meet the goals of the new community. Detailed environmental analysis, market study, financial forecasts, and social components studies are undertaken. These should lead to the initial programming of the number of housing units, and should form the background essential for shaping the final plan. They should also reveal those threshold problems of feasibility which were not revealed during the pre-application stage. A final plan is likely to be deficient if it is prepared without considering these detailed background studies, since the economic, social, environmental, and financial constraints of the site will not be known or fully appreciated.

A key point in the planning and development process is the stage where alternative plans and programs are examined and tested against stated objectives. Unfortunately, in the current state of the art of new community planning, we are most sophisticated in evaluating planning options against financial criteria. The computerized cash flow systems, such as the Columbia, Maryland, "economic model," permit all major development decisions to be measured in terms of their impact on the projected discounted rate of return on investment. Sensitivity runs can be made to determine how various plans affect financial feasibility. At least three different approaches to this testing process can be seen in three different HUD-sponsored research projects undertaken by Real Estate Research Corporation, Decision Sciences Corporation, and General Electric TEMPO.[3] Other leading consultants in new communities planning also have financial models.

It is far more difficult to assess different planning options against economic, environmental, social, and governmental constraints. In these areas, tools are far less sophisticated. We plan to undertake research to increase the capacity of HUD and developers to assess alternative plans against all these criteria. For example, HUD-sponsored research is underway with the National League of Cities and with Linton, Mields, and Coston to assess governance of new communities and relationships with local governments. Another contract is outstanding with the Decision Sciences Corporation, Real Estate Research, and the Match Institute to develop a complete interlocking series of models (NUCOMS, or "new community simulation system") which would show interrelationships among the economic growth of the region and regional sectors, the development pace of the new community, and the developer's cash flow and the fiscal impact of the new community on local government. Preliminary work has also been done by the Metropolitan Applied Research Center in New York in assessing difficult social issues in new communities. Additional research is under consideration in environmental planning, management, and other fields.

The ideal of testing options is not often achieved in the planning process of new communities. Too often the first plan that HUD sees is the developer's final plan, which he defends as "the best." A frequent criticism of environmental statements is that no real alternatives are presented in terms of their environmental impact, including the alternative of not building a new community at all.

Few items of the application process have generated so much controversy and public interest as the environmental impact statements and the analyses upon which they are based. In this age of ecological awareness, citizens, local groups, and governmental bodies are very concerned about the environmental impact of large-scale developments. Moreover, in most new community projects some environmental conflicts arise. Therefore, the developer is required to undertake continued environmental analysis through all stages of project development. Based upon this analysis and the federal government's own assessment, HUD prepares draft and final environmental impact statements. These statements describe the environment of the site before development, outline the proposed new community plan and alternatives to it, and assess the direct and indirect environmental impact of these alternative plans. All environmental impact statements are available from the National Technical Information Service (see Appendix 2).

The final environmental impact statements include all relevant comments from private citizens, local agencies, federal departments, and environmental experts, and must be issued before an offer of federal commitment for a loan guarantee can be made. Thus readers can judge for themselves the environmental issues involved. The more experience gained with undertaking environmental analyses, the more sophisticated the statement becomes.

However, the developer's early environmental analysis which forms the basis for creating alternative plans and programs and his early assessments of the environmental constraints of the site during the pre-application phase are probably more important in shaping actual decisions than the final environmental impact statement. The final statement provides an opportunity for public comment and increases the incentive for continuing developer and governmental concern for environmental issues. The existence of a few legal suits over inadequate statements places environmental questions on a higher plane than would normally have been the case.

Another outside check on the quality of new community planning and its relation to regional goals is the so-called A-95 procedure, based on the U.S. Office Management and Budget Circular A-95. This is designed to insure that regional clearinghouse agencies have an opportunity to comment on all major projects likely to receive federal assistance well before irrevocable federal action is taken. Even during the pre-application phase, initial notice of possible federal action is given to regional clearinghouses. A-95 reviews often serve as avenues for public discussion of environmental questions. The issues concerning the underground aquifer in the San Antonio Ranch new community, and the Thorn Creek Woods controversy in the case of Park Forest South, were first raised through regional A-95 review.

Once the HUD staff has determined that all requirements of the Act have been met, it prepares for the Community Development Corporation general manager a recommendation to the CDC board for project approval. The board frequently debates the issues on a specific project for several monthly meetings in a row before authorizing the secretary to issue an offer of commitment. When a commitment offer is made, it is often subject to certain conditions. For example, the developer is required to resolve some outstanding issues before accepting the offer. In the case of Soul City, a major condition was obtaining some commitment from industry to locate in the new community. In the case of San Antonio Ranch, the condition was that a positive finding be achieved and accepted by local authorities from a special study required regarding the pollution of the aquifer.

The developer has 120 days to accept the offer of commitment, although this period may be extended by the secretary. The offer permits the developer to make initial arrangements for permanent financing of the new community. Typically, a Wall Street underwriter or consortium of underwriters is chosen to float the bonds or debentures, although in at least one case (Maumelle, Arkansas) a

"private placement" to a single lender was made. Upon acceptance of the offer, the developer pays a commitment fee of 0.5 percent to HUD. This is based upon the total dollar amount of the commitment made.

When commitment conditions have been met and the commitment offer is accepted, the hard work of negotiating the project agreement and trust indenture begins. These documents define the rights and obligations of the developer and of the government for the life of the project. The trust indenture relates primarily to financial matters, including also a third party, the trustee, who holds in escrow the proceeds from the sale of bonds, which are drawn down upon certification of costs actually expended. The project agreement defines the conditions of performance default and other matters, and has appended a development plan which describes the plan to which the developer is legally committed for the life of the project. Both project agreements and trust indentures are available from the National Technical Information Service (see Appendix 2).

After the detailed negotiation is completed for the trust indenture and project agreement, the developer's bonds or debentures, usually bearing maturities of twenty years, are sold on the private market. Carrying the credit of the U.S. government, new community obligations generally bear interest rates from 7 to 7.5 percent. A list of bond sale prices and guarantee amounts is shown in Table 3. A guarantee fee of 3 percent of the financial obligations actually sold is paid by private developers to the federal government. The funds are placed in the new communities revolving fund, which had reached nearly $8 million as of December 1972. The revolving fund is invested and draws interest for the government.

Proceeds from the sale of bonds are placed in escrow with a trustee mutually acceptable to HUD and the developer. There is an initial draw down from escrow immediately after closing to pay for land acquisition and other expenditures which have already been made.

Major Problems and Achievements

There are many fundamental problems and potentials for achievement in new communities which are clearly apparent four years after passage of the original 1968 Act. Although time and space do not permit exploration of all of them here, among the central issues worth discussing are race and class, the establishment of an industrial base, and governance considerations.

Social Goals and Problems. The physical goals of developing a new community present a manageable problem to be overcome. However, the social goals represent fundamental problems, the solutions for which have few precedents. The basic social goal of the program is that new communities should be open to all Americans regardless of race or class. Furthermore, there should be adequate services and facilities to support these people. Jobs, community facilities, social services, health, education, transportation, recreation, and cultural facilities must be geared to the income and racial mixture in the new communities.

The statute defines no racial or class quotas. It merely says that there shall be a substantial amount of housing for persons of low and moderate income. Related civil rights legislation calls for compliance with laws and executive orders regarding provision of equal opportunities in jobs, housing, community facilities, and minority entrepreneurship. The new communities program simultaneously tackles the issues of race and class.

Table 2 shows the number of housing units which must serve persons and families of low and moderate income in fourteen approved new communities. Actual percentages of these units range from 16 percent to over 40 percent for individual projects, with most agreements requiring renegotiation of income mix after

five years, and periodically thereafter, to more closely resemble the income mix of the metropolitan area in which the new community is located. There are three factors which determine an acceptable income mix in any one project: the metropolitan area income profile, expected employment within the project, and supply and demand factors. Over 67,000 units of low and moderate income housing are projected for these fourteen new communities, which is 27 percent of the total of 245,000 units projected for twenty years. Housing mix formulae are now under reconsideration.

Early experience with racial integration in our new communities leads us to believe that new communities can approximate metropolitan racial and income profiles. Jonathan, Minnesota, has about 4 percent black population in its initial stage of development, corresponding with 3 percent in the metropolitan area; Park Forest South, Illinois, has a 19 percent black population.

What is the probability of success in attempting to provide truly open communities? There is probably no single answer to the question. It will depend upon the climate in the metropolitan area in which the new community is located; the skill of the developer in managing his enterprise; the flexibility and degree of support of the federal, state, and local governments; the attitude of the initial residents; and a host of other factors. I am cautiously optimistic about the outcome. That optimism is based upon general trends in American society pointing to a reduction in prejudice, particularly among younger people of both North and South. It is also based on the new communities movement which involves planning for total living environments. Because of their size and the fact that they are relatively undeveloped when the site is selected, new communities could become "neutral turf" which does not assume the coloration of a single race or class. Persons coming to a new community should know in advance that the settlement will encompass a complete spectrum of incomes and races.

In contrast, an effort to place low-income housing and achieve racial integration in existing highly segregated subdivisions and cities is more difficult, since patterns of race and class have already been defined in most major cities with sizeable minority populations. Where "integration" occurs in previously segregated areas, it often happens at the periphery of the black ghetto, in the center city, or in the inner suburbs. Because these areas are bottled up, they explode at the borders where "block busting" realtors use scare tactics to drive out white renters and homeowners. Efforts to place low-income housing in existing suburban or middle-class areas of the city have often met with violent resistance. However, current court cases and site selection criteria for subsidized housing all tend to move in the direction of dispersion as the basis for federal policy. Some progress has been made toward remedying these conditions, but it is slow and painful.

Despite the difficulties, the general attack on concentration of the poor and the minorities in the ghetto must proceed. Although a new community may set an example to follow, pressures on it will be immense if it is the only project in a metropolitan area to achieve genuine race and class integration. Already in one project realtors are referring minority buyers to the new community in a highly segregated metropolitan area to keep them out of predominantly white areas. It may be that new community projects in Chicago, Houston, Little Rock, and Dallas will be the only major developments to achieve integration by both race and class in the next several years. Concentrated federal efforts must insure that this exclusive situation does not last for long, since progress is easier when it occurs on all fronts.

Existing experience and research offer little guidance in predicting success or failure of simultaneous race and class integration. A major conclusion of a yet unpublished preliminary study by the Metropolitan Applied Research Center (MARC) in New York, on the social components of new communities, states that there is virtually no precedent in the United States or Europe for achieving racial and class integration simultaneously and on a large scale where significant minority populations are involved. Little documentation is available on the degree of race and class mixing in federal urban renewal projects, which constitute the largest parallel development offering a precedent comparable in scale and complexity to new communities.

Existing new communities or large developments initiated before Title VII are not generally integrated either by race or by class. An outstanding exception with regard to racial integration is Columbia, Maryland, which has about 17 percent black population. However, the average black income is higher than white income in Columbia, and there is less than 10 percent subsidized housing. It is, therefore, not a true test of race and class mixing. Many European new communities have a good cross-section of income, except for the very upper and very lower incomes. However, they are often racially homogeneous. Only Israeli new communities have dual integration. They "solve" the problem of class and cultural conflicts by placing immigrants from various countries according to their own wishes, in separate enclaves; they use segregation in the attempt to achieve integration later in a more natural course of events. These new towns are unified by a common national goal and a common religion. It is probable that this segregation is voluntary because immigrants feel most comfortable with persons of similar national origins in the early stage of their new lives.

The preliminary conclusions of the MARC study are echoed by a report to HUD written by a team of leading social scientists under the auspices of the National Academy of Sciences.[4] This committee concluded that as long as either race or class are held constant, each type of integration can be achieved; but when both are attempted simultaneously, there is less precedent upon which to be confident of success.

Among the variables affecting success or failure will be the location and management of low and moderate income housing in the new community, policies to insure balanced integration, quality of the affirmative action programs, success of development of the job base, and quality and quantity of social services.

Although a phenomenal amount of low and moderate income housing has been approved by HUD in the past four years (1.3 million units), a continued controversy has ensued about the location of this housing. Typically, it has been located in areas where minority and low-income concentrations already existed. This policy has been challenged by the courts. Revised site selection criteria have been sought to divert this housing away from existing ghettos.

Similarly, the policy with regard to new communities is a dispersion of low and moderate income housing within the new community. The unit of integration is the neighborhood. Primary school and neighborhood shops should serve a full range of incomes. This does not necessarily require placing a $15,000 house next to a $60,000 one; rather, there may be different income characteristics on different blocks. However, an attempt is made to eliminate "projectitis," where a development becomes identified by its residents and the town in general as subsidized housing, with an accompanying social stigma. Cedar Riverside in Minneapolis has become the first development in the country to achieve complete integration in the first stage of their 1,300 units. One complex contains FHA section 236 rentals, moderate-cost housing which receives reductions in property taxes by state law, leased public housing, and market rate units. Subsidized and nonsubsidized units are also planned within a single complex in Park Forest South,

near Chicago. Many developers have expressed interest in the housing allowance program which permits tying in subsidies with individuals rather than with houses, so that there would be no visible differences between subsidized and nonsubsidized housing. This is still in the experimental stage.

Accompanying the policy of income mix by neighborhood is the parallel policy of integration by race. Developers attempt to persuade blacks moving into their development not to resegregate themselves. This has been a problem in one project in that blacks, for social and other reasons, have tended to gravitate to areas in which black families are already living. James Rouse at Columbia faces a similar problem, since several of the teen centers have become identified as black centers. As a developer, he has opposed efforts of young blacks to have black dances, since this is against the policy of an open society.

In undertaking his initial analysis of the potential of integration in new communities, a leading sociologist, Herbert Gans, has predicted that there would be some voluntary segregation in new towns. Perhaps there is a difference between forced segregation and self-segregation, but HUD still does not encourage segregation in any form. In compliance with court guidelines on school integration, there will be integrated schools in new communities and elsewhere. I suspect that if voluntary segregation of neighborhoods were permitted, tensions in their integrated schools would increase. Automatically, racial differences will reinforce differences due to any territorial sense.

Some of the MARC interviews and certain expressions from black leadership in Detroit and elsewhere indicate that there may be a reluctance on the part of lower-income blacks to come to suburban new towns. Some would prefer new towns intown which are in their own "territory." This feeling of black leaders, expressed in a 1968 conference in St. Claire

Shores, led to the "paired new towns" concept of the Metropolitan Fund in which a new town intown would be matched with a suburban new town.[5] The black leaders were concerned about the dilution of their political base and doubted whether their constituents would be welcome in a suburban new town.

Researchers for the MARC team and others have argued for black new towns, particularly in the rural south, on the grounds that America is still not ready for integration on a large scale and that southern blacks should have an option in addition to that of moving to northern ghettos. In approving Soul City, HUD implicitly recognized that there may be minority-controlled projects which will have a special appeal to minorities. Of course, minority developers will have to apply the same affirmative action programs followed by majority developers. Therefore, it is highly unlikely that Soul City will be an all-black new town. In order to establish a strong industrial base, white as well as black firms will have to be attracted.

No one can fully predict the reaction of minorities to a given new town. However, developers must let minority groups know that they are welcome. This will help implement the basic policy that people have a right to live wherever they want to live. White real estate firms, banks, builders, and local governments are violating a basic human right when they determine where people can and cannot live. Many minority residents have moved to Columbia and to Park Forest South, not because they are seeking integrated living as an end in itself, but because they are seeking a better living environment at reasonable prices, sources of employment, and good schools. There are too few places in existing racial ghettos where these goals can be achieved.

A key part of achieving successful integration in a new community is the affirmative action program which all developers must follow. The program will necessarily vary with each new community, but it generally consists of advertising in publications which appeal to minority as well as majority audiences. It also includes meeting special goals for minority employment on the developer's staff and with all contractors and subcontractors employed in the new community. In the more recent programs, there have been efforts to encourage minority entrepreneurship.

All of these efforts are interrelated in that minorities certainly would also have a propensity to live near where they work. Often firms moving to the suburbs from the central cities have found that their minority employees have difficulty finding homes.

The most difficult questions relating to race are likely to arise where there are also class questions. I agree with Edward Banfield that the fundamental tension in American society comes from class conflict, not racial conflict, although issues become confused with high crime rates in black areas.[6] Similarly, the issue became confused during the first thirty years of this century when lower-class Italian and other immigrants had a higher crime rate than their numbers would have indicated. Anti-immigrant feeling ran high; it was based, in my opinion, on conflicts in lifestyle which were, in turn, based on class differences.[7] The white blue-collar workers and elderly persons living in the central cities who, along with the blacks themselves, share the brunt of crime problems, find difficulty in separating race and class issues.

Crime becomes a code word for class conflict which is only exacerbated by race. It will take decades of education, training, and achievement of steady employment and upward social and occupational mobility before "hard core" anti-social behavior often centered in ghettos can be overcome. The new communities program as it is presently constructed, with minimum federal subsidies, is not likely to be the sole weapon for attacking this problem. It must work closely with state and local antipoverty programs. However, new communities may well provide an avenue of upward mobility for those who are beginning to escape the cycle of poverty, despair, and crime. Rehabilitation does little good if the poor continue to be trapped in the same dismal environment which has been the early breeding ground for their anti-social behavior. New communities can make an important contribution to the larger effort to lessen crime and solve problems.

Employment Base. The degree to which the new community's ambitious goals of providing substantial amounts of low and moderate income housing are successful will depend largely on the number and composition of jobs which are created there and the speed with which industries are attracted.

Typically pre-Title VII new community developers have sought white-collar industry. As a matter of policy, Title VII developers are required to seek sources of employment using a full range of skills with opportunity for upward mobility. For large new towns, blue-collar industry is highly desirable in that it would insure sufficient demand to create a balanced new town. If only white-collar industry is attracted, it is unlikely that there would be sufficient demand in the new community for the large amount of low and moderate income housing, unless this new community were located adjacent to a major industrial center.

The policy of seeking other than white-collar industry creates some worries about possible conflict with the goal of ensuring air and water pollution control in new communities, since blue-collar industries often produce pollution. Perhaps experiments can be done to create systems in which these industries may share pollution control devices in order to achieve economies of scale. One developer is considering a noncontiguous site for heavy industry, within easy reach of the new community.

The job mix is important in a new commu-

nity because, although we can require developers to prepare sites for low and moderate income housing and even require a subsidiary to build it with federal subsidies, there is no way to force lower-income persons to seek homes in the new community if there are no jobs for which they are qualified nearby. If vacancy rates are high in this housing, its pace of development must be reduced until sufficient demand can be generated. Some argue that there is such a shortage of housing for low and moderate income persons that there will be demand anywhere. Nonetheless, local demand for this housing is likely to be increased if the new community has a substantial job base with skill requirements which can be attained by persons of low and moderate income. In existing suburbs and some new communities, there is an excess of demand for low and moderate housing. For example, many workers in the GE plant in Columbia and in the industrial facilities in Irvine Ranch, California, have to commute long distances because they cannot find housing within their price range in the new community. I shall discuss the special problems of attracting industry to nonmetropolitan locations in the section dealing with national growth policy.

Governance and Intergovernmental Relations. In planning and developing a new community, two of the most troublesome issues are related to governance: first, how to provide the necessary services for the new community itself; and second, how to get along with the existing local units of government which have jurisdiction over the new community. Unless developers give these twin issues careful attention, they may not succeed in their enterprise. Many vital components of the new communities must be provided by or undertaken under the supervision of governmental or quasi-governmental units.

The issue would not be so difficult if it were not for the ambitious social objectives of the program. However, considering the substantial number of low and moderate income families projected for the new community, the hopes for full citizen participation, and the goal of provision of a high level of services, the resulting problem of finding the most democratic, equitable, and efficient method of supplying these services is difficult indeed. In the long run, assuming successful industrial and commercial development in the new community, adequate services can probably be provided because of the strong tax base. In the short run, however, tensions may develop, especially when the immediate impact of the new community on the school system is felt. The Public Service Grant program authorized in the Act would have helped solve this transitional problem; it would have provided funds for essential services during the initial three years of the new community. However, the program was not funded, and new communities assisted under the Act (and their local governments) will have to get along without it.

There are several prototype approaches to providing services in a new community: municipal incorporation or annexation, special districts, homes associations, community associations, the "dual developer," or any combination of these. Each approach has its advantages and disadvantages.

Municipal incorporation was the governance route taken by Park Forest South. In this plan, as the developer purchases additional land, he petitions that it be included within the municipal jurisdiction of the village of Park Forest South, which was created only when the new town idea was conceived. The plan for the newly annexed land is included within the zoning scheme of the village. Any changes in the plan must be approved by the village board. The advantage of incorporation is that it encourages general purpose units of governments. Federal policy discourages local fragmentation by special purpose units. The disadvantage of incorporation is that the "pio-

neers" of the new community may gain control of the village board and frustrate continued development of the new community plan. Furthermore, in many jurisdictions municipal incorporation is impossible. In Reston, for example, it was impossible to incorporate, since the new community is located in an urban county where new incorporations are not permitted.

Jonathan relied upon annexation to the existing small town of Chaska (population 2,500) in the far suburbs of Minneapolis. San Antonio Ranch may eventually be annexed by San Antonio. The disadvantage of annexation or reliance upon existing larger units of government, without an intervening entity providing services, is that the new community usually calls for a higher level of services on a "pre-serviced" basis, not available at that level in the jurisdiction at large.

Formation of a special district was the predominant technique by which many services were financed in the pre-Title VII California new towns. This plan has the advantage of offering tax-free financing and removing "front end" costs from the price of the lot. Some speculate that the little interest shown by California developers in the new community program is due to the fact that interest rates on borrowing through these special districts is more favorable than that of Title VII financing, which must rely on the private bond market at non-tax-exempt rates. Consideration is being given to the use of Municipal Utility Districts (MUD) with special controls by local government in the Texas new communities, such as Flower Mound near Dallas. The disadvantage of this approach is that government is trying to discourage special purpose units of government in order to reduce fragmentation of these units in the United States.

The homes association is the most common form of delivering services in the thousands of cluster developments approved by the FHA. Homes associations are nongovernmental bodies with the primary function of managing recreation facilities and common open space. Capital facilities owned by the associations are generally turned over without cost by the developer, who pays for the facilities by increasing the prices of the lots he sells to residents of the development. Operating costs are received from assessments running with the land, secured by a lien on the property, enforced by covenants placed on the land to which the homeowner must agree when he purchases property in the new community. Often the assessments are flat fees, rather than assessments based on property value, but this is not necessarily the case. These associations have performed their function well for developments of subdivision size, which are homogeneous by family income and, generally, by racial composition. However, unless they are modified, they are less suited to provide services for an entire new community. They tend to drive the price of the land and housing up so that it may be difficult to provide a full range of low and moderate income housing. In addition, in a recent symposium, residents of Reston complained about the level of services compared with that of Columbia, which is governed by a community association.[8]

The community association typified by the Columbia Park and Recreation Association includes provision for assessments not only of private homes, but also of commercial and industrial and other developed property. Assessments are progressive and based on property value. This approach was initiated by Columbia, Maryland, and is considered by many to offer advantages over the homes association. In the first place, it is a better source of financing in that commercial and industrial properties are included which increase in value over time. By contrast, some preliminary studies by the Virginia Polytechnic Institute New Communities Study Center have indicated that Reston generates more tax dollars than it re-

ceives in educational services and more than comparable residential suburban developments.[9] Thus it has fewer funds than the Columbia Association for "pre-serviced" facilities. An advantage of the Columbia variable assessments scheme over the flat fee approach is that persons are assessed partly on their ability to pay. This feature makes the technique advantageous where substantial numbers of low and moderate income families are present. Unfortunately for Columbia, the huge General Electric plant is not included within the Columbia Park and Recreation Association's jurisdiction; all these tax dollars go to the county. Opponents of the Columbia approach point out that consumers may not take into account the stream of future assessments and pay double (or at least more) for the same facilities, providing developer "windfalls." In addition, they argue that payments for facilities in lot prices permits deduction of interest payments on income tax.

Complicating matters, it is possible to combine parts of both the Reston and Columbia approaches: namely, pay for facilities in the lot price and, at the same time, have a variable assessment and assessment of industrial and commercial properties.

A totally new approach is offered by the proposed new community of Newfields (near Dayton, Ohio), approved in 1973. The developer proposed a "dual developer," one public and one private, with HUD guaranteeing the bonds of both entities. This is the only form of governance proposed, other than municipal incorporation or annexation, where the developer does not control the entity by majority vote during the early years. The developer retains a minority vote, with a majority exercised by representatives of local governing bodies and private citizens. In addition, the public authority has progressive income tax power to help raise funds. It may also sell tax-exempt bonds. However, the same objections may be leveled at this form of service delivery as against the community association: the potential exists for the developer to gain a windfall by failing to pass on all of the savings generated by public financing to the lot purchaser. With this technique the developer could also reduce his equity requirement. Space does not permit a full exposition of all the issues of new community governance; however, a major point is that there is not a single or clear solution to this complex problem, and continued experiments are needed.

The second half of the problem of governance deals with establishing and maintaining good relations with local government. The problem is illustrated by the new community of St. Charles in Charles County, Maryland. Although at the time of commitment there was a general statement from the county board of supervisors concerning the desirability of the new community, it took several years before specific governmental approvals could be obtained to actually proceed with the development. It took a year before a Planned Unit Development ordinance was passed, and another year before that ordinance was applied to the new community. To avoid repetition of this problem, the current draft HUD regulations require not only that the local governing body should pass a general resolution approving in concept the whole new community, but also that the initial stages of development should actually be covered by zoning to permit the new community to begin without delay.

To allay local government's legitimate fears about the impact of the new community, the developer, as part of his regular application, must prepare and submit a fiscal impact statement. He must demonstrate that the long-term financial impact of the new community on the local government is positive. Typically, suburban jurisdictions impacted by new communities are merely trading one form of development for another; seldom does a suburban jurisdiction have the option of no development. Land use controls have not yet been applied which can stop development altogether, although they may postpone it.

New communities must provide a better alternative to traditional suburban development from the viewpoint of social, environmental, and fiscal impact. They should bring in high tax-paying industries and commercial enterprises to balance residential development, with its demand for schools and other social services. In addition, due to their large size and capacity to control density configurations, the potential exists for reducing costs of water, sewers, and streets on a per capita basis. Studies in Howard County, Maryland, and Staten Island, New York, have projected substantial tax advantages for cost savings over a long period if the option of the location is chosen, as opposed to unplanned urban sprawl.[10] Thus, in the long run, the interests of a carefully planned new community and the suburban jurisdiction should coincide. In the short run, there may be some problems to be worked out.

Part of the new community's impact on the local jurisdiction is handled by direct federal grants. As of fall 1972, some $17 million in federal basic and supplemental grant assistance had been granted or obligated to local jurisdictions impacted by new communities. This was largely in the form of assistance for construction of water, sewer, and waste treatment facilities, and the purchase and development of parks. Aid is also now under consideration for hospitals and other public facilities.

NATIONAL URBAN GROWTH POLICY

While Part B of the Act covers new communities and has formed the basis for the above discussion, Part A of the Act treats the question of a national urban growth policy, called "national growth policy" in the 1972 Annual Growth Report, to cover both urban and rural development. This pairing indicates that new communities are seen as major instruments of national growth policy.

In South America, notably in Brazil and Venezuela; in Europe, particularly in England, France, Sweden, and Finland; and in Russia, Israel, Japan, and India, new communities are regarded as major instruments of the federal government to create new national settlement patterns. Brasilia, now with a population of over 500,000, was a wedge to open the vast and undeveloped hinterland of Brazil; Ciudad Guiana in Venezuela was designed to create new industrial centers away from Caracas; and the Soviet Union has created the most massive new community program in the world to develop industry and population beyond the Urals in the Asian heartland. In part, its aim was to seek the protection of distance from future possible European invasion and to obtain Great Russian ethnic domination over the scattered ethnic minorities of Soviet Asia. No comprehensive evaluation of the costs and benefits of these national urban growth policies has ever been done, although Lloyd Rodwin did write an excellent book exploring some of the issues implied by such developments.[11]

In contrast, the United States has not yet embraced the new communities movement as an instrument of some single national plan to reshape a national settlement pattern. The first official work on the subject was the national growth report published in February 1972. This report rejected the federal "grand design," arguing that "it is not feasible for the highest level of government to design policies for development that can operate successfully in all parts of the Nation."[12] The report indicated that settlement patterns can best be determined if the decisions are made at the state and local levels with local objectives taken into account.

Even though a single national plan has been explicitly rejected, this does not mean that various state and federal policies are not directed at shaping growth patterns. Over the years various legislation has been passed to solve specific problems associated with excessive or inadequate growth in the United States. This body of legislation, added to state and local policies, constitutes a national growth policy, evolving and changing as new items are added or subtracted. Only a few illustrations of these policies need to be cited: tens of billions have been spent on urban renewal and model cities programs to revitalize decaying small towns and center cities; over $1 billion has been spent on the development of the Appalachian region, as well as on depressed areas under the jurisdiction of the Economic Development Administration; hundreds of millions have been spent on the urban planning assistance program ("701" program) which has provided states, multistate regions, metropolitan planning areas, counties, and localities with means for controlling growth or dealing with the problems generated by economic and population growth or decline; hundreds of millions have been spent, loaned, or lost in foregone tax dollars by state and local industrial location incentives in order to attract industry; tens of billions have been spent for water and highway public works which affect the development of whole states or regions; military and other federal installations have been located and preserved in a manner which has promoted the development of or at least maintenance of existing development in states and regions; and military procurement policies have had a profound impact on national growth patterns. Although some policies have been working at cross-purposes, it is a fact that these programs and policies have had a lasting and significant impact on the course of urban settlement in the United States, regardless of whether or not this was included in their originally stated objectives.

The current role of new communities in the United States in promoting national growth policy is consistent with the pragmatic and decentralized nature of that policy (or collection of policies). Wherever new communities are located, whether in the suburbs, center cities, small towns, or rural areas, they can work in tandem with other policies and programs already operating in these areas. In each case, a HUD-approved new community must be consistent with areawide planning in its locale. Any description of this variable role of the new community may best be broken down into operations within and outside metropolitan areas.

Metropolitan Areas

Eleven of the fourteen new communities approved as of December 1972 were in the suburbs. Their major function is to channel growth which would have occurred in any event into more efficient patterns of settlement. The suburbs have served as the major focus of industrial, commercial, and residential growth. In the absence of any national policy to provide for industrial location incentives and controls, this course of action is probably the only practical one. It is difficult to predict the economic feasibility of a large-scale development without control or strong advance influence over the creation of a job base upon which freestanding or rural new communities will entirely depend. Even if industrial incentives were to be instituted by the federal government, there is little agreement on how effective they would be.

In terms of density alone, the new communities approved under the Act should provide a more compact and efficient settlement pattern in their metropolitan areas. The average residential density of the fourteen new communities approved under the Act is twenty-three persons projected per residential acre, compared with from five to fifteen persons for normal suburban development outside existing cities and fourteen for Columbia and Ir-

vine Ranch. Although some argue that considerably higher densities, along the lines of European new communities, would be appropriate, the desirability of containing urban sprawl with compact development must be weighed against personal preference and must continue to parallel popular demand for fairly low density living.

One goal of national urban growth policy in suburban areas is conservation. In the fourteen new communities approved as of December 1972, some 18,336 acres had been designated for permanent open space out of a total of 78,558 acres. This is 24 percent of the total acreage or twenty-three acres per 1,000 persons at peak development. By contrast, a 1968 analysis of some 43 cities and counties which had received open space grants revealed that fourteen of these municipalities had less than 2.5 usable open space acres per 1,000 population; twelve had from 2.5 to 5; twelve had from 5 to 10; and only five had more than 10 acres per 1,000.[13] This picture may have improved since then with federal open space acquisition, particularly for suburban areas where land is still available. It is improbable that the center city situation has changed much. Although there is considerable vacant land in these cities, it is not to be confused with usable open space.

Contrast with European new towns is also interesting. Typical British new towns call for 20 percent open space. Runcorn, Harlow, and Cumbernauld run between 19.2 and 22.4 acres per 1,000 population. Continental new towns are more parsimonious in allocation of open space. Typical large-scale German developments run less than 5 acres per 1,000. An average of some seventeen Continental and British new towns was 14.2 acres per 1,000. The total population for the U.S. developments is 869,000; it is served by 12,341 acres of open space within the new communities.

Free movement of people, regardless of

race or income, is also part of the goal of national growth policy. The contribution of new communities to opening up new opportunities for low and moderate income persons and minorities has already been discussed.

Part of the challenge of controlling growth in metropolitan areas is the revitalization of center cities, both large and small. The last decade has witnessed a continued shift in the percentage of jobs from the center city to the suburbs; in ten large metropolitan areas selected by the *New York Times,* 72 percent of the persons who lived in the suburbs also worked there. In some major metropolitan centers, not only did the percent of jobs decline, but also the absolute number of these jobs. This has been a contributing factor to the financial trouble of many of our large cities. Problem urban populations multiply faster than the tax resources to help them.

Against such a massive problem as center city decline, the New Communities Program alone, as it is presently constituted, is not likely to have a significant and widespread impact. Experience to date has indicated that substantial subsidies are required to make most new towns intown viable. Even Fort Lincoln, which is on low-cost vacant surplus federal land, is requiring a federal renewal expenditure of over $20 million. Even massive programs such as urban renewal and model cities, which together have resulted in expenditures of billions of dollars, have not halted the enormous forces of decline in such cities as Cleveland, Philadelphia, Camden, Newark, Detroit, St. Louis, and many sections of New York City.

Yet the potential for some variation of the new communities program, or a combination of state Urban Development Corporation-type activities in conjunction with the development of new communities, could be one instrument of urban revitalization which holds great potential for the future. Operating under the Mitchell-Llama program of the state of New York, Co-op City was built to provide moderate cost housing for 45,000 people without major renewal subsidies. It was built in about four years, which is in itself a substantial achievement.

The core of this approach would be urban development of land which is vacant, underutilized, and has great potential for balanced development—rather than the removal of slums, which is the emphasis of urban renewal. The new approach should yield certain favorable results in that minimum relocation and faster development would be possible at lower per capita cost for new jobs and dwelling units. A research effort at UCLA sponsored by HUD is investigating the potential of new towns intown as part of an overall urban revitalization strategy.

Nonmetropolitan Development
From 1970 to 1973 the New Communities Program gave priority to nonmetropolitan projects, but it was acting only on a pilot basis in nonmetropolitan areas. Soul City in rural and poor Warren County, North Carolina, is the only freestanding new community for which a federal guarantee has been offered. Others are under consideration, but, generally speaking, they will be approved under special circumstances and are not likely to occur often without a strong policy of industrial controls and incentives, as well as coordination of federal and state efforts on genuine rural development in nonmetropolitan areas.

Interagency Regional Approach
For center cities and suburban and metropolitan areas, the degree of success new communities will enjoy in attacking urban growth problems will depend largely on whether or not we can succeed in getting various federal, state, and local programs moving in the same direction, with some consistency of purpose, and without dilution of efforts.

Secretary George Romney has echoed this theme in his attempt to get the TACLE (Total American Community Living Environment) program approved. This is an attempt to undertake large-scale solutions to urban problems in selected metropolitan and rural regions. It has several characteristics, involving both the private and public sectors, and attacks many problems simultaneously. The approach is on a multi-jurisdictional, regionwide basis. Romney also uses the term "real city" approach. Both concepts recognize that urban problems cannot be solved by operating independently in single jurisdictions.

New communities can be part of this regional approach in both metropolitan and rural areas. Stockholm, Paris, and other major metropolitan centers in Europe have tied new communities into such a broad approach. In these large urban regions, rapid transit was planned simultaneously with new communities, helping to make transit feasible and to facilitate the development of the new communities. The innovative and speedy aerotrain is tied in with Cergy Pontoise, a large new town in the Paris region, while most Swedish satellite cities, such as Farsta, are tied into the Stockholm regional transit system. At the same time, large areas of open space are protected from development either by government landbanking or by freezing development. In not a single metropolitan area of the United States has such a three-part approach been implemented on a significant scale. Park Forest South is the only new town which has a definite commitment for transit tied to a central city in the United States. It is on the Illinois Central railroad, which is itself a partner in that new community development.

Part of the regionwide approach is the tying together of model cities, urban renewal, housing subsidy assistance, and new communities —all planned comprehensively on a multi-jurisdictional basis. Both renewal and model cities programs have great potential in urban

revitalization, whether directed at the federal, state, or local level.[14] However, their effectiveness is reduced if operated within a single political jurisdiction which has a declining or static tax base and is limited in land available for space-hungry industries.

One great obstacle to achievement of coordination among programs with differing functions on a multi-jurisdictional basis is the departmentalization of functions at the federal and state levels and the fragmentation of power at the local level. Transportation agencies seek their goals with little thought to the vast potential for creating unwanted urban sprawl on the one hand, or for using transit as an instrument of controlling urban growth on the other. Three laws sought recently by the administration would pave the way for a more unified approach in tackling both urban and rural regional development. The first involves consolidation of grants. This should reduce the rigid requirements of hundreds of programs which make it a nightmare to apply unified assistance to any one location. Trips to other federal agencies for assistance to new communities too often result in dead ends because funds have already been allocated to the states and, in turn, to the localities. And the states receiving the funds too often find that for one reason or another assistance cannot be provided for the new community.

A second action is the consolidation of agencies into broader "super departments." The proposed Department of Community Affairs would have within its jurisdiction rapid transit, poverty programs, housing, community facilities, rural development, and as many other programs as needed to mount a unified effort toward control of urban growth and to provide for rural development in a coordinated fashion. A third proposal would provide assistance to states for increased land-use control and planning. Congress has not acted upon these proposals, and steps have been taken to accomplish some of the goals administratively by creating some cabinet posts which are "more equal than others."

In the meantime, modest progress is being made in working with the Department of Transportation (DOT) and the Department of Health Education and Welfare (HEW) to seek a coordinated approach to new communities development. Even in the absence of federal reorganization, interagency agreements, if enforced at a high enough level, could accomplish significant goals in national urban growth policy. The coordination of the New Communities Program, the Rural Development Act administered by the Farmers Home Administration, the rural development highway program, some (Economic Development Agency) industrial development programs, and some HEW health and welfare programs could concentrate together on forty or fifty development centers. This would have significant impact on rural development in the United States without major new legislation. The same goal could be accomplished in urban areas with proper coordination among different state agencies and regional planning bodies. For example, a regional transit system could be planned simultaneously with a regional new town and an open space system.

These goals could be accomplished with minimum modification of the current program by funding provisions of the Act which have been authorized, but not yet funded, and making certain modest legislative improvements along the lines suggested in the House version of the 1972 Housing Act which was never passed. Among the changes which have been suggested, but not yet acted upon, is the creation of a federally chartered private bank which would offer loans to developers once the federal government had approved them for compliance with the social requirements of the Act. The bank would support only those projects which were deemed to be good business risks. The government would continue to guarantee projects which were financially feas-

ible but with somewhat high risks. Together, these programs would considerably extend the number of new communities in the United States. Another suggested change involves strengthening the role of the states in the new communities movement by making administrative grants to state land development agencies for the first several years. There is little doubt that agencies as strong as the Urban Development Corporation in New York, with or without power to override local government zoning, could play a key role in both urban and rural development.

Maximum use could be made of existing federal regional councils and existing interagency organizations at regional office levels in order to coordinate federal efforts in a genuine regional approach to problem-solving. The approach suggested here is closely related to the concept employed by the "Hartford Process," which includes suburban new communities and new towns intown as part of a regional public-private attack on the problems of Hartford, Connecticut. On a more limited basis, the regional approach is seen in the "paired new towns" approach suggested by the Metropolitan Fund of Detroit. This process would develop a new town intown simultaneously with a suburban new town and connect the two with a rapid transit system, so that they might share facilities and services. The pairing concept would be an attempt to "build bridges" between city and suburb on a pilot basis.

The regional approach to new communities suggested here aims at one of the greatest potential problems of the new communities movement in the United States today. This is the center cities' fear and concern that new communities will compete with them for jobs, businesses, human resources, and federal dollars. The initial opposition of the mayors, along with the small builders, defeated the early proposals to create new town legislation in 1964 and 1965 during the Robert Weaver administration of HHFA. This opposition was partly diffused by insistence in the legislative history of both the 1968 and the 1970 legislation that "additions to existing communities" and new towns intown could be undertaken in the Act. This concern about competition has also led to specific proposals for annexation of suburban new towns by central cities and at least two of the existing "paired" new towns intown as complements to satellite communities.

I find this fear of competition greatly exaggerated. New towns are capturing suburban growth that would occur in any event, and generally no more than 5 percent of the growth in large urban areas and no more than 15 or 20 percent in smaller metropolitan areas. Jobs are moving out of central cities because of space shortage, high taxes, high crime, urban deterioration, poor services, and the abundance of cheap land in the suburbs. People move out for many of the same reasons. New communities are not accelerating this growth, but capturing it and putting it into somewhat more orderly patterns. Even more important, the new communities are providing an "escape valve" for many low and moderate income residents and minority groups who have been systematically blocked from the suburbs.

Even though fears may be exaggerated, they are real, and they may be exacerbated once new towns achieve greater success with commercial and industrial enterprises. This makes a balanced regional strategy imperative. Urban renewal, new towns intown, and social programs must continue (even if under local control), along with revenue-sharing and tax reform to insure that services can continue at existing levels or improve without confiscatory taxes. At the same time, progress in undertaking transit systems and suburban new towns should be made. This would be aimed at taking some of the spillover population generated by renewal activities, thus paralleling the European approach to the problem. One reason

why urban renewal problems are so acute is that there is a shortage of good areas in which to relocate people. Although safe and sanitary housing may exist, this does not mean that it is located in a quality environment. Miracles cannot be expected with the regional approach, considering the suburban political limitations described earlier, but some progress may be made.

Some may object that the regional approach described here is much too modest, and that there should be a more sweeping "grant national design" of large, freestanding new towns far away from existing urban centers based on a radical new approach to urban development. I would argue that such an approach is escapist, largely impractical, and very expensive, if only in that billions of dollars in infrastructure would have to be created from scratch. The more modest approach described here is incremental, building one brick at a time upon the edifice which has already been established, upon economic forces which are already in motion, and upon decentralized regional and state decision-making, in response to a diversity of local needs, desires, problems, and capabilities.

The regional approach is logically the next step for urban development and for the new communities movement. During the fifties and sixties, the various components of urban development were improved by such entities as the Urban Land Institute, the National Association of Homes Builders, HUD, and state and local governments. They have all encouraged more attractive and better-planned industrial parks, shopping centers, and Planned Unit Developments as residential developments. In the late sixties and early seventies, new communities began to make a real impression on the thinking of the land development industry. New communities tied these various urban components together into a better package and included more ambitious social objectives. This movement toward larger development will probably continue, even when federal assistance is not involved. The next logical step for urban development and new communities is a genuine regional approach, not only for planning, but also for implementation.

Another decade may pass before the more difficult, politically risky, and costly components of a genuine rural and urban regional approach can be organized effectively. Particularly difficult is the establishment of zones in which no development or minimum development should occur. This will require some fresh thinking on land-use law concepts and on the role of government in the purchase and resale of land. Some form of land-banking and techniques to recapture unearned increment of value should be experimented with to reduce political opposition. Similarly, regional transit tied in with new towns will require rethinking of the structure of regional transit and planning agencies, as well as techniques for justifying and funding transit systems. Nevertheless, in light of the growing national consensus on the seriousness of the environmental crisis, air pollution from private automobiles, and the growing shortage of fossil fuels, the day of regional new town planning and development may be closer than we think.

Table 1. Population and Land Use Acres in New Communities (December 1972)

	Population	Jobs	Residential	%	Industrial	%	Commercial	%	Schools	%	Open space & recreation	%	Roads	%	Other	%	Total
Flower Mound	64,141	16,454	2,989	(49)	427	(7)	262	(4)	260	(4)	1,456	(23)	345	(6)	417	(7)	6,156
Woodlands	150,000	40,000	6,339	(37)	2,000	(12)	466	(3)	—		4,000	(23)	1,6491	(8)	2,6942	(16)	16,939
Riverton	25,632	11,180	1,046	(49)	400	(19)	170	(8)	75	(3)	4343	(20)	—		—		2,125
Jonathan	49,996	18,152	2,436	(30)	1,989	(24)	230	(3)	292	(4)	1,705	(21)	465	(6)	1,0734	(13)	8,194
Park Forest South	110,000	—	4,871	(60)	1,012	(12)	348	(4)	269	(3)	8925	(10)	—		7716	(9)	8,163
Cedar-Riverside	31,250	4,609	83	(83)	—		17	(17)	—7		—8		—		—		100
Lysander9	18,355	—	910	(34)	795	(30)	16810	(6)	—		597	(22)	—		200	(7)	2,670
Maumelle11	45,000	—	2,044	(38)	1,071	(20)	86	(2)	238	(4)	1,700	(31)	184	(3)	—		5,319
St. Charles	79,145	14,890	4,320	(62)	40212	(6)	214	(3)	108	(2)	1,516	(21)	330	(5)	—		6,980
Harbison9	21,343	6,100	732	(42)	196	(11)	85	(5)	64	(4)	224	(12)	201	(11)	235	(14)	1,739
Soul City9	44,000	18,000	1,705	(33)	928	(18)	29813	(6)	453	(9)	1,495	(28)	200	(4)	101	(2)	5,180
Gananda	55,808	12,890	2,470	(51)	250	(5)	174	(4)	293	(6)	1,010	(21)	480	(10)	54	(1)	4,733
Welfare Island9	17,000	7,500	40	(27)	—		—18		—7		49	(34)	33	(20)	2119	(15)	143
San Antonio Ranch9	87,972	17,990	4,249	(46)	1,234	(12)	160	(2)	330	(4)	2,203	(24)	642	(7)	50016	(5)	9,318
	800,513	197,68917	33,933	(43)							18,336	(24)					78,558

Source: HUD
Revised December 1972

1 Includes schools, roads, and other infrastructure.
2 Includes an 1,800-acre reserve and 400-acre university.
3 "Community space" which includes open space and roads but not schools.
4 Church uses, plus agriculture and recreation reserves.
5 Residential areas including major open space. Counting 50% of university and schools and residential clusters, total open space is 2,247 or 27%.
6 All but 17 acres are for Governor's State University campus.
7 Schools included in high-rise buildings and not listed separately.
8 Open space is elevated over streets and not computed separately.
9 No project agreement signed. Statistics subject to change.
10 Acreage includes schools and other community facilities
11 Project agreement covers 12-year development program only. Land use statistics cover 20-year development period and include 633-acre golf course and 241-acre proposed commercial park, which is owned by an affiliate company and not covered in the project agreement. This land is included in the total plan.
12 Excludes 400 acres for industrial land not now acquired, but committed to acquire.
13 Includes medical and institutional as well as retail uses.
14 Excludes "primary reserve" and 1,113 acres and "land bank" of 4,026 acres.
15 Includes industrial preserve.
16 Other community facilities and supporting services.
17 Total employment computed by taking those projects for which there were no total employment estimates and applying to them the average ratio of jobs to total population for all projects for which statistics are available.
18 Commercial included in other structures.
19 Hospital

Table 2. Low and Moderate Income Housing in New Communities (December 1972)

Project	Low income		Moderate income		Combined low/moderate		Middle income		Total dwelling units
Maumelle	378	(7%)[1]	842	(16%)[2]	1,220	(23%)[3]	1,214	(23%)	5,293
Park Forest South[4]	—[5]	—	—	—	5,800	(16%)[6]	—	—	37,200
Cedar-Riverside[4]	1,754	(14%)[5]	3,785	(30%)[6]	5,539	(44%)	4,450	(34%)	12,500
Riverton[4]	799[5]	(10%)	2,405	(30%)	3,204	(40%)	—	—	8,010
St. Charles	10% of rents[1]		—	—	4,946[7]	(20%)	14,838[8]	(60%)	24,730
Flower Mound[4]	—	—	—	—	3,667[10]	(20%)	4,333[9]	(24%)	18,326
Jonathan	—	—	—	—	3,874[11]	(25%)	3,876[12]	(25%)	15,405
Woodlands[4]	6,072	(13%)	6,866	(14%)	12,938	(27%)	—	—	47,375
Gananda	1,245	(7.2%)	2,490	—	3,735	(21%)	—	—	17,200
San Antonio Ranch	2,948	(10%)	7,366	(20%)	10,314	(35%)	—	—	29,476
Harbison[13]	—	—	—	—	2,135	(35%)[14]	—	—	6,100
Soul City[13]	—	—	—	—	4,980	(37%)	—	—	13,326
Lysander[13]	1,500	(30%)	1,000	(25%)	2,500	(50%)	1,250	(25%)	5,000
Welfare Island[13]	1,500	—	1,250	—	2,750	—	1,000	—	5,000
Total	16,196		26,004		67,502		30,961		245,441

Source: HUD
December 1972

[1] Less than $5,000

[2] Figures for Maumelle cover a 12-year period only to 1984. Total d.u.'s are 14,390 per entire development period with percent of low and moderate income housing remaining constant. From $5,000–$7,000 considered moderate income within this project.

[3] $7,000 to $10,000

[4] Subject to renegotiation periodically to ensure their responsiveness to metropolitan income profile.

[5] Rent supplement or public housing level. In Park Forest South, it will constitute 20% of all 236 housing in project.

[6] Includes exception limits not to exceed 15% of subsidized housing in Cedar-Riverside and 40% of subsidized housing in Park Forest South.

[7] Less than $7,500

[8] $7,500 to $10,000

[9] Above 235–236 limits, but below $11,000

[10] 8% yearly below $7,000

[11] Below $7,800

[12] $7,800 to $10,500

[13] Project agreement not yet signed.

[14] Estimated time of offer of commitment. Final figure subject to change.

Table 3. Summary of Guarantees for New Communities Approved by HUD (December 1972)*
(Dollars in Thousands)

No.	Community name	Guarantee commitment Amount	Date	Guarantees issued Amount	Date	Interest rate
1	Jonathan, Minn.	$21,000	2/70	$ 8,000	10/70[a]	8.50%
				$13,000	6/72[a]	7.20%
2	St. Charles Communities, Md.	$24,000	6/70	$18,500	12/70[a]	7.58%
3	Park Forest South, Ill.	$30,000	5/70	$30,000	3/71	7.00%
4	Flower Mound, Tex.	$18,000	12/70	$14,000	10/71	7.60%
5	Maumelle, Ark.	$ 7,500	12/70	$ 2,500	12/71	7.625%
				$ 2,000	6/72	7.625%
				$ 1,200	12/72	7.625%
6	Cedar-Riverside, Minn.	$24,000	6/71	$24,000	12/71	7.20%
7	Riverton, N.Y.	$12,000	12/71	$12,000	5/72	7.125%
8	San Antonio Ranch, Tex.	$18,000	2/72	—		—
9	Woodlands, Tex.	$50,000	4/72	$50,000	8/72	7.10%
10	Gananda, N.Y.	$22,000	4/72	$22,000	12/72	7.20%
11	Soul City, N.C.	$14,000	6/72	—		—
12	Lysander, N.Y.	State land development agency project; obligations will not be guaranteed by HUD, but project eligible for other program benefits. Approved 6/72.					
13	Harbison, S.C.	$13,000	10/72	—		—
14	Welfare Island, N.Y.	State land development agency project; obligations will not be guaranteed by HUD, but project eligible for other program benefits. Approved 12/72.					

[a] Guaranteed under Title IV; all other guarantees under Title VII.
* Shenandoah, a planned new community to be located 35 miles south of Atlanta, was also approved by HUD in February 1973. Commitments were also offered on Newfields, Ohio, and Beckett, N.J.

Appendix 1.

Supplementary Information on Balanced New Communities Listed in
"Survey & Analysis of Large Development & New Communities"

Name	Developer	Location	Major milestones	Population	Other information
Arizona					
Litchfield Park	Litchfield Park Properties	Maricopa Co. 18 miles west of Phoenix	1965 major planning started	N.A.	600 acre industrial park
Lake Havasu City	McCulloch Properties (subsidiary of McCulloch Oil)	153 miles from Las Vegas, Nev.	Started 1963	8,500(1972)	320 acres for industry; only free-standing project in U.S.
California					
Foster City	T. Jack Foster & Sons, Inc. (sold interest recently)	18 miles south of San Francisco	Started 1963	14,000(1972)	Dense development on landfill in S.F. Bay
Irvine Ranch	Irvine Co.	40 miles south of Los Angeles	Plan 1960	25,000(1970) 276 industrial firms (1970)	
Janss (Conejo/Janss)	Janss Corp.	45 miles north of Los Angeles downtown		5,800(1972)	
Laguna Niguel	Laguna Niguel Corp. AVCO purchased in 1969	50 miles south of Los Angeles		5,000(1968)	800 acre industrial park
Mission Viejo Rancho Bernado	Mission Viejo Co. AVCO Community Developers, Inc.			11,000(1970)	
San Ramon Village	San Ramon Village Corporation (subsidiary of Property Research Corp., Westwood, Calif.)	24 miles east of Oakland	Started 1969	17,500(1969)	432 acre industrial park
Valencia		30 miles north of Los Angeles	Plan 1966	2,000(1968)	
Westlake Village	American Hawaiian Co.	10 miles north of Los Angeles	Started 1966		
Colorado					
Montbello	KLC Ventures Ltd.	near Denver	Started 1966	230(1969)	
Florida					
Palm Beach Gardens	John P. MacArthur	Palm Beach County	Plan 1968		
Georgia					
Peachtree City	Phipps Land Co.	20 miles south of Atlanta	Started 1963	275(1969)	Major industrial development

Name	Developer	Location	Major milestones	Population	Other information
Illinois					
Elk Grove	Centex Corp.	near O'Hare Airport, 20 miles from Chicago			
Park Forest	Philip Klutznick	30 miles south of Chicago	1950(?)	34,000(1972)	Industry never developed
Maryland					
Columbia	Howard Research & Development Corp.	25 miles from Washington D.C.		20,000(1972)	Major industry established
Virginia					
Reston	Gulf Reston	20 miles from Washington, D.C.		17,500(1972)	Major industry established

Source: Office of New Communities, HUD
May 1972

Appendix 2.
Listing of New Communities Documents in the
National Technical Information Services

*The following New Communities Development Program documents have been published by the National
Technical Information Service (NTIS), Department of Commerce.*

Title	Access code	Title	Access code
1 New Communities—Annotated Bibliography, Decision Sciences Corp.	PB-206-880	United States of America and Cedar-Riverside Land Company	
2 New Communities—Survey of the State of the Art, Decision Sciences Corp.	PB-206-883	14 Indenture of Mortgage and Deed of Trust—Cedar-Riverside and Company to First Trust Company of St. Paul	PB-206-478
3 New Communities—Systems for Planning and Evaluation, Decision Sciences Corp.	PB-206-882	15 Indenture of Mortgage and Deed of Trust—Maumelle Land Development, Inc., to the First National Bank of Little Rock, Trustee	PB-207-044
4 Economic and Financial Feasibility Models for New Community Development, Real Estate Research Corp.	PB-206-925	16 Final Environmental Statement —Flower Mound New Town, Tex.	PB-202-338-F
5 Project Agreement between the United States of America and Jonathan Development Corp.	PB-206-466	17 Project Agreement between the United States of America and Maumelle Land Development, Inc.	PB-207-624
6 Indenture of Mortgage and Deed of Trust—Jonathan Development Corp. to First Trust Company of St. Paul	PB-206-422	18 Final Environmental Statement, Maumelle New Town, Ark.	PB-200-236-F
7 Indenture of Mortgage and Deed of Trust—Interstate Land Development Company, Inc., to the Equitable Trust Company	PB-206-421	19 Final Environmental Statement, Cedar-Riverside, Minn.	PB-201-378-F
		20 Final Environmental Statement, Riverton, N.Y.	PB-201-391-F
8 Project Agreement between the United States of America and Interstate Land Development Company, Inc.	PB-206-467	21 Final Environmental Statement, San Antonio Ranch, Tex.	PB-202-588-F
		22 Final Environmental Statement, Soul City, N.C.	PB-203-088-F
9 Project Agreement between the United States of America and Park Forest South Development Company	PB-206-465	23 Final Environmental Statement, The Woodlands, Tex.	PB-204-498-F
		24 Final Environmental Statement, Gananda, N.Y.	PB-204-845-F
10 Indenture of Mortgage and Deed of Trust—Park Forest South Development Company to Continental Illinois National Bank and Trust Company of Chicago	PB-206-471	25 Developing a Methodology for the Evaluation of Proposed New Communities	PB-207-719
11 Project Agreement between the United States of America and Flower Mound New Town, Ltd.	PB-206-609	26 Project Agreement between the United States of America and Riverton Properties, Inc.	PB-209-555
12 Indenture of Mortgage and Deed of Trust—Flower Mound New Town, Ltd., to First National Bank in Dallas	PB-206-608	27 Indenture of Mortgage and Deed of Trust—Riverton Properties, Inc., to Marine Midland Band—Rochester	PB-209-554
13 Project Agreement between the	PB-206-477	28 Indenture of Mortgage and Deed of Trust—Woodlands Development Corporation to the Chase	PB-213-066

Appendix 2. (Continued)

Title	*Access code*
Manhattan Bank (National Association)	
29 Project Agreement between the United States of America and The Woodlands Development Corporation	PB-213-044
30 Project Agreement between the United States of America and Gananda Development Corporation	PB-213637
31 Indenture of Mortgage and Deed of Trust—Gananda Develop-	PB-213700

Access Code	*Title*
	ment Corporation to the Chase Manhattan Bank (National Association)
PB-207-740-F	32 Final Environmental Statement, Welfare Island, N.Y.
GA-72-5718-F	33 Final Environmental Statement, Shenandoah, Ga.
SC-72-4622-F	34 Final Environmental Statement, Harbison, S.C.
NY-4620-F	35 Final Environmental Statement, Lysander, N.Y.

NOTES

1 By June 1973 the supplemental grant program had been terminated by the Administration, as had the basic grant programs in HUD. However, Congress was in the process of requiring an extension of the supplemental grant program. At this writing the outcome of the difference of opinion has not been fully resolved.

2 These programs provide for an interest subsidy to enable lower-income persons to purchase a single-family home or to rent an apartment. They are currently being phased out, and a study commission is under way to replace them with some other form of assistance.

3 Reports on the use of financial models in Phase I, as well as on the development of a method for undertaking a more complicated economic model in Phase II, may be obtained by ordering items 1, 2, 3, 4, and 25 on the list in Appendix 2 from the National Technical Information Service.

4 National Academy of Sciences, National Academy of Engineering Advisory Committee, "Freedom of Choice in Housing: Opportunities and Constraints," Report to the Department of Housing and Urban Development, 1972.

5 For a fuller description of the concept, see Metropolitan Fund, "Regional New Town Design: A Paired Community for Southeast Michigan" (Detroit: Metropolitan Fund, 1971).

6 Edward Banfield, *The Unheavenly City* (Boston: Little, Brown, 1970).

7 For a fuller exposition of this issue of race and class as related to intergroup conflict, see Jack Underhill's "The Italian Immigrants and the American Negroes in the Urban North: Comparisons of Group Adjustment," seminar paper (1969), Ken-

nedy School of Government, Harvard University. The study concludes that there are more similarities than differences between the problems of the blacks in the urban North since World War II and those of the Italian immigrants since their arrival at the turn of the century.

8 Royce Hanson, *Managing Services for New Communities,* report of the symposium on the management of new communities, Washington Center for Metropolitan Studies and New Communities Study, Virginia Polytechnic Institute and State University (Washington, D.C.: Washington Center for Metropolitan Studies, 1972).

9 Ida Cutherbertson, "Education Expenditures and Real Estate Tax Revenues in New Town and Suburb," *New Communities Research Bulletin,* New Communities Study Center, Virginia Polytechnic Institute and State University, 1973.

10 Howard County [Md.] Planning Commission, *Howard County 1985: General Plan, Technical Report No. 1,* April 1967.

11 Lloyd Rodwin, *Nations and Cities: A Comparison of Strategies for Urban Growth* (Boston: Houghton Mifflin, 1970).

12 United States, Department of Housing and Urban Development, Domestic Council Committee on National Growth, *Report on National Growth 1972* (Washington, D.C.: U.S. Government Printing Office, 1972), p. 31.

13 Jack A. Underhill, "Open Space in the City as a System: A Broader Approach to Program Budgeting," seminar paper (1968), Kennedy School of Government, Harvard University. (See Table 1, p. 89). Per capita figures based upon the *1966 Park and Recreation Yearbook.* Information on European

new towns derived from unpublished report of Cornell University to UDC in 1971.

14 The model cities and urban renewal programs are being consolidated into a single block grant, along with other HUD programs in the administration's proposed Better Communities Act.

READING LIST

Alonso, William. "The Mirage of New Towns." *Public Interest,* no. 19 (Spring 1970), pp. 3–17.

American Institute of Architects. "Toward a New Chapter in Urban Growth." *American Institute of Architects Journal* 54 (November 1970): 27.

Ashley, Thomas L. "A New Urban Growth Strategy for the United States." *Urban and Social Change Review* (Spring 1971): 50–52.

Banfield, Edward. *The Unheavenly City.* Boston: Little, Brown, 1970.

Baranov, N. V. "Building New Towns." In *Planning of Metropolitan Areas and New Towns.* New York: United Nations Publications, 2967, pp. 209–215.

Beckman, Norman. "Development of a National Urban Growth Policy: Legislative Review, 1970." *American Institute of Planners Journal* 27, no. 5 (1971).

Belser, Joseph. "The Corporate Role in New Town Development." University of North Carolina New Towns Research Seminar, Series 1, Fall 1969.

Birch, David L. "Toward a Stage Theory of Urban Growth." *American Institute of Planners Journal* 37 (March 1971): 78–87.

Bodnar, Donald J., and Mark Wassenich. *Implementation: A Critical Limit on the Planner's Role in Planned Community Development.* Chapel Hill: Center for Urban and Regional Studies, University of North Carolina, 1970.

Brooks, Douglas L. "Environmental Quality Control: A Statement of the Problem." Address at the American Institute of Biological Sciences Plenary Session, 28 August 1967.

Cutherbertson, Ida. "Education Expenditures and Real Estate Tax Revenues in New Town and Suburb." *New Communities Research Bulletin.* Reston, Va.: New Communities Study Center, Virginia Polytechnic Institute, 1973.

David, Philip. *New Towns: The Development Process.* Washington, D.C.: American Institute of Architects New Communities Conference, 3–6 November 1971.

Downs, Anthony. "Creating the Institutional Framework for Encouraging New Cities." In *Regional New Towns: Alternative in Urban Growth for Southeast Michigan.* Detroit: Metropolitan Fund, 1970.

Eichler, Edward P. "The Larger Concerns of New Community Building." Seminar, Center for Urban and Regional Studies, University of North Carolina, 1970.

————, and Marshall Kaplan. *The Community Builders.* Berkeley and Los Angeles: University of California Press, 1967.

Feiss, Carl. "Development Incentives and Controls for New Communities: An Overview." Washington, D.C.: American Institute of Architects New Communities Conference, 3–6 November 1971.

Fitch, Lyle C. "National Development and National Policy." In *Environment and Policy: The Next Fifty Years,* ed. William R. Ewald, Jr. Bloomington: Indiana University Press, 1968.

Foer, Albert A. "Democracy in the New Towns: The Limits of Private Government." *University of Chicago Law Review* 36 (Winter 1969): 379–412.

Friedman, John. "The Feasibility of a National Settlement Policy for the USA." *Ekistics* 32 (November 1971): 320–322.

Gobar, Alfred. "PUDs as Alternatives to New Towns." *Real Estate Review* 2 (Summer 1971): 72–75.

Godschalk, David. "Comparative New Community Design." In "Creating New Communities: A Symposium on Process and Product." *American Institute of Planners Journal* 33 (November 1967): 371–387, and *Ekistics* 25 (May 1968): 306–315.

"Governmental Organization for the Minnesota Experimental City." *Minnesota Experimental City (MXC).* Vol. 1: A Compendium of Publications Relating to Socio-Cultural Aspects, pp. 199–201. Minneapolis: University of Minnesota/Experimental City Project, 1969.

Graves, Clifford Wayne. "Public New Town Corporations for California." Master's thesis, University of California, 1961.

Gross, Edward, and George Donohue. "Some Aspects of Urban Organization Reconsidered." *Minnesota Experimental City (MXC).* Vol. 1: A Compendium of Publications Relating to Socio-Cultural Aspects, pp. 205–213. Minneapolis: University of Minnesota/Experimental City Project, 1969.

Hanson, Royce. *Managing Services for New Communities.* Report of the symposium on the management of new communities, Washington Center for Metropolitan Studies and New Communities

Center Study, Virginia Polytechnic Institute and State University. Washington, D.C.: Washington Center for Metropolitan Studies, 1972.

―――. *New Towns: Laboratories for Democracy.* Report of the Twentieth Century Fund Task Force on Governance of New Towns. New York: Twentieth Century Fund, 1971.

Hoppenfield, Morton. "Considerations on Developing New Towns." *Minnesota Experimental City (MXC).* Vol. 2: Economic and Physical Aspects, pp. 189–204. Minneapolis: University of Minnesota/Experimental City Project, 1969.

Howard County [Md.] Planning Commission. *Howard County 1985: General Plan, Technical Report No. 1.* Maryland: Howard County Planning Commission, April 1967.

Jacobs, Peter. "The Site Planning Process: Activity Allocation at the Urban Fringe." *Environmental Design: Research and Practice: Proceedings of the EDRA 3/AR 8 Conference,* ed. William J. Mitchell. Los Angeles: University of California, 1972, p. 161.

Kaplan, Marshall. "The Roles of the Planner and Developer in the New Community." In *New Towns and Planned Communities.* New York: Practicing Law Institute, 1971.

Kelly, Michael. "Planning the Government of a New Town." Paper, Yale Law School, 1967.

LeRoyer, Ann M. "The New Towns Movement in Great Britain and the United States." *Urban and Social Change Review,* Spring 1971, pp. 53–58.

Logue, Edward J. "The Need for Urban Growth Policies." *American Institute of Architects Journal* 55 (May 1971): 18–22.

McKellar, James. *Public Control versus Public Action: Legitimizing the Public Role in New Community Development.* Washington, D.C.: American Institute of Architects New Communities Conference, 3–6 November 1971.

Metropolitan Fund. "Regional New Town Design: A Paired Community for Southeast Michigan." Detroit: Metropolitan Fund, 1971.

Morely and Geraughty, Architects and Planners. *Metro/Center: A New Town in Town.* Kansas City, Mo.: Kansas City Region Metropolitan Planning Commission, October 1971.

Moynihan, Daniel P., ed. *Toward a National Urban Policy.* New York and London: Basic Books, 1970.

National Academy of Sciences, National Academy of Engineering Advisory Committee. "Freedom of Choice in Housing: Opportunities and Constraints." Report to the Department of Housing and Urban Development, 1972.

National Committee on Urban Growth Policy. *The New City,* ed. Donald Canty. New York: Frederick A. Praeger, 1969.

New York State Urban Development Corporation. *Goals, Guidelines, Concerns of the New York State Urban Development Corporation.* New York: New York State Urban Development Corporation, 1971.

Osborn, F. J. *Greenbelt Cities: The British Conurbation.* London: Faber & Faber, 1946. Revised ed., London: Evelyn, Adams & Mackay, 1969, and New York: Schoken Books, 1969.

―――, and Arnold Whittick. *The New Towns: The Answer to Megalopolis.* New York: McGraw-Hill, 1963.

"Policy Considerations: Governmental, Political." *Minnesota Experimental City (MXC).* Vol. 2: Economic and Physical Aspects, pp. 81–87. Minneapolis: University of Minnesota/Experimental City Project, 1969.

Rodwin, Lloyd. *The British New Towns Policy: Problems and Implications.* Cambridge, Mass.: Harvard University Press, 1956.

―――. *Nations and Cities: A Comparison of Strategies for Urban Growth.* Boston: Houghton Mifflin, 1970.

Schtuchter, Arnold. *White Power/Black Freedom.* Boston: Beacon Press, 1968.

Scott, Stanley. "New Towns Development and the Role of Government." *Public Affairs Report.* Berkeley: University of California, Institute of Government Studies, 1964.

Self, Peter. "New Towns, Greenbelts, and the Urban Region." Paper presented at "The Metropolitan Future" Conference, Berkeley Calif., September 1963.

Simon, Robert E. "Problems of the New Town Developer." *Building Research* 6 (January/February 1966): 16–17.

Thompson, Stephen G. "Techniques of Land Acquisition and Finance." *Building Research* 6 (October/December 1969): 29–31.

Underhill, Jack A. "The Italian Immigrants and the American Negroes in the Urban North: Comparisons of Group Adjustment." Seminar paper (1969), Kennedy School of Government, Harvard University.

―――. "Open Space in the City as a System: A Broader Approach to Program Budgeting." Seminar paper (1968), Kennedy School of Government, Harvard University.

————. *Proposal for Strengthening the Role of New Communities in Implementing National Urban Growth Strategy*. Washington, D.C.: Department of Housing and Urban Development, 27 October 1971.

United States, Congress, House. *Urban Growth and New Community Development Act of 1970*. Congressional Record, S.3640, 25 March 1970.

United States, Department of Commerce, New Communities Development Program Documents. *Project Agreement between United States of America and Inter-State Land Development Company, Inc.* Springfield, Va.: National Technical Information Service, 1972.

United States, Department of Housing and Urban Development, Domestic Council Committee on National Growth. *Report on National Growth 1972*. Washington, D.C.: U.S. Government Printing Office, 1972.

Wendt, Paul F. "Large-scale Community Development." *Journal of Finance* 22 (May 1967): 220–239.

Opportunities for Innovative Local Government

Royce Hanson

The governance of new towns is generally neglected in the planning stages. Most people think: "We'll get it built, people will move in, and somehow it'll get governed." They think the processes of participation, representation, and decision-making will take care of themselves. This ignores a basic philosophical objective of new towns, which is to make them new as social entities and as communities as well as structures in a built environment. With this in mind, I would like to offer some ideas about the governance of new towns which may be useful to achitectural, social, and economic planners.

Local government in the United States has not distinguished itself as our most brilliant invention. We could use experimentation with new forms, processes, and practices of governance, if we are to help shape new towns as communities, and if we are to learn some things from the new towns movement which could substantially influence the overall process of urbanization in this country.

Too little emphasis has thus far been placed on that latter point. Over the next thirty years most development in this country will not be in new towns. In fact, for the next twenty years, most commitments on the land and other resources have already been made. There will not be enough new towns built to materially alter the general shape of urbanization. But new towns can influence development practices beyond their own immediate situation. If we can learn some things about building, planning, community, government, and various kinds of service systems through the opportunity that new towns give us to create, then we may have our most exciting opportunity yet to reshape some of our existing cities, and even to improve much suburban development.

Governance can be viewed in two ways. It can be a series of services and facilities which the government provides; it can also be a set of civic institutions. By "institution," I do not mean organization. Rather, I mean organized and reasonably consistent patterns of behavior. The legal system, for instance, is an institution, and within this frame of reference the regulation of land use is an institution; the market is an institution. Participation and representation come together as processes which form institutions of formal and informal government. The party system and pressure groups, for instance, are institutions.

Either of these two basic interpretations of governance may be adopted for the development of new communities, regardless of Title VII. In fact, it makes very little difference, from the local government point of view, whether or not there is a Title VII. Title VII means only that the local government has to deal with federal bureaucrats whom it might not otherwise have encountered, and that it has to do some things it might not really want to do. On the other hand, Title VII makes a lot of difference to the developer, not only because he saves about 2 percent in interest rates, but also because of what he has to do in the way of institutional engineering to convince the Department of Housing and Urban Development (HUD) that he is meeting its guidelines. Most significantly, HUD requires a certain minimum percentage of low and moderate income housing, which immediately sets in motion the need to provide other sorts of social and governmental institutions for the people who will occupy this housing.

Because a large percentage of the new town population will be renters, the developer's ability to covenant the land and to establish homeowners associations as means of providing services is modified. Since low and moderate income people do not have much income above that required for the necessities of life, which includes their rent, they probably cannot pay an additional set of dues or user fees for community facilities. Yet, if the developer wants his new town to function, he must find a way for all the people in that new town to participate in its public life, and to use the full range of its public facilities and services. Since these requirements make such a substantial difference to the developer's plan for social and governmental institutions, let us deal first with local government, since it is overlaid with the federal situation.

A developer will usually find that there is no state or local governmental policy which is explicitly aimed at new towns, although he may find a great deal of public policy which will encourage or inhibit (normally, inhibit) the development of new communities. Usually, no area has been designated by the local planning jurisdiction or by the state planning department as a suitable location for a new town. Thus land prices have been affected not by public planning, but by market situations. The fact that local or state government has not designated any site as a potential new town, but has left this entirely to the market, means that neither has it planned to provide any services to those sites. The developer, then, reaps the benefit of no inflation in land values as a result of no planning for development; but he also incurs the cost of providing services which may include major roads, certainly sanitary systems, and possibly other services, such as health systems. Columbia, for instance, found that in order to achieve proper access to its site, it had to build a good piece of state road system—roads that should have been built by the county or the state, if the state had been undertaking a conscious policy of encouraging people to settle in that area. Because access is an absolute necessity, state highway locations and the capital improvement program are vital. Highways may well be the key to the developability of new towns, depending on the adequacy of the market.

Almost anybody who owns a tract of land near an interstate highway is beginning to visualize it as a new town, whether there is a market for that land or not. However, part of ripening the market depends on where else local government is going to permit development. If development continues to sprawl out around the fringes of the entire metropolitan area, it will soak up much of the market which could otherwise be displaced and put into a new town location.

Usually there are no state institutions capable of actively assisting development, or of directing state public investments into new communities. Most public officials regard everything that the government spends as simply expenditures, rather than as investments in development, although this spending is essential to the developability of an area. Consequently, our major capital investments—highways, schools, health facilities, sewer and water systems—are often financed backward. They are partially financed by special assessments levied after the development has already occurred, rather than built in the first instance as investments in the developability of that particular area with the assumption that, given public investment, there should be a return in public benefits. In the case of the new town, the benefit could be a pattern of development, bringing with it an advantageous economic distribution of population. One fails to think of capital improvements as investments; consequently, they rarely pay for themselves, from either an economic or a social point of view, and one normally finds that each generation of new residents in a community not only pays for its own bad development, but also helps to subsidize each future bad development that occurs in an area.

State and local taxation and assessment systems also greatly influence the develop-

ability of new towns. They often work in combination with a system of land use control. To illustrate, Reston is being developed under what is known as the Residential Planned Communities (RPC) zone. This means that the master plan prepared for Reston was adopted as an amendment to the public master plan for that section of Fairfax County, Virginia. The difficulty is that, under the law, master plans do not determine zones; they are only a guide for zoning. This is generally true of all states. The Reston master plan calls for all residential areas to be zoned RPC, although by 1972 only 2,500 of its 8,000 acres had been so zoned. It is not possible to zone all of Reston RPC at one time, even though this would greatly cut down on the time spent processing individual zoning applications for each piece of land to be developed, because under Virginia tax laws rezoning requires reassessment. Rezoning land from low to higher density, therefore, greatly increases the annual tax. Possession of an 8,000-acre piece of land over a twenty-year period means that for at least ten years the developer would be carrying an average of 4,000 acres which he has no immediate intention of developing, while he would be forced to pay the higher assessment on it. This would come at a time when he is also paying the heaviest interest on his loan on the land, and his construction loan. Since these carrying costs (his "front end" costs) escalate very rapidly during this period, he would probably be driven into bankruptcy.

Because all the land cannot be zoned at once, the county, the developer, the citizens of Reston, and the citizens who live in the rest of the county are kept in a state of constant warfare; they wonder, for example, "Is Gulf really going to use the rest of the land for a new town, or are they going to sell it off to someone else who would come in with a conventional subdivision?" Since the undeveloped land is zoned not for a new town, but at conventional suburban densities, if Gulf should sell it to somebody else, it could be built upon without going back to the county for any further action, such as site plan review, and without any of the architectural and design controls that are obtained under the RPC zoning. The alternative to the Reston experience is to rezone the entire tract at one time, and then to reassess at the time of subdivision. This is done in some jurisdictions; a developer comes in for approval of his subdivision plans when he is ready to file for his building permits.

Columbia has worked a bit differently. All of the land was rezoned at one time. However, Maryland has a preferential farmland assessment law; it says in effect that if your land is zoned industrial and you keep a cow on it, it has to be assessed for agriculture. So it has been possible, as a result of a law that works badly everywhere else in this state, to go ahead and zone the land and have a development program scheduled for Columbia. Until the land's use has been converted, it will not be reassessed at its market value for urban development. There should be a state policy relating to new towns which would allow land in approved new towns to be reassessed when it comes on line for development, rather than when it is first zoned. This would avoid the sham of preferential farmland assessment, which elsewhere generally means that the public is subsidizing (in my county to the tune of over ten million dollars a year) speculators in holding land off the market. Although economic pressure is lacking, the land ought to be converted because its real market value has actually increased.

Problems of zoning and assessment are crucial and are often overlooked in discussions about new town financing, planning, and development. Moreover, a change in state and local development policy is necessary, because a new town requires from the state and the locality a commitment that certain things are going to remain stable throughout the development period. Almost all of our local land regulatory institutions are geared to the "quick buck artist." They are designed to regulate him. The small-tract builder will be in with his rezoning application and out with all of his houses sold in five years. The new town developer will be in for twenty years; he may never get completely out, because of his equity in some of the high-yield property such as a shopping center, town center, apartment buildings, and industrial land. In fact, some new town developers argue that the equity in the new town is, in the long run, of far more financial significance to them than the sale of the land or structures.

The concept of regulation must be changed so that a "contract" of mutual assistance can be made between local government and the developer as continuing institutions. This will preclude one of the developer's constant worries: say that, when he decided to develop his new town, the board of supervisors and the planning board thought it was a great idea; but the new council or board about to be elected thinks it is the worst thing that has ever happened, and they have decided to turn off the water and withhold sewer taps because they did not like the most recent site plan. This means inestimable economic damage for the developer.

This policy aspect is only one part of the whole governmental context of new town development. We should be equally concerned with the institutional side of new town governance and management. First, when we talk about governance and management, we are talking about both public and private government; private government has begun to matter a great deal, particularly in new towns.

Among the developer's first concerns is whether or not the key local government agencies have the capacity to perform on schedule, and with integrity. Often they do not. Furthermore, the "front end" costs of a new town development are such that corruption cannot be an economic possibility, because it is too erratic and too difficult to cope with. Any new town developer who is willing to pay off a local government in order to operate is out of his mind, because ultimately he will not be able to develop. Local governments must be able to do their jobs well. The governing body and the chief administrators must have some understanding of new town development. The staff must be capable of doing the government's work.

Many potential sites for new towns are in rural settings where this is not the case. Therefore, if the state is going to promote a new town development policy, it should also make initial technical assistance available to the local governments where new towns are being established. The governing body, chief administrators, and the planning and zoning authorities must be able to operate well. Capacity is particularly needed in the school system. If capacity is not already there, the developer must provide it himself, or at least stimulate its provision. Columbia caused Howard County to rethink its entire educational system and program; the result was a much better system of public education than the county had ever had before.

Stimulating the provision of governmental capacity depends largely on the political circumstances. If a developer goes into an area that is already substantially developed when there is great pressure for schools elsewhere in the county, the fact that the new community has been chosen to get the new schools will immediately raise political problems of immense proportions. After all, until a new community is built, people will not live in it; when the bond issues have to be voted for schools in the new town, parents of children in the old schools resent paying "their taxes" to support all of those "invaders" who do not come from

their own county. The utilities system must also be good, as well as the transportation and revenue systems.

Other important community institutions or services are useful in developing the new community. Such catalysts might be churches and religious groups; institutions for higher education, such as community colleges or four-year colleges; graduate schools, depending on the kind of industry and people to be attracted to the new community; various cultural groups; and other associations such as labor unions, chambers of commerce, health service centers, and mental health organizations. If these can be established and built upon, they will be important resources for rapid community expansion.

Another wise and important action, whatever the state policy and existing institutions might be, is to assess the general political situation as it applies to new community development. Again, this must be done relevant to a twenty-year investment. The existing party system, factions, and leaders must be identified. In Columbia, a careful analysis was made of all political activity which had occurred in Howard County over the past 300 years. As a result some very good decisions were made in the early development of Columbia; the right people were brought into the process and were told what was being done, so they became committed politically to the development of the new community.

Unfortunately, this practice must continue throughout the whole development period, since the injection of a new town into a community brings about basic political changes. Because the social structure will inevitably be altered by the new community, a developer must be sensitive to what this social structure has traditionally been. Furthermore, a new town makes large demands on the market. Right now in Fairfax County, Virginia, close to a fifth of all the new houses are being built in Reston. This is great for Reston, but for a builder who does not build in Reston, it is not so good. He would like to see the politics of the county shift the emphasis to other places where it is easier for him to get land.

To cope with local people's resentment, the developer must move slowly. In Charles County, Maryland, where St. Charles City is proposed for development, the present developers went in and bought a piece of land on which a tract development had been in financial difficulty. Without consulting the local county commissioners, they announced that they were going to build a new community for 75,000 people. There was an immediate and strong negative response. After a long time, the county commissioners adopted a Planned Unit Development (PUD) ordinance. Moreover, the state government is very unfriendly to St. Charles City, partly because it feels that it is not going to be an economically sound development.

One of the most serious problems new towns face is parasitic growth which produces an overuse of facilities originally planned for a specific population. This type of growth inevitably reduces the quality of life which was the original objective of the new town. Depending in part on the kind of policy the county will permit, the new town may or may not generate additional growth in its immediate vicinity. The key to this could be sewer connections and zoning policy. If the county will not permit additional sewer connections around the development of the new town, then the new town will not stimulate additional growth. Local zoning policy usually says, "Let nature take its course." When nature takes its course, the fact that a developer must build a trunk sewer, a major extension of the highway system, a high school, and secondary and intermediate schools, all for the new town, means that the town will indeed stimulate new growth.

The solution is governmental policy to provide for a large number of new towns to absorb the market. Until we reach that point, however, we will continue to have problems. Columbia provides a good illustration: it is planned for a population of 115,000, for a certain kind of industrial and business base, and for a particular mix of activities. However, it was also proposed as a great site for Marriott's "Great American Playland," which is supposed to be the Middle Atlantic's Disneyland. Such a development would probably have caused traffic to back up on I-95 both to Baltimore and to Washington, particularly during holiday seasons. It could have inundated Howard County, and nearby Anne Arundel and Prince George's counties, with demands for restaurants, pasture camps, hotels, and motels; and it probably would have attracted more people to Columbia's recreation systems than Columbia could have absorbed. Conceivably, Playland could be redesigned—but to do that, much larger public investment would be required. Howard County ultimately rejected the proposal. The whole theory of planning investments, making decisions on them, and trying to limit the size of facilities to absorb a particular kind of population or market means that the regional elements of the situation must also be carefully considered.

Economic feasibility is a very important consideration in planning a new town. Levitt proposed to develop a planned community in Loudoun County, but the board of supervisors denied his rezoning application on the grounds that the project would cost more than they would ever gain from it in revenue. They cited the experience of Sterling Park, a nearby large-scale tract development. However, the legal question is intriguing. Can a community deny a rezoning application because public costs are going to be greater than public benefits? If so, we may be in a situation where a fiscal feasibility study will ultimately be required of new town developers prior to zoning. I think it should be required in any event. If a developer is going to commit a county to twenty years of public investments, he ought to be able to demonstrate that he has a feasible project. He has to do so to get Title VII guarantees now, and HUD looks hardest at the economic feasibility study. If the project is not feasible, they will not agree to underwrite his debt. And why should a local government underwrite a debt in terms of the kinds of public investments it will have to make, if the project is not going to be financially feasible?

We have studied the fiscal impact of Reston on Fairfax County as compared with West Springfield, a conventional subdivision developed at about the same time as Reston. In 1971 (our base year) the two had a difference of only 1,000 in population. We have discovered so far in our analysis of the real estate tax, which is the principal local revenue source, that Reston has produced about $70 more per capita than the average amount for the county, and it has produced about $50 more per capita than another high-quality new subdivision. We are just getting into the expenditure aspects, but I think we may also demonstrate that, in terms of net expenditures to local government, Reston probably costs less than other subdivisions. All lands for public institutions are dedicated. There is no need for public acquisition and maintenance of a park system in Reston, and financing of other major public facilities (such as fire stations and police stations) is being done by lease-purchase to the government, rather than by requiring the government to go into debt by financing bonds.

Politically, however, there is a lag. People in the rest of Fairfax County have the impression that Reston is soaking the county, because the growth rate makes its needs quite obvious. When most new schools have to go into one place, there is resentment of the new town dwellers. People object to seeing their tax money go elsewhere, especially when their own

local twenty-year-old high school needs repair. Here again, the institutional setup may be very important. If bond issues must be voted, it is bad for the developer, whereas if bond issues can be approved without a referendum, he is in a better position.

There is also a need to think about establishing new town districts which can either capitalize the value of the land and build their own public improvements, or be allowed to use the county's tax base to finance services. This would help in the initial period of development, before the population arrives and when the developer is overbuilding facilities. At the building stage, no assessable base exists in the new town to pay for the facilities. The developer needs either to borrow money from the state or to obtain credit from the state or the local government, to be repaid over some agreed period of time. Essentially this is what is being done in the private services. In Columbia, the concept of "pre-servicing" is based on the idea of building more swimming pools and more village centers than are actually needed for the population that will first use them. They will be in place when the first people move into the village or the neighborhood, so they will improve the quality and increase the marketability of the land and, in turn, make it possible to accelerate the development process. Anything done to accelerate the development process improves the cash flow; when the cash flow is improved, the interest is paid off faster, and more can be done with the total operation of the development. The Columbia Park and Recreation Association was established, and lent money by the developer, so that it could go ahead and build the necessary community facilities. Now, with Columbia only about one-fifth complete, almost half of the village recreational facilities are already in place. This means that people will have to pay off that debt over a longer period of time, but it also means a better community over that whole period. This plan precludes waiting for the whole community to develop before beginning to acquire the land and building the facilities in less choice locations and for more money. It also means that recreational facilities are only going to increase by 50 percent over the remainder of the development period, while population will increase 400 percent.

A strong local government, on the other hand, may cause the developer many serious problems. For example, Irvine Ranch, California, has a unique problem. It is probably the biggest planned development underway in the country right now; ultimately, it will have almost half a million people on the 53,000 acres of the old Irvine Ranch. All the land was in Orange County, but as development began, five different bordering municipalities decided to annex parts of the development. The developer was then faced with the prospect of having to work with five different master plans, zoning boards, and public service systems in order to carry out his development. He was also faced with an Orange County Planning Board that was beginning to look with more and more skepticism at his proposed development. In self-defense, he decided to incorporate. Things went along well until the election of the mayor and council, when the citizens (13,000 of the ultimate 450,000 people) elected a city council and mayor who are not aligned politically with the developer. So he now finds himself with an incorporated city, an elected city government, an appointed planning commission, no adopted master plan, no zoning ordinance, and no staff. The city will ultimately have a staff, but this will set back development for a year or so. Fortunately, the operation is probably large enough to survive the delay.

In the early stages, the developers of Riverton had some difficulty with the local government in Henrietta Township outside Rochester, New York. They finally persuaded these people that Riverton would be a good thing.

This nurturing process has to be undertaken, particularly if the developer is coming in from outside. Less difficulty was encountered in Chaska, Minnesota, by the developers of the Jonathan new town. Henry McKnight, the (late) president of the development corporation, and Julius Smith, the vice-president, grew up in that area and knew everybody; as a result, they were able to bring the town along much faster. But the town still drove some hard bargains with them regarding sewage and water costs and their repayment. Even in friendly situations, a tedious and delicate process must be negotiated.

A nonprofit organization could also be used for some (but not all) aspects of governance. Homeowners associations, for instance, are nonprofit in the provision of services. Some services probably ought to be provided by nonprofit groups, but this should come as part of a general governmental plan produced when the physical plan, the economic feasibility study, and the social program for the new community are developed.

The governmental plan of Reston is going to change, as will others, because a plan of governance cannot be made and kept for twenty years. It must frequently be adjusted to market changes and family lifestyle changes. Just look at our changing perception of the "right size" family, and the impact of this on the last decade's housing market. Look at the change in lifestyle, and the impact this is having on whether people want to buy or rent. These elements have to be read back into the economic feasibility program, along with the fact that, when the first village is built, there are no people living there, and what the developer thinks they would like must be provided. When he develops the next increment of a new town, he must take into account the feelings, frustrations, and ideas of the people who bought the first units, and their thoughts about the second stage.

The developer's nightmare is that, if he incorporates his new community, the first people who move in will abrogate his plan. When my hometown, Guthrie, Oklahoma, was settled after the great run in 1889, it was a new town, and 10,000 people were there overnight. The first public act of the citizens of Guthrie was to elect an organizing committee to create a town government; their second act was to repudiate the plan for the site that had been drawn by the Army Corps of Engineers. If the developer does what might be a socially responsible thing by providing a system of government for the new community that could have real authority over the planning and zoning process, the first thing the community will say is, "We don't like that. We don't want any industry in our town." The sale of industrial land is a key part of the developer's economic programs; if he cannot sell that, he cannot build the rest. The people might say, "Great! We don't want the rest. We like it the way it is. We know the master plan envisions an office tower and a shopping center, and a big complex of commerce here, but we'd rather have the woods." That puts the developer in a rather embarrassing position with his bankers. He must be wary of running headlong into any kind of new governmental arrangement, and he must weigh several factors carefully before deciding on incorporation.

Some developers believe in incorporation, and in some states there are good reasons. It creates an assessable base which can be used for taxation. If a developer does not incorporate, he will have to pay fully for many of the public improvements himself: streets, water systems, and sewer systems. If he does incorporate, even though he may not have a sufficient assessable base, he can work out an arrangement with the local government, which he will probably control initially, whereby these services can be provided. The local government can then pay back the developer over a period of time. From an economic point of view, incorporation makes the development eligible for all kinds of state and federal assistance which a private developer cannot receive, such as water and sewer grants, and various kinds of construction grants. These grants act as cash flow because they are money that the developer does not have to put out. In addition, an assessable base is made available immediately and can be used as a basis for issuing bonds. This again operates as cash flow when the revenue is obtained from bonds coming in, and it may be used to finance facilities that would otherwise have to be paid for from the construction development loans. So incorporation may have attractions, if the developer is in a state where incorporation is viewed favorably by the state and local governments as a way of resolving problems. In California, some authorities think that the only way to govern a development is through incorporation; that is simply because that is how it is done in California. In Maryland and Virginia, I think incorporation would be quite unfortunate, at least initially. There the county is the principal instrument of local government, and the developer wants the county tax base to rely on. In addition, he wants the expertise of county officials and staff to assist in much of the process because, if won over, they can be extremely helpful. But where there is a weak county, some way must be devised to circumvent the county rules.

A developer must look at each situation as it arises and make some judgments. He must examine the circumstances that will lead him into a particular governmental arrangement. Then one of the most interesting problems about new towns occurs—how is the developer to avoid getting stuck in a governmental arrangement which was necessary for him initially, but which has become inappropriate at a subsequent stage of development?

A complex system of local government may not be needed during the first five years when there are few people in residence. But by the time the population reaches 25,000, or 40,000, or 100,000 people, a different kind of government is needed. The community must begin to resolve some of the basic problems of government that have existed in older cities and in suburbs, which we in the new towns movement like to think can be improved upon.

Many things must be considered in order to make a new town government operative. Whether he is a private, nonprofit, or public developer, such as the New York State Urban Development Corporation, the developer must plan his operation to accomplish a series of specific tasks. He must assemble the land, often from diverse ownerships. This is one of the critical governmental problems, and maybe the most important single aspect, of new town development. If a developer must assemble the land from hundred-acre farms, the costs of assembly will be high, and he may not be able to get a complete unit. It would be useful to have some kind of governmental organization which has the power to locate new towns in terms of their consistency with overall development policy for the state or the region, and then to assemble the land, either permitting private owners to come into a joint venture, or using eminent domain for that kind of land assemblage. The developer must then produce a plan that is acceptable to local authorities; secure the necessary development permissions, arrange financing, and secure the commitments for public facilities or provide them himself; undertake a development and marketing program; arrange for extra services and facilities (such as better recreation programs) so that his development will be more attractive than others; work with the residents of the new town, maintain good relationships with local authorities, and make money if he is a private developer.

As I said earlier, the mere injection of a new community into the area changes the political order in many jurisdictions. The developer must be prepared to deal with rapidly changing political pressures and circumstances from new residents and businesses, as well as from the residents and officials of neighboring jurisdictions. The existence of the new town itself can be expected to become a major political issue in the area.

In the Reston case, when Robert Simon acquired the land, it was clear to him that it could not be developed as a new town under existing zoning, because it was zoned one acre, and an exciting community cannot be built on one-acre lots. So he had to have a new zoning ordinance written. He needed a water system, and Fairfax County was acting as though it was not going to give him one, so he threatened to incorporate by attempting to revive a charter for a town which had been granted an unused charter in the early 1900's. This was an idle threat, but it was also a political ploy to get the county to agree to provide water and sewage systems. Finally, he had to agree that he would not incorporate, because in Virginia an incorporated town can become a first-class city when the population reaches 5,000. If a town becomes a first-class city, all the land within its boundaries comes off the tax roll of the county. So Fairfax County was not the least bit interested in seeing Reston incorporate after it had spent its money in helping meet the "front end" needs of that community. It wanted the economic benefits of Reston to come back into the county, rather than to be separated from it. Simon also had to agree that he would dedicate the elementary school sites, and that he would permit the county to purchase the secondary school sites wherever they wished. He had to agree that a large percentage of land would remain in open space. But since the county did not want to maintain that open space because of its cost, he had to figure out a way to dedicate and maintain the open space himself. Therefore, he created a homeowners association.

He also had to make a contribution to extend the sewer trunk from its present location. Although Simon had to pay the full cost of the sewer extension, the county will repay him as other people downstream from Reston hook into the sewer and pay their tap fees. That is a general practice with sewer agencies. I dislike it because it means leapfrog development and filling in that the planners do not want. There ought to be a better way to finance that kind of sewer extension, if the new town is desirable. Limited access sewers should be made possible, and other people should not be permitted to hook onto them.

In Reston both homeowners associations and cluster associations provide services. Cluster associations are formed where there are townhouses, and they maintain the common areas. The homeowners association is also basically a maintenance organization, but it maintains all master plan items in Reston—the major open space, walkways, pools, tennis courts, multi-use courts, and one golf course. The major recreation facilities in Reston are dedicated debt-free by the developer to the homeowners association, and the homeowners association then maintains and operates those items based on dues and users fees from the members of the association. Dues are not graduated based on property assessment. Apartment owners pay the fee for the renters in their building, because the owners are members of the homeowners association. The fee then is generally calculated into the rent and passed on to the renter. Renters do not vote in the Reston Homeowners Association. One of the reasons for the association was Federal Housing Administration (FHA) policy. FHA's idea was that a homeowners association is a home *owners'* association, and other people should not be in it.

FHA did approve the Columbia Park and Recreation Association, but it maintained afterward that it would never approve another one. In Columbia the private government is substantially different. The Columbia Park and Recreation Association has a broader mandate; it oversees the operation of programs

as well as maintenance of facilities. Instead of having the developer build and dedicate the facilities in Columbia, the Columbia Association buys the land from the developer and develops the facilities itself. These are paid for through debt financing from the loan made by the developer to the association, which is being amortized. The dues structure in Columbia is also different, in that dues are based on the assessable value of property. Moreover, in Columbia, all property-owners pay an assessment, including owners of industrial and commercial property, on the theory that the programs and facilities provided by the Columbia Association are benefits to employers and make the community more attractive when they recruit employees. This builds a larger financial base for the activities of the association than is provided in Reston, where the assessable base is essentially residential property.

In considering the institutional context for local government, two broad ideas are important. First, when the institutions of local government and the institutional context of government for new towns are examined, thought must be given to the production functions, to the things that people consume. This leads to the second consideration, that of the civic functions of local government. This is the most important part of the entire question. The production functions present problems that are solvable. The civic functions have only proximate solutions, because they are basically unsolvable problems.

I shall repeat some of the things I tried to say in the Twentieth Century Fund report,[1] because they require emphasis. One is that if new towns are to perform a useful governmental role, we should look on them as opportunities to perfect the democratic experience in an urban environment. When we talk about the civic function of the democratic experience, we essentially mean making citizens out of inhabitants. Theories of city government or local government can come from two sources:

the Greek concept of the city, in which the citizens shared responsibility for the city; or the city management tradition, in which the city is an administrative subdivision of the state. I prefer the former, in which the civic function of local government makes possible the development of a public life, as distinguished from a private life.

Local government is not necessary for the administration of services. If you look for the basic rationale for local government, you come back to its civic function, that of giving people an opportunity to acquire intimate personal experience with self-government. Most people's non-local government experience is vicarious —except for the few individuals who run for state and national public office, or who serve in state and national bureaucracies. Local government provides an opportunity for direct experience, and that is its greatest reason for being. Therein, also, has been our greatest failure in local government; however, now an opportunity exists for new towns to revive or make available much wider experiences in self-government.

Most of us have developed considerable private skills throughout our education. I see this even among people who are trained in public administration, city planning, urban design, and other public services. I know fine public administrators who can run an agency, but who are unable to cope with public issues and public problems because they have been unable to deal organically with the process of self-government.

By "organic" I mean that things are related to each other. They are not separated so that government becomes simply something that people in government do. Government should relate to the full social and cultural experience of the population, rather than being a subject for political scientists, with a particular set of mysteries to which only they are a party. The governance of a community involves the full range of community activities, and particularly its public activities.

There is no inconsistency between centralization and decentralization; they are not antithetical. In fact, one could argue that in order to have decentralization you first must have centralization. In a new community, you can tier your governmental organization in such a way that each neighborhood within the town has a system of government based on delegated powers, and at the same time have a townwide central government. In fact, the tiering of general government is one thing we should definitely experiment with, in new towns and elsewhere. I abhor special purpose districts because they make it very difficult for people to know what is going on and to keep account of it, and they force us away from making hard choices about public policy. But there is no reason why there cannot be, in each community or village, an organic structure of government which is fairly general in its scope of activities, but which permits people at the village level to deal with the village aspects of government. I do not think, for instance, that government can be neatly divided into village, town, and regional functions. Take education, for an example—there are aspects of education that are regional, and there are aspects of it that concern the neighborhood. A community should be organized to deal with those different aspects. The system should permit various minorities and majorities to be represented, and to have their interests aggregated differently at various levels. They could combine in various ways to deal at a larger level with problems that simply cannot be handled at a smaller level, and vice versa.

John Dewey's *The Public and Its Problems*[2] is relevant to much of today's discussion about community, belonging, and meaningful participation in public life. The "civic function" of local government is based on the philosophical principle of converting residents into citizens. Dewey and others as far back as Aristotle have pointed out that a citizen is an official. There cannot be government without officials, and there cannot be a public without officials, because it is through officials that publics govern. The purpose of government, ultimately, is the authoritative allocation of values. Values may be allocated, but only government may authoritatively allocate them. If government authoritatively allocates values, and if government acts through officials, it becomes important to have officials to represent publics, and it becomes important also to understand that officials in the Aristotelian sense, and in Dewey's sense, are more than elected representatives or appointed functionaries.

One official act of government is voting. Every voter in this sense is an official, and if one begins to take the notion that citizenship is an official act, then one begins to say that the citizen is an official and every citizen who acts in his office as a citizen shares responsibility for the development of his community.

An act is public when it is a shared experience. The association of two people to do something to or with others that requires the acts of officials for it to be done, becomes a public act. The civic function of local government, therefore, includes helping people obtain experience in the performance of public duties and responsibilities.

Part of the present problem is that we do not know how to develop the civic experience. Some of the reluctance regarding the use of referenda, for example, is related to the issue of shared experience which also involves shared responsibility. There is no particular objection to referenda via cable TV, if these referenda should come at the end of a useful discussion of the problems shared by the people who have to vote on the matter.

Democracy is a unique kind of system; it cannot be "taught." There is no unified theory that says democracy follows certain rules. It grows from the experience of the people and has its operational and ethical aspects. If the democratic experience says to people, "It does not matter what you do, everything is fixed anyway," then its results are alienation, apathy, disengagement from the political system, and withdrawal from the sharing of responsibility.

One thing that people on both sides of the citizen participation argument fail to understand is that, for participation to be useful, it must provide real experience, which means experience that may result in mistakes. One notion of local government is to have it on a scale small enough so that if you make a mistake, it does not hurt too many people. To believe in democracy, you must merely believe that 51 percent of the people will do the right thing 51 percent of the time. A 49 percent margin of error is very generous; furthermore, if an error is made in the location of a park or some facility, it probably does not make all that much difference anyway. It is well worth it to give people the experience. However, planners, developers, and planning commission members feel very possessive of the plans they have produced.

For democracy to be workable, and at the same time to provide this shared experience, there must be ethical considerations. Democracy is not just a process of voting or finding out how many people you can bring to the meeting. In the operational sense, however, democracy is often merely an exercise in the stacking of meetings. Democracy demands a free flow of information, so people who get into the meeting can know whether it is stacked or not and can understand the problems involved. It also demands toleration of ideas that are antagonistic even within the system. It demands that someone learn to honor the views of the developer. It does not mean that he has to agree with him; it means that he has to appreciate the existence of views that represent interests which ought to be heard and weighed fairly.

In the new towns context, it is fair to assess big city government as having failed in providing a democratic experience for most residents. Sharing experiences and meaningfully participating is becoming something of a forlorn hope. By and large, we are reduced to more useful vicarious methods such as computer voting, town meetings, telethons, and letters to the editor. The suburbs provide a civic experience of limited utility. Although there is a great deal more direct contact in many suburbs than in most large cities, the populations are often homogeneous; no really valuable civic experience is developed in the management of conflict. Democracy tries to provide a means for managing conflict within some reasonable rules of the game. If everyone agreed on the basics, like keeping out poor folks, citizens would never have to deal with some of the real conflicts of an urban society. The new town, by providing a heterogeneous population and a large range of economic activities in a relatively small area and for a relatively small total population, provides an opportunity for much more face-to-face experience and contact with a wide variety of interest groups. More experience may be gained in accommodating views and in resolving social conflicts. The new town offers ways of dealing with reality in urban life at the neighborhood, community, and regional levels.

The new town can also provide some experience in the operation of a polity. This raises questions of representative functions, aggregation of interests, management of conflicts, and legitimation of authority. For example, how is the new town represented as an interest in itself, within the larger jurisdiction? How are interests aggregated internally and represented? We still have a lot to do with the development of viable representative systems in this country. The reapportionment revolution was really only laying the constitutional basis for developing a usable system of representa-tion. One man–one vote is not, by itself, a good system of representation; it is the constitutional basis for it. Management of conflict and the legitimation of authority remain the functions of government. Legitimacy depends ultimately on acceptance, not on force; acceptance depends on experience. Is the government honest? Competent? Representative? Are governmental process and officials accountable? Each function is closely related to the capacity to govern.

A state commission of some sort should probably be established to constantly review the stages of growth of given new towns, to make specific recommendations about whether new governmental powers are needed, and to say whether a new system of representation, a new structure, ought to be included at a particular time in the development stage. We probably ought to think of setting up some kind of catalytic organization in each new town. A university would be helpful in providing some of the research necessary to keep the public and private institutions of the new town under review. It would try to anticipate about three years in advance, because that is the minimum time needed to change institutions. To give an example, we had a conference at Reston last June. Reston now has about 19,000 people in it. In three years it will have 42,000 people. We are asking, "What kind of institutions are you going to need in 1975?" rather than merely, "What do you need now that you don't have?" Columbia will have almost 60,000 people in 1976. We are moving rapidly during a crucial period, and we do not want to end up with cities of 80-100,000 people which have governments that are adequate for only 4,000.

The plan for a new community ought to consider the basic political and social purposes which it can serve, as well as its architectural, design, and environmental purposes. These are all elements of an organic system. The physical design of a community can enhance certain kinds of governmental activities. Places can be provided for people to meet, spaces that will encourage a certain kind of social and political intercourse. But this will only happen if you know what kind of social and political intercourse you want to encourage and should be trying to encourage. The physical design should be kept flexible enough to take feedback from the original citizens who get into the process and say, "We're not using the meeting hall, and we don't like the town square. It is a dead space instead of the lively space we learned in architecture school that town squares were supposed to be. And there are reasons for that. Now, maybe we need a different kind of space or a different kind of circulation system that will bring people into contact with each other." These are just small elements of the total design process for a new community. If talk is not only about the civic functions, but also about the many social functions of a new community, an even broader context for design and development of a community will be achieved.

Several issues should be mentioned which may become central political issues regarding new town governance. Most of the current rudimentary approaches are inadequate. These can be characterized as government by the developer, of the developer, and usually for the developer—a "benevolent despotism" where the developer does everything. The next stage would be private government, such as the homeowners associations and the community associations; municipalities, which could include townships or boroughs; and counties, with special districts. We toyed in the southeastern Michigan study with the idea of a new town district,[3] a creature of the state, which would permit some of the flexibility discussed earlier. Experimentation in these forms is definitely necessary. We need to avoid being locked into existing forms of local government unless those forms can perform the kinds of

production and civic functions that I have been talking about.

A second issue is that of citizenship versus consumerism. I am for consumerism when it comes to making sure that people provide what they claim they are providing, that what you buy works, and that it does not cost too much. But if we look at new towns simply as ways of satisfying an important segment of the housing market, and if the people who live in new towns view themselves essentially as consumers of the houses, parks, playgrounds, recreation facilities, and government services there, new towns will not be any better than our existing cities and suburbs. The consumerism approach states, "You produced it, and you owe me what I bought." The obverse to this challenges, "If you don't like it, you can sell it and move." When one goes into a new community, he has as much of a stake in that new community as the developer himself, and he has not only a right but also an obligation to share with the developer the responsibility for its proper development. That means not that he will agree with him all of the time, or even most of the time, but that he has a shared responsibility for the ultimate development and control of his environment.

A third issue regarding new town governance is the extent of resident and nonresident participation in the physical and institutional development processes. There are people who will not live in the new town, yet who will use it, particularly if it is to be an instrument of development policy for states and regions. They have some rights regarding the new town; just what these are, as contrasted with those of the citizens who live there, must be determined.

I have mentioned phasing several times in relating institutional development to the stages of physical and population growth. Here again, institutions must be provided to review, assess, and develop programs.

John Dewey once stated that the new age

of human relationships has no political agencies worthy of it. The democratic public is still unorganized.[4] The new town offers an opportunity to meet this exciting challenge.

·NOTES

1 Royce Hanson, *New Towns: Laboratories for Democracy*. Report of the Twentieth Century Fund Task Force on Governance of New Towns (New York: Twentieth Century Fund, 1971).
2 John Dewey, *The Public and Its Problems* (Denver: Henry Holt, 1927).
3 Metropolitan Fund, *Regional New Town: Alternative in Urban Growth for Southeast Michigan*. Research project of Metropolitan Fund, Detroit, 1970.
4 Dewey, *The Public and Its Problems,* p. 31.

READING LIST

Clark, Ruben, and Paul J. Mode, Jr. "Transfer of Power in New Communities." Seminar, Center for Urban and Regional Studies, University of North Carolina, 1969.
Committee for Economic Development. *Modernizing Local Government to Secure a Balanced Federalism.* New York: Committee for Economic Development, 1966.
Conkin, Paul. *Tomorrow a New World: The New Deal Community Program.* Ithaca, N.Y.: Cornell University Press, The American Historical Association, 1969.
Connell, Kathleen M. *Regional New Towns and Intergovernmental Relations: Four Case Studies.* Detroit: Metropolitan Fund, 1972.
Cowley, R. J. "Communal Facilities on High Density Estates." *Housing Review* 10 (May/June 1961): 85–91.
"Democracy in the New Towns: The Limits of Private Government." *University of Chicago Law Review* (Winter 1969): 379–412.
Dewey, John. *The Public and Its Problems.* Denver: Henry Holt, 1927.
Downs, Anthony. "Creating the Institutional Framework for Encouraging New Cities." In Metropolitan Fund, *Regional New Town: Alternative in Urban Growth for Southeast Michigan.* Detroit: Metropolitan Fund, May 1970.
Eckardt, Wolf Von. "Planning for 'Public Concern.' " *Arts in Virginia,* Winter 1967, pp. 16–29.
First Annual Columbia Conference on Community Governance. Columbia, Md., 24–25 March 1972.

Flaxman, Fred. "Can a New Town Be Democratic?" *Restonian* 1 (October 1969): 22–26.
Gans, Herbert J. "Political Participation and Apathy." Master's thesis, Divisional Program in the Social Sciences, University of Chicago, 1950.
Hanson, Royce. *Managing Services for New Communities.* Report of the Symposium on the Management of New Communities, Washington Center for Metropolitan Studies and New Communities Study, Virginia Polytechnic Institute and State University. Washington, D.C.: Washington Center for Metropolitan Studies, 1972.
———. *New Towns: Laboratories for Democracy.* Report of the Twentieth Century Fund Task Force on Governance of New Towns. New York: Twentieth Century Fund, 1971.
"How Columbia Manages Its Amenities While Gearing for Public Control." *Columbia Today,* March 1971, pp. 11–15.
Kelly, Michael. "Planning the Government of a New Town." Paper, Yale Law School, February 1967.
Larsen, C. L., and R. D. Andrews. *The Government of Greenbelt.* College Park, Md.: University of Maryland, Bureau of Public Administration, 1951.
Meltzer, Jack. "Administrative Problems of New Towns." In *Planning.* pp. 71–81. Chicago: American Society of Planning Officials, 1952.
Metropolitan Fund. *Regional New Town: Alternative in Urban Growth for Southeast Michigan.* A Research Project of Metropolitan Fund, Detroit, 1970.
Mields, Hugh, Jr. "Federal Performance: Local Needs." Address given at the American Society of Planning Officials 1972 National Planning Conference, Detroit, 19 April 1972. Mimeographed.
Myers, Phyllis. "Communities: Columbia's Carefully Cultivated Institutions are Beginning to Bear Fruit." *City* 3 (October 1969): 33–38.
Noland, Richard, et al. *Local Government and Preplanned Communities in San Diego County.* San Diego: San Diego State College Public Affairs Research Institute, 1968.
Ricks, R. Bruce. "A Tool for Managerial Analysis in Land Development." *American Institute of Planners Journal* 33 (March 1967): 117–120.
Scott, Stanley. *The Large New Communities: Ultimate Self-Government and Other Problems.* A Public Affairs Report. Berkeley: University of California, 1965.
———. *New Towns Development and the Role of Government.* A Public Affairs Report. Berkeley: University of California, 1964.
Steadman, Robert F. "Government for Modern

Needs." Seminar, Center for Urban Studies, University of Chicago, 1967.

Urban Land Institute. *Planning Community Facilities for Basic Employment Expansion.* Washington, D.C.: Urban Land Institute, Technical Bulletin no. 16, 1951.

"Who's Going to Make the Hot Chestnut Decisions?: The Second NAHB Conference on Environmental Design." *National Association of Home Builders Journal* 19 (December 1965): 38–41.

New Communities:
Issues and Implementation

Hugh Mields, Jr.

This discussion of new communities legislation in the United States will review the federal government's involvement in new communities and discuss the legislative aspects of new communities at the federal level. Special attention will be given to the new communities program of the Department of Housing and Urban Development (HUD). It will also examine this program's prospects for the future.

Aside from 1917 to 1918, when the United States Housing Corporation tried to create permanent homes and communities in response to severe war industry housing shortages, the first substantive federal involvement in planned communities came in the mid-thirties when President Roosevelt used the Emergency Relief Appropriation Act to establish the Greenbelt program.[1] Although the Act did not specifically provide for support of new community activity, it did provide the President with the general powers to establish the Resettlement Administration. One primary responsibility of this administration was to develop eight new communities, intended to provide employment opportunities as well as to test some of the same planning concepts and new ideas that had been attempted at Sunnyside and Radburn.[2] The towns were to be built by workers on relief and were to provide low-income housing in high densities within a pleasant, open setting. Each town was to be an experiment, and technicians were given the full opportunity to develop new ideas and approaches in their assignments.

Plans to build the eight communities were changed when Congress appropriated $31 million rather than the $68 million requested. The number of communities was reduced further by a court decision which blocked the development of Greenbrook in Franklin Township, New Jersey, and by the opposition of the St. Louis Plan Commission, which stopped a development that was not even near enough to completion to have deserved a name.[3] The three communities that were finally developed were Greenbelt (thirteen miles north of Washington, D.C.), Greenhills (five miles north of Cincinnati), and Greendale (seven miles from downtown Milwaukee). The Greenbelt program was a totally federal new community program. The Resettlement Administration selected the sites, acquired the land, planned, financed, built, and managed the communities. The sites were selected because they were near major cities which had stable job bases and optimistic projections for future employment opportunities. No provisions were made for local review of the sites, and no consistent concern was expressed for regional development goals. Most of the land was acquired at the outset of the development process; since the federal government was the sole owner of the property, there was no need for development controls.[4] The Resettlement Administration provided all residential and commercial facilities, including schools, fire and police stations, roads, sewage systems, and even water, gas, and electric utilities.

The governments of the Greenbelt communities were conditioned by their unique local-federal relationships. Federal land was not subject to local zoning restrictions, and there was no local taxing power. Congress authorized payments in lieu of taxes, in amounts equal to the cost of the municipal services provided. Eventually all three communities incorporated under their respective state laws—Greenhills in 1949, Greenbelt in 1952, and Greendale in 1953.

Unfortunately, this first federal effort to support new community development did not prove entirely successful. World War II diverted the concern and effort needed to develop the towns into something more than garden suburbs. While the first neighborhoods in each of the communities had been completed by 1938, less than 1,000 housing units were built by the federal government in each community, and only a few educational, commercial, and community facilities were actually completed. Furthermore, interest in new communities was not revitalized after the war. From 1949 to 1953 the government liquidated its assets in these developments by selling the undeveloped land to private developers.

Today the Greenbelt communities are still distinguishable from other communities. When the government withdrew, Greendale's development was guided by a public investment group consisting of several Milwaukee businessmen, and the spirit of the original concept was retained. There was, however, no evidence of a balanced socioeconomic population mix. In 1953 Greenbelt adopted a cooperative housing system, and in 1970 the population of this community was approximately 19,000, the largest of the three Greenbelt towns.

In the fifties, as a result of the Housing Act of 1949, local and state governments became concerned about housing for low and moderate income families, and especially for low-income families. Urban redevelopment then meant clearance programs designed to raze slums, eliminate blight, and thereby provide cleared areas which could be reused for various purposes, including housing, industry, and commerce. However, some fairly large-scale redevelopment was initiated during this period. In southwest Washington, D.C., 1,000 acres were cleared. This is a good example of a project started in the mid-fifties and still in the process of development.

Urban redevelopment is essentially a renewal process which continues to be practiced as a program. The local public agency acquires land, clears it, and holds it until it can find a private developer willing to accept and assume the risk of rebuilding the area. The redevelopment program, renamed "renewal" by the Eisenhower administration in 1954, has suffered considerably—first as a result of the inadequate ability to relocate displaced families, and second because of the impact it has had on minority groups, particularly on blacks in the central city. Even now in many communities the program is referred to as "Negro removal."

Renewal in its latter and present stages is, nevertheless, more frequently a device for providing sites for residential reuse by low and moderate income families. Early antagonism toward the program developed because many communities were thought to have unduly concentrated their efforts and money on renewing central business districts, instead of providing housing for the poor. Considerable controversy resulted in Congress about the amount of urban renewal funds allocated for nonresidential renewal. However, the federal response since the mid-sixties has been in favor of projects emphasizing housing for low and moderate income families. The federal government's urban renewal focus has been on the major central cities, although between 1949 and 1971 about 25 percent of the money went to cities of 50,000 or less.[5]

The Housing Act of 1949 has itself undergone significant change since its enactment. The Housing Act of 1954 made several major revisions: it provided federal grants for planning (Section 701), enlarged and renamed the redevelopment program to "urban renewal," required localities to develop comprehensive and workable programs for development, and established an insurance program for families in private housing displaced by urban renewal. The Housing Act of 1961 expanded the categories of loans eligible for Federal Housing Administration (FHA) mortgage insurance, authorized grants for mass transportation facilities, increased the federal share of urban renewal grants for communities of 50,000 or less, and authorized grants to create open space. The Department of Housing and Urban Development was established in 1965.

That same year the Housing and Urban Development Act authorized federal rent supplements to low-income families; provided rehabilitation grants for substandard housing in urban renewal areas; authorized grants to municipalities and counties for code enforcement in deteriorating areas; facilitated purchase of existing ("turnkey") housing for public housing use; authorized grants for financing basic water and sewer facilities and neighborhood health, recreation and community service centers; and (in Title X of the 1965 Act) provided for short-term loan guarantees to the developers for the "front end" money needed for infrastructure to support large-scale residential development.

In 1966 the Demonstration Cities and Metropolitan Development Act provided grants and technical assistance to help communities plan and carry out model city programs. The Housing and Urban Development Act of 1968 established home ownership assistance programs for low and moderate income families who had never before qualified. It also authorized the guarantee of bonds and other obligations issued by private developers of new communities (Title IV); grants for water, sewer, and open space projects in new communities; and a new program of financial assistance for "neighborhood development programs" under which urban renewal projects could be planned and carried out annually. The 1970 Urban Growth and New Community Development Act called for the formulation of a national urban growth policy and increased the means of assistance for new community developers.

All these changes were offered as "perfecting amendments." Each advocate of an amendment thought that his might make the program better. Each tried to provide that new factor, or inject that new aspect, that new level of assistance, that new approach which would make it possible to solve the compounding problems of urban growth in America.

The recent "new towns" concept in the United States began around 1961, when the Housing and Home Finance Agency administrator, Robert Weaver, an economist with a long and abiding interest in new towns, decided to try to get the federal government involved. He felt, as did some of his colleagues in the housing agency, as well as many other urbanists and planners throughout the United States, that the federal government ought to get into the business of supporting, or at least encouraging, large-scale community developments. Weaver recognized that part of the problem with the development of the major cities was disorderly peripheral growth. This growth was inefficient, uneconomical, and encouraged segregated housing for the affluent. Weaver, his colleagues, and other new town advocates felt that if the federal government could help encourage large-scale development, they could then insist that developers provide housing for a greater range of income groups and insure that the result would be open, integrated communities. As early as 1961 Weaver had recommended mortgage insurance for land to the Congress, but it was not until August 1965 that Weaver, who was to become secretary of the Department of Housing and Urban Development a month later, managed to persuade Congress to accept the program which eventually became, through amendment, Title X of the National Housing Act. In 1966 Title X was amended to provide for mortgage insurance on land to be developed as new communities, and in 1968 the first new communities act was approved by the Congress as Title IV of the Housing and Urban Development Act of 1968.

Title IV of the 1968 Act was designed exclusively for private developers: it provides loan guarantees for up to thirty years. Through Title IV, loans to the developer are insured to cover land acquisition and the provision of infrastructure, as the basis for development of a new community. The legislation, as passed in 1968, never managed to capture the support of major interest groups such as the National League of Cities, the National Association of County Officials, or the state governments. About the only organization which publicly supported the idea of new towns was the National Association of Housing and Development Officials. Other public interest groups followed the lead of the mayors, who then argued that any federal program providing assistance for new community development would divert resources from the central city to the suburbs, encourage white middle-class families to leave for the open turf of a wonderful new community, and simply exacerbate the flight to the suburbs. These mayors felt strongly enough about the issue to urge opposition to all efforts to enact new communities legislation in Congress.

Although there was active opposition in both the Senate and the House, Secretary Weaver had convinced President Johnson of the importance of new communities legislation. The president was a close friend of Wright Patman, chairman of the House Banking and Currency Committee. When the 1968 housing bill went into conference to resolve the differences between the House and the Senate versions, Patman insisted that Title IV, which had been eliminated from of the Senate bill, be passed, even over the opposition of the city lobbies. Unfortunately, 1968 was the year for a change in administration, which inevitably affects program continuity. That, plus the newness of the program, meant that for its first two years the new communities program was understaffed, and little attention was paid to it.

During the same two-year period, however, other things were stirring in Congress and among professional and public interest groups. Some people began to feel that there might be more to the idea of new communities than they had supposed. The problems in the inner city were not being solved on any significant scale. Officials were finding that they frequently could not move major capital improvement programs, such as interstate highways and freeways, through their communities because of inadequate relocation resources. The housing shortage for low and moderate income groups was a difficult burden, not only for these groups but also for the cities whose important capital improvement programs were delayed as a result.

Furthermore, in the late sixties, the trend toward large-scale abandonment of cities began to surface in New York, St. Louis, Chicago, Philadelphia, Boston, and other cities. It was hoped that new communities might offer solutions, particularly in situations where the city itself might control new town development. Utilizing basically vacant sites within the city itself, the new town would provide housing without a massive relocation load, and an opportunity to demonstrate the potential for at least socially, if not economically, integrated housing, as well as an opportunity to deal with the problem of the housing need and the problem of segregation on a scale which would have some reasonable impact.

In 1968 a group of individuals met with Laurance G. Henderson, who had been staff director of the Senate's small business committee during the Truman administration. Henderson had gained important experience by organizing, in 1965, the Special Committee on Historic Preservation, which led to legislation in this area.[6] He thought he might be able to do much the same kind of job in developing the basis for an expanded federal new town program. The result of Henderson's efforts was the National Committee on Urban Growth Policy, which had the support of the National League of Cities and the United States Conference of Mayors.[7]

Henderson obtained support from the Ford Foundation and organized a two-and-a-half-

week study tour to Europe in November 1968 so senators and congressmen could study new towns and growth policy in Western Europe. Meetings held during and after the trip led to agreement on the substance of a bill providing for a federal direct long-term loan program. The bill, as recommended, made public agencies eligible for loans and grants. It encouraged them not only to build freestanding new towns, satellite cities, and accelerated growth centers, but with respect to new towns intown, it provided reinforcing linkages with the urban renewal program.

The accelerated growth centers were designed specifically to please and to meet the needs of senators with a more rural orientation. It was the first time this terminology had ever been used in any legislation. Basically, it described a modification of a set of concepts developed by Ted Aschman of Barton-Aschman Associates in a policy paper prepared for Charles Haar, then assistant secretary for metropolitan development with the Department of Housing and Urban Development.

The National Committee on Urban Growth Policy simply said that the growth center concept relates to small towns in predominantly rural areas. It was hoped that growth centers would offer potential for experimentation and support for encouraging growth in some very small American towns. The bill provided for the four kinds of developments described in the Committee's report, *The New City*.[8]

The first title of the bill dealt with the creation of a Council of Urban Growth Advisors for the president, modeled after the Council of Economic Advisors. The council was to be a statutory advisory committee at the national level concerned with the importance of growth and the implementation of a growth policy, although in a generalized form. This legislation also provided planning assistance to the states and to regional agencies to help them decide how they wanted their individual areas to develop. It was thought not that national policy would be an aggregate of fifty state policies, but that the federal government had a much more positive role to play in encouraging rational growth.

The rest of the bill dealt with titles for the provision of loan funds and planning assistance. It provided that the federal government develop some new communities on its own, and that the Community Development Corporation be the key agency for all federal agencies engaging in large-scale developments. This would mean that all these agencies would be required to go to HUD for advice and counsel on the manner, location, and basis for their developments. It would even mean that the Department of Defense could not locate a major installation just anywhere—if their proposed development was to have any impact in a community sense, it would have to be cleared through HUD.

As a result of the interest generated by the National Committee on Urban Growth Policy and his own growing concern about the future growth and development of the United States, Congressman Thomas L. Ashley of Ohio persuaded Wright Patman of the House Banking and Currency Committee and William Barrett of the Housing Subcommittee to agree to the creation of an ad hoc subcommittee on urban growth, and to fund its work for one year.

Ashley retained Henderson to staff the subcommittee's work and began hearings in June 1969. From 3 June 1969 to 3 December 1970 the ad hoc subcommittee on urban growth took testimony from over fifty witnesses, including Margaret Mead; Gunnar Myrdal; Robert F. Hastings, president of the American Institute of Architects; Barbara Ward (Lady Jackson); A. L. Bethel, vice-president of Westinghouse Electric Corporation; Jay W. Forrester of the Massachusetts Institute of Technology; William H. Whyte of the American Conservation Association; Sir Hugh Wil-

son of the Royal Institute of British Architects; Philip M. Hauser from the University of Chicago; and Leo F. Schnore of the University of Wisconsin. The hearings were published in three volumes: *Population Trends, The Quality of Urban Life,* and *Industrial Location Policy.*[9] They constitute one of the best series of commentaries on urban problems ever assembled, and they provide a solid basis of support for the Title VII new communities program.

While the National Committee on Urban Growth Policy was considering the possibilities of a new communities program, the administration was toying with new towns legislation of its own. Fortunately, several members of HUD felt that the two efforts were not basically in conflict. These HUD members included Samuel Jackson, assistant secretary for Community Management, who later became general manager of the Community Development Corporation; William Nicoson, the former director of the Office of New Communities Development (which was subsequently renamed as the New Communities Administration); and Floyd Hyde, then assistant secretary for Community Development, later undersecretary of HUD. Thus the bill before Congress had some chance of being considered as a bipartisan effort. Early in 1970, however, the administration decided it was not going to introduce new communities legislation. When the Ashley bill, the Housing and Urban Development Act of 1970, was finally introduced in the Senate and the House, the administration (to the chagrin of some of the Republican advocates of the program) started to oppose it. The administration was particularly unhappy about the Council of Urban Growth Advisors, arguing that it would be enough to say that the president would be responsible for examining growth issues and making recommendations about the creation of such a policy. The Republican bill was fairly similar, at least in terms of new towns, to the one that had been introduced by the Democrats. The Republican (administration) draft provided the same levels of assistance. One early draft went well beyond the Democratic bill in that it gave HUD the power of eminent domain, enabling it to acquire land on behalf of local developers. Nevertheless, and despite the strong efforts of the Office of New Communities Development staff led by its director William Nicoson, in early 1970 the basic policy decision was made that the Nixon administration would not become heavily involved in new towns as envisaged by the legislation then pending. But it soon became clear to the administration that a bill would be passed by the Congress, and HUD was ordered to negotiate the best possible deal. Hilbert Fefferman, HUD associate general counsel for legislation, was ordered into the breach to work with both Senate and House committee staffs.

The compromise produced a bill that everybody agreed would be relatively ideal under the circumstances. The big change was that there were to be no direct loans, as had been originally proposed. The loan guarantees have worked out reasonably well, however, and they seem to have proven adequate substitutes for direct loans. The House bill went to the floor, and since the new town provisions were in the first title, they were the first area subject to debate. Some minor amendments were added to the legislation when Republican Gerry Brown moved to strike the whole first title of the bill. This happened at a time when there were few Democrats on the floor, and the title was lost on a teller vote. Everything that the proponents had worked for, the whole new communities title, was eliminated from the House bill. Furthermore, House leadership decided that no effort would be made to resurrect it later in the debate. Thus the bill that passed the House did not have new communities legislation in it. The Senate bill passed earlier did have a new communities title, and when the two versions of the housing bill went to con-

ference, the new communities title was restored. Moreover, the Senate agreed to include some of the provisions which were part of the final House version. Therefore, the bill in its final form was a combination of the Senate proposals and what were considered desirable aspects of the New Communities Title which had been eliminated from the passed House bill.

After a long and difficult battle, the legislation was at last on the books. However, sometimes the executive branch of government chooses not to administer legislation as Congress intended, and so far Congress has not discovered a way in which it can force the executive branch to perform according to its own standards. Presidents have long asserted that they do not have to spend appropriated money and that they do not have to fund programs, even though Congress may make money available. The executive branch usually responds by performing in those programs where the constituency is putting the pressure, and the new communities program has a remarkably small constituency. It does not have strength at the state and local levels, and only a very limited number of private developers are ready to support it in the higher reaches of the Republican party. Also there are few if any who will appear voluntarily before congressional committees to support it. Local and state governments appear reasonably concerned about the new communities program and seem to like the idea, but they always feel that they have more important legislative issues to attend to, either through special revenue-sharing, general tax-sharing, or other programs that involve more resources.

One other provision in the Title VII legislation that had not been part of Title IV was the creation of the Community Development Corporation. The corporation was created as one way of giving the program visibility and substance within the administration. It was originally set up as a corporation "within HUD"

Table 1. HUD New Communities Program Activity for Developer
Loan Guarantees Assistance[10]

Present activity stage	Number of projects	Satellite	Type of new community		
			New town intown	Growth center	Freestanding
Approved guarantees/commitments	13	10	1	1	1
Applications in preparation	9	5	3	—	1
Full applications in house	6	4	2	—	—
Active pre-applications	24	12	5	2	5
Pre-application unlikely to sustain ONCD review	10	5	1	4	—
Total	62	36	12	7	7

to handle all new communities business, and it was very broadly defined. It was to operate pretty much as an independent entity, making the program as responsive as the support and interest on the outside could make it. Secretary George Romney opposed the formation of the corporation, because he feared that he would have a problem controlling it. The compromise here was that the secretary of HUD was appointed chairman of the board of the corporation with the power to appoint members of the board, except the general manager, who by law is a presidential appointee. In addition, the legislation called for a general manager equivalent in rank and status to any of the existing secretaries to run the Community Development Corporation program within HUD. The idea was to create an instant administration, and to do it in such a way that HUD itself could not completely control it. That was the theory—but planning the corporation was one thing, and making it work efficiently was another, particularly since the administration was not especially excited about the concept.

When the bill passed, there were fewer than twenty professionals working for the Office of New Communities Development (ONCD) within HUD. Although the number went up to about thirty within a year, the office never achieved its authorized strength of fifty. ONCD has had to make do with fewer than forty pro-

fessionals, and thus it has been unable to deal with its backlog and to work efficiently with the processing load for the new communities in the application process. Table 1 is included to show the status of new communities program activity as of November 1972. [See also the Underhill article, Table 3, page 60, for new communities approved by HUD.]

Unfortunately, the administration has not tried to fund all aid programs available under the law. Special planning assistance was authorized for innovative social planning and for the utilization of new technology. Congress actually gave HUD $5 million in 1971, yet the Office of Management and Budget has not yet made that money available to eligible sponsors. Public service grants were authorized to provide necessary social, educational, health, and public safety assistance to new communities during the start-up period, when the new communities' own resources would not adequately support a reasonable level of services.

The administration has not asked Congress for an appropriation. In addition, the interest differential grants have never been authorized. Such grants were to be made available to public bodies to make up the difference in interest payments between a taxable federally guaranteed bond, which would be used in Title VII, and a local tax-exempt bond which might otherwise have been used to finance the improvement involved. Proposals for funding these grants need not even go to the Appropriations Committee. HUD has contract authority in this case, but refuses to use it. Furthermore, HUD is authorized to provide technical assistance out of its own resources to help both public and private developers. HUD has done none of this; it has made no effort to justify any level of effort with the Appropriations Committee to carry out needed technical assistance. In the new communities title of the 1972 Housing Act, HUD would have received another $500 million in guaranteed authority which would have brought the total authorization up to $1 billion, and it could easily have requested and received another $1 billion. Securing additional authorization for loan guarantees for new communities from Congress does not appear to be a problem. The legislators view loan guarantees somewhat differently from direct loans. Because of this, there is potential for significant funding of new community developments if the basic idea takes hold. HUD could easily review about twenty or thirty proposals a year, at least in terms of the potential market. HUD's present conservatism is understandable because of the problems it is having within the administration itself. All HUD is really doing now, however, is providing for the guarantees, and making quite a bit of money in the process through the fees it charges. The service charges and fees run about 7.5 percent over the aggregate of the total amount guaranteed. There is also a 3 percent fee due immediately upon issuance of the bonds. HUD maintains a revolving fund, and as of 27 December 1972 the cash value of the securities held in the fund was $7,614,598. This certainly must exceed their cost of administration so far.

HUD is now running a program that makes money for the federal government. The paradox is that HUD and the new communities people are interested in making the program effective and expanding it. Yet their efforts are constantly frustrated by the Office of Management and Budget, the White House, and the president. There seems to be no real hope, at least at this moment, that the president will change his mind, or that the White House will instruct the Office of Management and Budget to give this program more support.

In addition, HUD's budget report for fiscal 1973 is interesting because it contains some baffling contradictions. HUD projects that it will do three times the amount of business it did in fiscal 1972, yet it asks for no additional staff and no additional funds to cover the cost of managing the expanded program. Right now, ONCD is simply putting off potential developers, public and private, who are asking for pre-application interviews. Therefore, given no change in the attitude of this administration (or the next), and given that the administrative staff at HUD is not sizeably increased, any realistic view of the program would show that there will probably be a diminution of potential developers. Developers cannot afford the long, discouraging wait for their interviews, application reviews, and processing. So the new communities program could conceivably find itself in a situation where it would actually be doing far less business.

Nevertheless, as the list of new communities approved by HUD illustrates, the Title VII program is in fact functioning and trying to help meet the housing needs of all Americans in the context of communities, rather than simply tracts of homogenized housing. The new communities program has made a beginning in the thirteen new communities approved so far, with jobs and housing in two, a major housing complex underway in a third, lots developed and sold in a fourth, and major infrastructures installed in others. The number of units in these thirteen new communities at maturity is expected to be 244,000, serving a population of about 750,000.

For the first thirteen new communities to go under commitment, about 62,000 dwelling units are planned for low and moderate income families involving about 250,000 people. At the current average of 55,000 population per each new community project under Title VII, and considering workload and pipeline as it existed in October 1972, Secretary Samuel Jackson estimated that over 9 million people could be housed within these communities, including 2.25 million of low and moderate income.

In any event, the program's ability to grow and produce high quality communities in significant volume will depend on a substantially increased level of federal grants for infrastructure; on positive commitments from HUD for housing subsidies needed to meet the communities' low and moderate income housing targets over the full projected development period; on the release of special planning and public service grant funds already authorized; on augmented staff; and on a considerably higher priority for action in the Nixon administration. The program's advocates, clients, and constructive critics must support a bold and flexible program—one which will encourage a variety of approaches consistent with regional needs and lifestyles; they must also experiment and take calculated risks. No program of this complexity can be flawlessly conceived and executed, nor should it be applied uniformly throughout the nation.

The federal New Communities Program provides a unique opportunity to demonstrate, on a large scale, the potential viability of a community which is deliberately planned to take advantage of the best available technology for safeguarding its environment, to develop a full complement of effective service delivery systems, and (possibly more important) to accept social, economic, and ethnic integration as a stated goal. Federally assisted new communities are the only major American development efforts where such goals are accepted as essential elements of the community-building process. If there is any hope that we will

be able to build better communities with safe and attractive living environments equitably for all out citizens, I think that hope lies most clearly with the federal new communities program.

NOTES

1 For a more detailed discussion of the history of American new towns and federal involvement in such efforts, see United States, Advisory Commission on Intergovernmental Relations, *Urban and Rural America: Policies for Future Growth,* Report A–32 (Washington, D.C.: U.S. Government Printing Office, April 1968).

2 In the twenties Sunnyside, N.Y., and Radburn, N.J., were attempts to transfer the English garden city to the United States. They can be considered as the first private effort to develop new towns. Sunnyside planned to house 1,200 families on 56 acres and was relatively successful. Radburn was planned to house 25,000 people on two square miles and failed (partly due to the Depression), although the concepts involved were very successful.

3 In the Greenbrook case (*Franklin Township* v. *Tugwell,* 85F.2nd 208, D.C. Cir. 1936), the president's power to build new communities under the Emergency Relief Appropriation Act was challenged as an unconstitutional delegation of authority to the president because the grant of powers was too broad. The decision was limited to Greenbrook.

4 When the Farm Security Administration succeeded the Resettlement Administration, private builders were permitted. However, the homes they constructed were subject to an FSA review.

5 Analysis of the distribution of urban renewal projects and funds to communities during the calendar year 1971 shows that slightly more than half the projects and three-fourths of the funds went to cities with populations above 50,000. The higher allocation of funds to the larger communities reflects the greater workloads and the higher unit costs of operations in these areas.

6 *With Heritage So Rich* (New York: Random House, 1966) is a report of a Special Committee on Historic Preservation under the auspices of the U.S. Conference of Mayors. Committee members were Albert Rains, chairman; Laurance G. Henderson, director; Edmund C. Muskie, William B. Widnall, Philip H. Hoff, Raymond R. Tucker, and Gordon Gray. Ex-officio members were Stewart L. Udall (alternates Walter I. Pozen and George B. Hartzog, Jr.), John T. Connor (alternate Rex T. Whitton),

Robert C. Weaver (alternate William L. Slayton), and Lawson B. Knott, Jr. (alternate William A. Schmidt).

7 Members of the National Committee on Urban Growth Policy included Albert Rains, chairman; Hale Boggs, congressman from Louisiana; William B. Widnall, congressman from New Jersey; Thomas Ludlow Ashley, congressman from Ohio; Albert W. Johnson, congressman from Pennsylvania; Henry S. Reuss, congressman from Wisconsin; Robert G. Stephens, Jr., congressman from Georgia; Henry Maier, mayor of Milwaukee; John Sparkman, senator from Alabama; Raymond Shafer, governor of Pennsylvania; Philip Hoff, former governor of Vermont; Floyd Hyde, assistant secretary, Department of Housing and Urban Development, and former mayor of Fresno, Calif.; James Aldredge, commissioner, Fulton County, Ga.; Laurance G. Henderson, director; Frank DeStefano, assistant director; and John G. Tower, senator from Texas. Consultants were John Gunther, executive director, U.S. Conference of Mayors; Patrick Healy, executive director, National League of Cities; Bernard F. Hillenbrand, executive director, National Association of Counties; William L. Slayton, executive director, Urban America, Inc.; Casey Ireland, minority staff member, Housing Subcommittee, House Banking and Currency Committee; Hamilton Richardson, investment banker; Dallas; Hugh Mields, urban affairs consultant; John Garvey, Jr., deputy executive director, National League of Cities; Gillis Long, lawyer and investment banker, Alexandria, La.; Carl A. S. Coan, staff director, Housing Subcommittee, Senate Banking and Currency Committee.

8 *The New City*, ed. Donald Canty (New York: Frederick A. Praeger, 1969), is the report of the National Committee on Urban Growth Policy.

9 Committee on Banking and Currency, Hearings before the ad hoc Subcommittee on Urban Growth, House of Representatives, 91st Cong., 1 and 2 sess., 30 September 1968–24 June 1970. Part I: *Population Trends* (1969), Part II: *The Quality of Urban Life* (1970), and Part III: *Industrial Location Policy* (1971).

10 Loan guarantees of assistance are given according to the Urban Growth and New Community Development Act of 1970 (Title VII, Housing and Urban Development Act of 1970). Entire table based on information then available from HUD.

READING LIST

Anderson, Robert M., and Bruce B. Roswig. *Planning, Zoning, and Subdivision: A Summary of Statutory Law in the Fifty States.* New York: New York Federation of Official Planning Organizations, 1966.

Babcock, Richard F. "Suggested Legislation with Commentary." In *Legal Aspects of Planned Unit Residential Development with Suggested Legislation.* Washington, D.C.: Urban Land Institute, Technical Bulletin no. 52, 1965 (reprinted 1970).

Commission on Population Growth and the American Future. *Population and the American Future.* New York: New American Library, Signet Books, 1972.

"Congress Realizes New Towns Need Help." *Engineering News-Record*, 1 August 1968, p. 106.

Davis, Georgia K. "Title VII: A Spur to the Building of New Communities." *American Institute of Architects Journal* 56 (August 1971): 41–43.

Edwards, Gordon. "The Greenbelt Towns and the American New Towns." *American Institute of Planners Journal* 32 (July 1966): 225–228.

Faltermeyer, Edward K. *Redoing America: A Nationwide Report on How to Make Our Cities and Suburbs Livable.* New York: Harper & Row, 1968.

"A Firmer Foundation for New Towns." *Business Week*, 9 January 1971, p. 22.

Herbers, John. "White House Blocks Bill Creating New Cities." *New York Times*, 7 June 1970.

Keegan, John E., and William Rutzick. "Private Developers and the New Communities Act of 1968." *Georgetown Law Journal* 57 (June 1969): 1019–1058.

Krasnowiecki, Jan. "The Legal Aspects." In *Legal Aspects of Planned Unit Residential Development with Suggested Legislation.* Washington, D.C.: Urban Land Institute, Technical Bulletin no. 52, 1965 (reprinted 1970).

"Land Legislation: Inflationary Time Bomb?" *House and Home* 25 (April 1964): 105.

Liston, Linda. "Need for New Towns Spurs State Legislative Action." *Industrial Development*, November/December 1969, pp. 15–18.

Mandelker, Daniel R. "The Role of Law in the Planning Process." *Land Use Controls* 1 (1967): 55–66.

———. "Some Policy Considerations in the Drafting of New Town Legislation." In *New Towns and Planned Communities*, ed. James A. Lyons et al. New York: Practicing Law Institute, 1971.

McCallum, Donald V. "Legal Requirements Shaping Land Development Methods." *Building Research* 7 (January/March 1970): 115–116.

McFarland, John R. "The Administration of the New Deal Greenbelt Towns." *American Institute of Planners Journal* 32 (July 1966): 217–228.

Mayer, Albert. "Greenbelt Towns Revisited." Washington, D.C.: Department of Housing and Urban Development, Urban Planning Research and Demonstration, October 1968.

National Committee on Urban Growth Policy. *The New City,* ed. Donald Canty. New York: Frederick A. Praeger, 1969.

New York State Urban Development Corporation. *New York State Urban Development Acts of 1968: Summary.* New York: New York State Urban Development Corporation, 1968.

———. *New York State Urban Development Corporation Act: As Amended through June 1971.* New York: New York State Urban Development Corporation, n.d.

Paul, Robert M. "The New Communities Act of 1968." *Building Research,* January/March 1970, pp. 97–98.

"Planning Urban Development: Legislative Review 1968–1969." *American Institute of Planners Journal* 36 (September 1970): 355–356.

Reilly, William K., and S. J. Schulman. "The State Urban Development Corporation: New York's Innovation." *Urban Lawyer* 1 (Summer 1969): 129–146.

Slayton, W. L. "A Critical Evaluation of New Towns Legislation." *Planning,* American Society of Planning Officials, 1967, pp. 171–174.

Special Committee on Historic Preservation. *With Heritage So Rich.* New York: Random House, 1966.

Stein, Clarence S. "Toward New Towns for America." Cambridge, Mass.: MIT Press, 1957.

United States, Advisory Commission on Intergovernmental Relations. *1970 Cumulative: ACIR State Legislative Program.* Washington, D.C.: U.S. Government Printing Office, August 1969.

———. *Urban and Rural America: Policies for Future Growth.* Commission Report A–32. Washington, D.C.: U.S. Government Printing Office, April 1968.

United States, Congress. *United States Housing and Urban Development Act of 1970, Title VII: Urban Growth and New Communities.* Public Law 91–609. Washington, D.C.: U.S. Government Printing Office. (Law enacted 31 December 1970).

United States, Congress, House. *Drafts of Bills Relating to Housing: Message from the President of the United States Relative to Drafts of Bills Relating to Housing.* 88 Cong., 2 sess., 1964, Doc. no. 206. Washington, D.C.: U.S. Government Printing Office, 1964.

———. *Housing and Community Development Legislation: Hearings before the Subcommittee on Housing of the Committee on Banking and Currency,* 88 Cong., 2 sess., Doc. no. 206. Washington, D.C.: U.S. Government Printing Office, 1964.

United States, Congress, House, Committee on Banking and Currency. *Basic Laws and Authorities on Housing and Urban Development.* Washington, D.C.: U.S. Government Printing Office, 1969.

———. Hearings before ad hoc Subcommittee on Urban Growth. Part 1: *Population Trends* (1969). Part 2: *The Quality of Urban Life* (1970). Part 3: *Industrial Location Policy* (1971). 91 Cong., 1 and 2 sess., 30 September 1969—24 June 1970.

United States, Congress, Senate. *Introduction of Balanced Urbanization Policy and Planning Act: S.3228.* 91 Cong., 1 sess., 10 December 1969.

United States, Congress, Senate, Committee on Banking and Currency. *Housing Legislation of 1964.* Washington, D.C.: U.S. Government Printing Office, 1964.

———. *Housing and Urban Development Legislation of 1968.* 2 vols. Washington, D.C.: U.S. Government Printing Office, 1968.

United States, Congress, Senate, Subcommittee on Intergovernmental Relations. *Balanced Urbanization Policy and Planning Act: S.3228.* 91 Cong., 1 sess., 7 December 1969.

United States, Department of Housing and Urban Development. *Draft Regulations: Urban Growth and New Community Development Act of 1970.* Washington, D.C.: Department of Housing and Urban Development, 31 July 1971.

———. *Excerpts from Urban Growth and New Community Development Act of 1970.* Washington, D.C.: U.S. Government Printing Office, 31 December 1971.

———. *Initial Policies and Procedures: New Communities Act of 1968.* Washington, D.C.: Department of Housing and Urban Development, 27 January 1969, pp. 1–19.

———. *New Communities Act of 1968: Title IV of the Housing and Urban Development Act of 1968.* Washington, D.C.: Department of Housing and Urban Development, 1968.

———. *Questions and Answers on the Urban Development Bill.* Washington, D.C.: Department of Housing and Urban Development, 1966. Mimeographed.

United States, Department of Housing and Urban

Development, Office of New Communities Development. *Outline of New Communities Assistance Programs.* Washington, D.C.: Department of Housing and Urban Development, January 1971.

United States, Department of Housing and Urban Development, Domestic Council Committee on National Growth. *Report on National Growth: 1972.* Washington, D.C.: U.S. Government Printing Office, 1972.

United States, Housing and Home Finance Agency.

New Towns Act, 1959. Washington, D.C.: Commission for the New Towns, 31 March 1963.

Wehrly, Max. S. "Urban and Rural America: Policies for Future Growth." *Urban Land News and Trends in City Development* 28 (May 1970): 3–10.

Wise, H. F., and Associates. *State Greenbelt Legislation and the Problem of Urban Encroachment on California Agriculture.* Sacramento: Assembly of the State of California, 1957.

Social Planning and Research in New Communities

Robert W. Marans and Robert B. Zehner

Since the early history of the contemporary new towns movement, promoters of planned communities have tended to emphasize the presumed beneficial aspects of their communities for residents and society. Ebenezer Howard, in setting forth the rationale for garden cities, modestly suggested that "out of [the] joyous union [of town and country in garden cities] will spring a new hope, a new life, [and] a new civilization."[1] Furthermore, he noted that this path of reform promised to "lead society on to a far higher destiny than it has ever yet ventured to hope for. . . ."[2]

While Letchworth and Welwyn have had a more limited impact on civilization than Howard had hoped, his planning and rhetoric have been models for much that has transpired in twentieth-century new town planning. By the sixties, for example, prominent American developers had refined the promise of life in a planned community to place a greater stress on the virtues of the planning for the residents, particularly in comparison with traditional incremental suburban development, which was characterized as wasteful, inconvenient, unpleasant, and expensive. Promotional material for Columbia, Maryland, presented the community as: ". . . a symphony in the woods on a summer evening, a horseback ride on a wooded trail, a dip in a pool, a golf or a tennis match. It is a place of beauty where nature has been preserved and enhanced. It is acres of green meadows, trees, lakes, streams, and rolling hills. It is a place where the smile of a friend and the nod from a neighbor give it meaning and purpose. . . . It is designed for people. It is people."[3]

The pastoral ethic with the opportunity to escape the pressures of urban life is but one attraction of new community life. Another key attribute is the array of facilities and services customarily provided. Although some developers spend more time and money planning amenities than others, the range and variety that are eventually included in a community plan are often cited as one indication of the developer's commitment to "social planning." The siting, variety, and quality of facilities vary across planned communities, just as they do in less-planned areas, but the general aims of most developers are quite similar. For example, "Litchfield Park will provide a complete range of civic, cultural, business, industrial, educational, medical and recreation facilities for a population of nearly 100,000,"[4] just as Reston will provide "the fullest possible range of opportunities for the residents including employment, recreation and cultural opportunities as well as the simple opportunity to get away from it all and commune with nature."[5]

Associated with plans to provide a complete array of facilities and services in the new towns is the desire to include a wide range of housing types and costs. In part, the attraction of higher density dwelling units for a land developer is that they offer a high enough rate of return to offset the cost of providing "undeveloped" open space and other amenities for the community. For some developers, however, plans for a housing mix have also been an important factor in fostering a socially balanced community with regard to socioeconomic status, race, and family life cycle. According to William Finley, former vice-president of the Rouse Company, "Columbia must be a truly balanced community so that everyone who lives there will be able to work there and everyone who works there will be able to live there. This, of necessity, requires a broad spectrum of housing prices, types and styles, a true city of variety."[6] Later in this paper we will consider Columbia and Reston, the two new towns we have studied most thoroughly,

in terms of their success in becoming socially "balanced" communities.[7]

Developers also want to provide more to residents than a selection of physical facilities. The attempts to maintain a "people" focus occur in a variety of guises. For instance, to offset the persistent view that communities of 70,000 to 100,000 people can become impersonal warrens of isolated individuals, new town plans invariably emphasize a well-articulated hierarchy of neighborhoods and villages within the overall community so as to encourage residents to identify not only with the community as a whole, but also with a smaller and more comprehensible residential unit. To enhance the sense of a comfortably scaled environment, paths and walkways designed to keep vehicles and pedestrians safely separated within the village or neighborhood are laid out to encourage walking and bicycling in and around the area near schools, convenience stores, and recreation facilities. For example, the aim of Litchfield Park, a Goodyear Rubber Corporation new town, is "to provide its residents with safety, convenience, beauty, and a sense of personal identity—each with his own small village—that are rarely available in our urban life today."[8]

The effort to encourage a sense of community and a matrix of formal and informal interpersonal ties usually consists of more than pathways and a community hierarchy. Everything from attractive street signs and imaginative names to community meeting rooms, bulletin boards, outdoor sculpture, newspapers, cable television, and community health plans (as in Columbia, Maryland) are seen as amenities that can facilitate social linkages or otherwise open residents' opportunities in the community. Finally, and possibly most central to the twin goals of encouraging residents to identify with and participate in the neighborhood and the community, residents' associations are invariably established to provide a formal mechanism for participation in governance and decision-making in the community, and to furnish a channel for communication with the developer.

From this brief overview of some aspects of new town planning that are designed to have a relatively direct impact on residents, it is apparent that our working definition of "social planning" has turned out to be very broad indeed. This is as it should be, since the *raison d'être* for most new community planning is to enhance the overall quality of the residents' lives. In that context, planning decisions concerning the location and quality of shopping facilities, open space, and transportation systems can have as important an effect on community life as the operation of more socially oriented institutions like homeowners associations and community newspapers.

Whether components of new communities contribute significantly (and positively) to the residents' participation in, and enjoyment of, their community is a good subject for research. The results of a study to determine the effects of some components of social planning form the basis of the next section.[9]

A STUDY OF RESIDENTIAL ENVIRONMENTS

A study of residential environments conducted at the University of Michigan's Survey Research Center attempted to assess people's attitudes and behavioral responses to new towns and other less-planned residential communities.[10] The study was designed to determine how living in a planned new town influences people's satisfaction and behavior with respect to the physical environment. Residents in ten communities in three metropolitan areas were interviewed.

The communities selected ranged from the highly planned new towns of Columbia, Maryland, and Reston, Virginia, to less-planned communities of a similar vintage in the Baltimore-Washington and Detroit regions. Two

central city newly developed communities were selected in order to observe the effects of community location on people's responses. Based on the personal interviews, attitudes and behaviors of people living in the ten communities were determined, including attitudes related to community and neighborhood satisfaction and patterns of social interaction. The study allowed us not only to observe relationships between people's responses and environmental conditions which existed in their communities, but also to compare responses between communities. We were able to see if the responses of people living in Columbia and Reston differed from those of people living in the more traditional suburban communities.

Residents' Levels of Satisfaction

We found that levels of satisfaction with one's community were highest in the new towns of Reston and Columbia, where 61 percent and 42 percent of the people rated their community as excellent. Lower levels of satisfaction were identified in the less-planned suburban developments of a similar age, where an average of 34 percent of the respondents gave their communities excellent ratings. When asked why they gave positive evaluations of their communities, residents of Columbia and Reston were more likely to mention the availability of facilities, the planning of the town, and the proximity of open space. On the other hand, having "friendly" and "desirable" neighbors and good schools were mentioned more often by people living in the more traditional suburban developments.

Similarly, when asked what attracted them to their community, the residents of Columbia and Reston cited the natural environment and the philosophy or image of the new town as prime motivating factors. For people living in the more traditionally built communities, characteristics of the individual dwelling or lot, including price and nearby good schools, were mentioned most often.[11]

It is interesting to note that ratings of the communities from the teenager's point of view indicated that new towns did not fare as well as the more traditional suburbs. An average of 22 percent of the residents in Columbia and Reston said the community was excellent for teenagers, but 45 percent of those living in two traditional subdivisions said their community was excellent from the same point of view. These responses may be different today, since more facilities and programs are now available in both Columbia and Reston for the teenage population.

Residents' ratings of their immediate neighborhoods were somewhat higher in the new towns. Furthermore, density of development was found to underlie many factors important to neighborhood satisfaction.[12] Important factors included privacy within the yard, the level of noise in the neighborhood, and the adequacy of outdoor space for family activities. The most important factor related to neighborhood satisfaction in all communities was how well the neighborhood was kept up.

Recreation and Travel in the Community
With respect to outdoor recreation, the study found that there were many more recreational facilities available in the new towns than in the less-planned communities. People living in the new towns participate considerably more in several forms of outdoor recreation—walking, hiking, swimming, tennis—than the people with the same socioeconomic background in communities which have been less planned. Actually, however, the most important predictors of participation in outdoor recreation irrespective of whether a person lived in a new town or in a suburb were age, income, and educational level.[13]

While we have not completely analyzed the relationship between outdoor recreation participation and community satisfaction, it appears that more opportunities for, and participation in, recreational activities in a community are associated with high levels of satisfaction. But this association is less important for satisfaction than conditions in the respondents' more immediate neighborhood.

The distance between people's homes and recreational facilities influences the extent to which these facilities are used. For example, people who live within a quarter-mile of a swimming pool or tennis court are more likely to use it than people who live farther away. With respect to water-based activities such as boating, the critical distance between where people live and a body of water suitable for navigation is approximately one-eighth of a mile. On the other hand, there is no relationship between how far people live from a golf course and how frequently they play golf. This is logical, because even if people live next door to a golf course or clubhouse, they still usually drive in transporting their golf clubs.

Walkway systems, which are often characteristic of new towns and other planned developments, were used extensively by community residents. The number of people who hiked or walked for recreation and shopping was much greater in the new towns than in the less-planned communities. However, these walkways had little influence on the extent to which adults bicycled for recreational or shopping purposes.

It had been expected that the high percentages of the population who walked in the planned communities would reduce the number of automobile trips, but the findings indicated otherwise. Although rates of automobile ownership were somewhat lower in the new towns, annual automobile mileage in new towns was comparable to that in the less-planned suburbs. The amounts of work travel and weekend travel were about equal. If anything, weekend travel was probably more extensive in Columbia and Reston. If we were to repeat our survey today in new towns, now that more facilities are available and the population has expanded considerably, we might find a reduction in mileage figures as well as in auto ownership per family.

Social Balance in the New Towns

Despite the goal of producing a balanced community where all those who worked could also live, experience to date has not been encouraging. At the time of our survey (fall 1969), for instance, the median incomes of families in both Columbia ($17,100) and Reston ($20,000) were over twice the national average. Furthermore, since the lowest-priced housing in Columbia (the less expensive of the two communities) was selling for over $30,000 in early 1973, it does not appear that market mechanisms will lead to a socioeconomic balance among resident families in the foreseeable future. Subsidized units in Columbia and Reston (under 500 units in each community at the end of 1972) provide housing for only small fractions of the residents, a proportion which seems destined to decrease.

Within the context of a socioeconomically homogeneous residential setting, however, both new towns have been able to attract black families as well as white. At the time of our study, about 6 percent of the respondents in Reston were black. In Columbia, on the other hand, where photographs in promotional materials and displays tended to stress the interracial nature of the community more frequently, roughly 14 percent of the respondents were black.

We did not attempt to determine if some neighborhoods in these communities were more homogeneous than others, or if some were becoming more homogeneous as the communities matured. It is interesting to note, however, that conscious attempts by the British government to mix different classes in new town neighborhoods have been only marginally successful. Families began to "re-sort" themselves to create more homogeneous neighborhoods.[14] In contrast, at least one experience in Israel suggests that experimentation in design and layout do provide possibilities for creating a viable social balance within planned communities.[15] At this juncture, however, it does not appear likely that American new towns will be able to attain more than a token socioeconomic balance among their residents without considerable government encouragement and economic support.[16]

Social Planning and Participation

Information was collected on citizen involvement and participation in organizations (PTA groups, bridge clubs, etc.) to measure organizational activity and to see if participation was related to satisfaction with the community as a whole. Although rates of membership tended to be high in all sample communities, analysis indicated little relationship between the extent to which people participated in organizations and became involved in community affairs, and their satisfaction with where they lived. In fact, we found relatively little difference between people in the less-planned communities and those living in Columbia and Reston, where residents were expected to be exceptionally active in civic activities.[17] This was surprising. It may reflect, in part, the fact that residents of the control communities as well as the new towns were largely upper-middle class, and therefore were more likely to be "joiners" than the population as a whole. It may also reflect a feeling among residents that in a new town one doesn't have to organize to solve problems since "the developer will do it" (or has already done it). In any case, data indicated that the extensive planning to facilitate social linkages in the new towns does not necessarily lead to much higher rates of involvement in community groups and organizations for most residents.

A FINAL PERSPECTIVE AND COMMENT ON SOCIAL RESEARCH

In 1969 the National Committee on Urban Growth Policy predicted that, by the year 2000,

America's urban population would have grown by 100 million.[18] It recommended that 100 new towns be built, each of at least 100,000 population, to help accommodate this growth. In addition, ten new cities of a million people each should be created.[19] This proposal of the committee, while appearing quite radical in terms of the number of new towns and new cities, would affect a small part of the future population of the United States. The committee pointed out that these new communities would accommodate 20 percent of the 100 million additional people expected over the next thirty years. However, this is only 7 percent of the predicted total population of 300 million people. Furthermore, if we accept the fact that a substantial portion of the present population in metropolitan areas will have to be rehoused, an even smaller percentage of the housing needs of the total population could be accounted for by such extensive new town development.[20]

It is difficult to gauge the number of new towns actually contemplated at this time. Defining a "new town" rigorously is not easy, and communities that have reached the planning stage often change or, in some cases, evaporate altogether. However, one can take as a base a list 142 developments compiled by the *Environment Monthly*. "Some are strictly single-family residential areas. Some, by design and circumstances, are limited in their appeal—usually to an upper middle class market. Some are second home vacation communities, while a few are just the opposite: high density, urban centered developments. . . . These community projects, good, bad, and horrendous, fairly represent the state of the art today in American environmental design."[21]

If all 128 projects for which data were available were to attain their target populations, they would hold less than half (8.85 million) of the 20 million people recommended by the National Committee on Urban Growth Policy.

Since the *Environment Monthly* list does not distinguish between highly planned "new towns" and traditional subdivision developments whose main trait is simply significant size, the number of residents that will be housed in communities with a serious commitment to social objectives will clearly be much smaller. The nine communities listed that were to receive Housing Urban Development Title VII assistance, although presumably more extensively planned developments than most on the *Environment Monthly* list, were expected to house only about 500,000 people when completed.[22]

New towns will not provide an instantaneous solution to all, or even most, of the country's housing problems. Still, the new communities which have been built and will be built in the next decade—either through the entrepreneurial efforts of private developers or with active government assistance—can be instrumental in shaping the future pattern of residential development. In order for this to occur, new town development must be viewed as a vehicle for experimentation and innovation, and as a means of upgrading the general level of residential development in the metropolitan areas in which they are developed.

One problem, of course, is the identification of specific innovations that can be pursued in a given environment. We have suggested the need to encourage a socioeconomic balance among residents in new communities. Innovations in community cable television, intracommunity transportation, provision for rapid transit to central cities, educational reform, community health services, modular home construction, and fuel from solid wastes are but a few other possible areas for experimentation.

A second and equally important problem is that techniques need to be developed to monitor the process and results of innovation so that the applicability of new (or traditional) techniques to other settings can be systematically estimated. Survey research focused on the residents would help to evaluate innovative contributions, and to determine whether social objectives are being fulfilled. The research could include the collection and analysis of data dealing with people's attitudes, aspirations, expectations, values, motives, and behaviors in relation to specific attributes of the community, so that these could be more precisely evaluated and their functions understood.

There are several related reasons for including an iterative plan of survey research in the design process. First, it can provide an important measure of the validity of the programs under which the planning and design of new environments take place—Model Cities, housing allowance programs, Operation Breakthrough, etc.—to determine if the programs are successfully meeting objectives at the consumer's level. Such research would allow for the testing of operating preconceptions (hypotheses) held by architects, planners, urban designers, and government officials regarding residential environments. If new designs and the residents can be monitored at successive stages of development (including points before and after residents arrive), they can become important sources of feedback for future design and development.

Second, regular studies of resident responses to environmental characteristics and community issues can help residents alert developers to the more widespread problems in their communities. Survey research should not, of course, provide the only source of data for environmental evaluation. Of comparable importance would be the collection of independent and objective data to be used in conjunction with attitude and behavioral information taken from surveys. Such objective data might include detailed characteristics of community facilities and services (shopping, recreation, transportation, etc.), as well as more delineated data drawn from maps or aerial photographs focusing on the resident's home, such

as the size of the dwelling or yard, the degree to which the latter is enclosed, the amounts and kinds of open space in the neighborhood, the layout of structures, and the gross dwelling unit density. Interviewers or observers can also be trained to make independent (if not necessarily objective) assessments of quantitative or qualitative attributes of the social and physical environments.

While observational information about attributes in the environment ranging from the use of parks and playgrounds to the amount of litter in the streets can tell the planners something about the behavior of people living in that environment, they may provide little insight into the human meaning attached to these conditions. What is accepted as good or bad by those who do the observing or use the information to make policy may appear different or completely irrelevant to the segments of the population whose lives are affected by such policies.

CONCLUSION

The pursuit of social objectives in planned communities has clearly been a multi-dimensional task. The aim has been to create better living environments than are found in alternate forms of development. Research has indicated that in some areas (such as recreation and overall satisfaction) American new towns have begun to fulfill their promise; in other areas (most notably, in attaining a socially balanced population mix) they have fallen significantly short of their objectives.

Whether the infusion of Housing and Urban Development assistance will alleviate these shortcomings remains to be seen. But it is apparent that the new community, no matter how it is financed, can offer an important opportunity to experiment with innovative solutions in this and other areas of residential development. Finally, an equal component of the innovation process should be a comparative assessment of both the innovative and the tradi-tional planning conceptions used in environmental designs, in order to provide focused feedback on the adequacy of those design solutions and their applicability for subsequent development.

NOTES

1 Ebenezer Howard, *Garden Cities of To-Morrow* (1920; reprinted, Cambridge: MIT Press, 1965), p. 48.

2 Ibid., p. 128.

3 "Columbia: American Dream in One Big Package," *Engineering News Record,* 21 November 1968, p. 26.

4 Litchfield Park Properties, "A New Kind of City" (Litchfield Park, Arizona, n.p., n.d.).

5 Robert E. Simon, Jr., "Problems of the New Town Developer," *Building Research* 3, no. 1 (January-February 1966): 16.

6 William E. Finley, "New Towns of the Future," *Building Research* 3, no. 1 (January-February 1966): 26.

7 The community which has probably been the subject of the most social planning to date is Columbia, Md. See, for example, the discussion in Morton Hoppenfeld, "A Sketch of the Planning-Building Process in Columbia," *Journal of the American Institute of Planners* 33, no. 6 (November 1967): 398–409; Edward Eichler and Marshall Kaplan, *The Community Builders* (Berkeley: University of California Press, 1967), pp. 61–69; Lowell E. Sunderland, "How Columbia Manages Its Amenities," *Columbia Today* 4, no. 2 (March 1971): 11–15; and Richard Brooks, "Social Planning in Columbia," *Journal of the American Institute of Planners* 37, no. 6 (November 1971): 373–379. For Reston, Va., see the Reston Virginia Foundation for Community Programs, Inc., *Social Planning and Programs for Reston, Virginia,* March 1967. Mimeographed.

8 Litchfield Park Properties.

9 Published reports of empirical research on residents of American new towns are not plentiful. In addition to the study summarized here, the reader might wish to refer to Carl Werthman, Jerry S. Mandel, and Ted Dienstfrey, *Planning and the Purchase Decision: Why People Buy in Planned Communities,* a prepublication of the Community Development Project (University of California at Berkeley: Institute of Regional Development, Center for Planners and Development Research, Preprint no. 10, July 1965); Carl Norcross, "Open Space Communities in the Market Place," *Urban Land Institute Technical Bulletin 57,* December 1966; Herbert J. Gans, *The Levittowners* (New York: Random House, 1967); and Francine F. Rabinovitz and James Lemare, *After Suburbia, What?: The New Communities Movement in Los Angeles* (Los Angeles: Institute of Government and Public Affairs, University of California, 1970).

10 John B. Lansing, Robert W. Marans, and Robert B. Zehner, *Planned Residential Environments* (Ann Arbor: Institute for Social Research, University of Michigan, 1970).

11 For a more thorough discussion of levels of satisfaction, see Robert B. Zehner, "Satisfaction with Neighborhoods: The Effects of Social Compatibility, Residential Density, and Site Planning," Ph.D. dissertation, University of Michigan, 1970; and "Neighborhood and Community Satisfaction in New Towns and Less Planned Suburbs," *Journal of the American Institute of Planners* 37, no. 6 (November 1971): 379–385.

12 For more detailed discussions of the effects of density for this sample of communities, see Robert W. Marans and Robert B. Zehner, "Some Observed Patterns of Residential Density and Social Interaction," *Housing: New Trends and Concepts,* ed. K. Bernhardt (Ann Arbor: Institute for Science and Technology, University of Michigan, 1972); and Robert B. Zehner and Robert W. Marans, "Residential Density, Planning Objectives, and Life in Planned Communities," *Journal of the American Institute of Planners* 39, no. 5 (September 1973): 337–345.

13 Recreation analyses are presented in Robert W. Marans, "Determinants of Participation in Outdoor Recreation in Residential Environments," Ph.D. dissertation, University of Michigan, 1971; see also "Outdoor Recreation Behavior in Residential Environments," *Environment and the Social Sciences: Prospectives and Applications,* ed. D. Carson and J. F. Wohlwill (Washington: American Psychological Association, 1972).

14 B. J. Heraud, "Social Class and the New Towns," *Urban Studies* 5, no. 1 (February 1968): 33–58.

15 Robert W. Marans, "Social and Cultural Influences in New Town Planning: An Israeli Experiment," *Journal of the Town Planning Institute* 26, no. 2 (February 1970): 60–65.

16 For recent more general discussions of the possibilities of socioeconomic and racial mixing in resi-

dential settings, see the report of the Social Science Panel of the Advisory Committee to the Department of Housing and Urban Development, *Freedom of Choice in Housing: Opportunities and Constraints* (Washington: National Academy of Sciences, 1972); and Herbert J. Gans, "The Possibilities of Social Integration in American Towns," a paper presented at a Conference on Human Factors in New Town Development, School of Architecture and Urban Planning, University of California at Los Angeles, June 1972.

17 Robert B. Zehner, "New Town Participation: Much Ado About. . . ." (Chapel Hill: Center for Urban and Regional Studies, University of North Carolina, 1971).

18 It should be pointed out that the Commission on Population Growth and the American Future in their report, *Population and the American Future* (New York: New American Library, 1972), presented to the president, indicated that the projected population growth by the turn of the century (2-child average) would be 66 million (p. 20).—Ed.

19 National Committee on Urban Growth Policy, "Key National Leaders Recommend Large Program of New Towns for the United States" (Washington: Urban American, Inc., 25 May 1969). Also in *The New City,* ed. Donald Canty (New York: Frederick A. Praeger, 1969), p. 172.

20 The argument against a major American new town commitment is developed more extensively by William Alonso in "The Mirage of New Towns," *Public Interest,* no. 19 (Spring 1970), pp. 3–17.

21 *Environment Monthly,* May 1972, p. 4.

22 The nine communities *Environment Monthly* noted were Maumelle, Ark.; St. Charles, Md.; Jonathan and Cedar-Riverside, Minn.; Gananda and Riverton, N.Y.; Flower Mound and San Antonio Ranch, Tex.; and Harbison, S.C. In addition, five other communities have since received guarantees and are planned to house an additional 300,000 people. The projects include Park Forest South, Ill.; Soul City, N.C.; Woodlands, Tex.; and Lysander and Welfare Island, N.Y.

For an overview of a project which will compare and evaluate thirteen private new towns, two Housing and Urban Development–assisted new towns, and a series of control communities on a number of dimensions, see Shirley F. Weiss, Raymond J. Burby et al., "New Community Development: A National Study of Environmental Preferences and the Quality of Life," *Research Previews,* Institute for Research in Social Science, University of North Carolina 20, no. 1 (April 1973): 5–15.

Several of the "General Criteria" for Housing and Urban Development assistance are comparable to the social objectives of planning which have been discussed in this paper. They include, for example: a) "It must be designed to create a newly built community or a major addition to an existing community which includes most, if not all, of the basic activities and facilities normally associated with a city or town . . ."; b) "It must combine these diverse activities in a well-planned and harmonious whole, so as to be economically sound and create an environment that is an attractive place to live, work, and play . . ."; c) "It must be designed to increase the available choices for living and working for the fullest possible range of people and families of different compositions and incomes . . ." (*Federal Register* 36, no. 148 [31 July 1971]: 14205–214).

READING LIST

Alonso, William. "The Mirage of New Towns." *Public Interest,* no. 19 (Spring 1970), pp. 3–17.

Brooks, Richard. "Social Planning in Columbia." *Journal of the American Institute of Planners* 37, no. 6 (November 1971): 373–379.

Canty, Donald, ed. *The New City.* New York: Frederick A. Praeger, 1969.

Cohen, Erik. "Social Images in an Israeli Development Town." *Human Relations* 21, no. 2 (May 1968): 163–176.

"Columbia: American Dream in One Big Package," *Engineering News Record,* 21 November 1968, pp. 26–29.

Downs, Anthony. "Alternative Forms of Future Urban Growth in the United States." *Journal of the American Institute of Planners* 36, no. 1 (January 1970): 3–11.

Eichler, Edward, and Marshall Kaplan. *The Community Builders.* Berkeley: University of California Press, 1967.

Environment Monthly, May 1972.

Finley, William E. "New Towns of the Future." *Building Research* 3, no. 1 (January–February 1966): 24–27, 33–34.

Gans, Herbert J. *People and Plans.* New York: Basic Books, 1968.

———. *The Levittowners.* New York: Random House, 1967.

———. "The Possibilities of Social Integration in American Towns." Paper presented at a Conference on Human Factors in New Towns Development, School of Architecture and Urban Planning, University of California at Los Angeles, June 1972.

Gutman, Robert. "Site Planning and Social Behavior." *Journal of Social Issues* 22, no. 4 (October 1966): 103–115.

Heraud, B. J. "Social Class and the New Towns." *Urban Studies* 5, no. 1 (February 1968): 33–58.

Hoppenfeld, Morton. "A Sketch of the Planning-Building Process in Columbia." *Journal of the American Institute of Planners* 33, no. 6 (November 1967): 398–409.

Howard, Ebenezer. *Garden Cities of To-Morrow.* 1902; reprinted, Cambridge: MIT Press, 1965.

Lansing, John B., Robert W. Marans, and Robert B. Zehner. *Planned Residential Environments.* Ann Arbor: Institute for Social Research, University of Michigan, 1970.

Lemkau, Paul V. "Human Factors in the New Town." *Building Research* 3, no. 1 (January–February 1966): 29–32.

Litchfield Park Properties. "A New Kind of City." Litchfield Park, Ariz.: n.p., n.d.

Marans, Robert W. "Determinants of Participation in Outdoor Recreation in Residential Environments." Ph.D. dissertation, University of Michigan, 1971.

———. "Outdoor Recreation Behavior in Residential Environments." *Environment and the Social Sciences: Prospectives and Applications,* ed. D. Carson and J. F. Wohlwill. Washington: American Psychological Association, 1972.

———. "A Prospectus on Survey Research for Environmental Planning." *Environmental Design Research,* ed. W. Preiser. Stroudsburg, Pa.: Dowden, Hutchinson and Ross, 1973.

———. "Research on New Community Development: Opportunities and Results." In *Housing Market Opportunities,* ed. K. Bernhardt. Ann Arbor: Institute for Science and Technology, University of Michigan, 1972.

———. "Social and Cultural Influences in New Town Planning: An Israeli Experiment." *Journal of the Town Planning Institute* 26, no. 2 (February 1970): 60–65.

———, and Robert B. Zehner. "Some Observed Patterns of Residential Density and Social Interaction." In *Housing: New Trends and Concepts,* ed. K. Bernhardt. Ann Arbor: Institute for Science and Technology, University of Michigan, 1972.

National Committee on Urban Growth Policy. "Key National Leaders Recommend Large Program of New Towns for the United States." Washington: Urban American, Inc., 25 May 1969.

———. *The New City.* Ed. Donald Canty. New York: Frederick A. Praeger, 1969.

Norcross, Carl, "Open Space Communities in the Market Place." *Urban and Land Institute Technical Bulletin 57,* December 1966.

Rabinovitz, Francine F., and James Lemare. *After Suburbia, What?: The New Communities Movement in Los Angeles.* Los Angeles: Institute of Government and Public Affairs, University of California, 1970.

Reston Virginia Foundation for Community Programs. *Social Planning and Programs for Reston, Virginia.* March 1967. Mimeographed.

Simon, Robert E., Jr. "Problems of the New Town Developer." *Building Research* 3, no. 1 (January–February 1966): 16–17, 21–23.

Social Science Panel, Advisory Committee to the Department of Housing and Urban Development. *Freedom of Choice in Housing: Opportunities and Constraints.* Washington: National Academy of Sciences, 1972.

Sunderland, Lowell E. "How Columbia Manages Its Amenities." *Columbia Today* 4, no. 2 (March 1971): 11–15.

United States. *Federal Register* 36, no. 148 (31 July 1971): 14205–214.

Weiss, Shirley F., Edward J. Kaiser, and Raymond J. Burby, eds. *New Community Development: Planning Process, Implementation, and Emerging Social Concerns.* Vols. 1 and 2. Chapel Hill: Center for Urban and Regional Studies, University of North Carolina, 1971.

Weiss, Shirley F., Raymond J. Burby III, Edward J. Kaiser, Thomas G. Donnelly, and Robert B. Zehner. "New Community Development: A National Study of Environmental Preferences and the Quality of Life." *Research Previews,* Institute for Research in Social Science, University of North Carolina 20, no. 1 (April 1973): 5–15.

Werthman, Carl, Jerry S. Mandel, and Ted Dienstfrey. *Planning and the Purchase Decisions: Why People Buy in Planned Communities.* A prepublication of the Community Development Project. University of California at Berkeley: Institute of Regional Development, Center for Planners and Development Research. Preprint no. 10, July 1965.

Zehner, Robert B. "Neighborhood and Community Satisfaction in New Towns and Less Planned Suburbs." *Journal of the American Institute of Planners* 37, no. 6 (November 1971): 379–385.

———. "New Town Participation: Much Ado About. . . ." Chapel Hill: Center for Urban and Regional Studies, University of North Carolina, 1971.

————. "Satisfaction with Neighborhoods: The Effects of Social Compatibility, Residential Density, and Site Planning." Ph.D. dissertation, University of Michigan, 1970.

————, and Robert W. Marans. "Residential Density, Planning Objectives, and Life in Planned Communities." *Journal of the American Institute of Planners* 39, no. 5 (September 1973): 337–345.

Jonathan, Chaska, Minnesota

Benjamin H. Cunningham

The new community of Jonathan, at Chaska, Minnesota, has a strange mixture of atmospheres. Located near the gateway to the upper northwest, it is much like a frontier area, where the people are self-reliant and basically conservative. Nevertheless, Minnesota ranks quite high in per capita state expenditures for education and welfare. The community's location in the Minneapolis-St. Paul area lends excitement and immediacy to the work of developing Jonathan as a new town for the partial solution to the problems of urban growth. "New town," when applied to Jonathan, really refers to a set of community relationships and not to a political jurisdiction. Jonathan sprawls over three areas. The central portion lies within the city limits of Chaska, Minnesota, creating constant but healthy tension between patriots of Chaska and those involved with the development. The northeast portion is in the community of Chanhassen, while the western section is in Victoria, a small community in the Laketown Township. Only time will tell how the political dynamics will operate; this is one of the more exciting aspects of the new town development process. We expect, however, that in ten or twelve years a super community will evolve, with Jonathan as the focus within this region.

Jonathan exists primarily because the time is right for it. Today people are talking about urban overgrowth, urban undergrowth, the ecology, or social problems, and there is strong public awareness of a need for alternate solutions. The new town is not a universal savior which will solve all the world's problems, but it can take care of a certain very small segment of the population in its own area. Successful new communities will illustrate the ideas and some aspects of the planning and development process, and will thereby influence and enhance future more conventionally produced developments. The term "new town" is very broad, and Jonathan itself has been variously classified as a diversified center, part of a rural growth center, a constellation city, and a satellite city. Originally, Jonathan was conceived of as a self-contained new community within the urban influence of the Twin Cities metropolitan area. Although this is our main emphasis, its proximity to the urban area and to the Cedar-Riverside new town intown development has stimulated our interest in the links between the new town intown and the diversified center or constellation city types of new towns. Jonathan is planned to be self-contained, nevertheless, with some parity between jobs and households, a very diversified land-use plan, and a commitment to a full income profile. Many variables exist to interfere with the artificial design of a programmed mix of people, and we concluded that the probability of success would be higher if we planned to duplicate the demographic and income profile of our metropolitan area, since the forces which operate there, operate universally.

Jonathan should offer choices in density, jobs, and lifestyles. How well it will succeed remains to be seen, and four or five years from now it will be interesting to see if these policies are actually operating. We have emphasized the preservation of natural features in the area, and have noted useful existing technologies. In fact, we are working in only two truly innovative areas. We are demonstrating the first duplex communication system in the United States, and we are working with some fun housing. We are committed to building a framework for people's self-realization. We hope to create an environment where people can do whatever suits them. This is already beginning to happen, and it is very exciting to watch.

Our planning parameter includes about 8,000 acres now. We expect to generate about 22,000 jobs, about 16,000 households, and to have a very broad income profile. We plan for more jobs than households, largely because of our position in the center of the southwest corridor of the metropolitan region. Even now the influence of Jonathan spreads beyond its own 8,000 acres. The communities on our periphery are beginning to pick up some of the kinds of things we are doing in the areas of housing and the environment, and we hope Jonathan will have a much stronger impact than we had originally anticipated. It will cost over $1 billion to build Jonathan. The investment from both public and private sources is estimated at between $20,000 and $30,000 per capita.

Jonathan is the first new community to be given a federal debt guarantee under Title IV of the Housing Act of 1968. We had reached the point where we needed a large infusion of capital. Although the money market in 1968 and 1969 was disastrous, we had several choices. One was to follow the Columbia-Reston model and join a large institutional lender. This choice was unacceptable to us because it implied various unwelcome obligations, and so we decided to test the 1968 Housing Act. After a strenuous year, because the HUD New Communities Program was new, we were successful in receiving the Title IV debt guarantees for some $21 million. I believe we were the first to receive a HUD guarantee—because we were persistent, and because our notion of what a new town should be closely resembled the model of what HUD thought a new town should be.

There are some advantages and disadvantages to working with HUD. Although some private developers fear federal bureaucracy and red tape, we have found no impossible problems in the new communities relationship. The things they want are the things we produce for our management anyway. The only danger is that the new communities office will become a sluggish bureaucracy. Title VII under the Housing Act of 1970 requires developers to process their planning and legal work a little more than is necessary to carry out successful development. There is no need to spend $500,000 planning an 8,000-acre new community before the developer actually knows whether or not he will build that new community; that much planning is not prudent at the beginning because many changes will necessarily be made later. Moreover, the legal costs are a little high. On the other hand, the HUD guarantee certainly helps with credibility. People who earlier had not wanted to do business with us came along to say that, if HUD had promised a debt guarantee for $21 million, there must be something to the idea and they would like to work with us. The HUD loan produces triple A, gold-plated debentures.

One of the least understood aspects of new town development in the United States is the fact that no new towns have effective or complete control over their own destinies. They all exist within counties, townships, or cities, and so operate within a whole series of existing political municipal layers. We in Jonathan work with no less than twenty-one different levels of jurisdictions. The state has a wide variety of regulatory bodies (the pollution control agency, the highway commission, the warehouse commission), and it is a daily effort to deal on all of these levels. We have an independent school district, and one of the innovations we introduced was encouraging the school board to send representatives to various planning meetings, so that it could be recognized that the schools were part of the basic community. They are doing that now, and community facilities, such as schools, are now indicated on the cities' comprehensive plan. Like most new communities, Jonathan does

not have control of all the municipal political constraints; we have to sell our concepts. We have a man at the weekly council meetings. Because of our present pace of development, we usually dominate the agenda at each meeting.

Our communications company can help us in this endeavor. Planning commissions and city councils, by law, must hold public meetings, but they generally schedule the more difficult questions toward the end of the agenda, so that by midnight most of the public has gone home and the officials can deal with Jonathan or whatever particularly tough problem they have. Our communications company can videotape all of the planning commission, school board, and city council meetings. When we have the communications network complete enough so that we may have a public service channel, the meetings will be available on prime time for anybody who wants to see what is happening. We are trying not to underestimate the effect of this in establishing a high quality of government.

The development corporation is a private company, owned essentially by local people. Henry T. McKnight [now deceased], a former state senator, conservationist, and civic leader, was the principal investor and prime mover. The fact that it is a private company means that most of the decisions are made quickly and daily. The company, organized with an eye toward action, is run by five people: the president, the executive vice-president (who is experienced primarily in real estate and financing), a vice-president for municipal and political affairs, a vice-president for money, and a vice-president for design. Since the inputs change daily, we feel that it is very important to have such in-house capabilities in a development company. Our people represent all the disciplines, so we hope to make fewer mistakes. Because talking to a consultant at the other end of the telephone is less effective, we have built this kind of organization. Second, because our work is very much a day-to-day process, we are not doing master planning. We are doing framework planning, and we hope that our process will produce a satisfactory community.

We started the Jonathan feasibility studies in 1965. They take a long time. We knew then that we would have either a large-scale development or a very expensive cow pasture. Since we thought the risk was worth taking, we started acquiring land. In June 1967, with the city's cooperation (because as yet there had been no public announcement of the new town), we received our first industrial center zoning and began industrial development. Part of our strategy was to initiate industrial development early, so that we could demonstrate our capability of producing jobs, and, therefore, a tax base and income for the community as a whole. We also wanted to create some of our own housing market, although the numbers are too small now for that to be a significant part of the endeavor. In August 1967 we made a public announcement of what we were doing, because of the many rumors. It was better to make our efforts and intentions completely public. However, since then we have received so much press coverage that we wish the media would just stay away and let us work for a couple of years. In October 1968 the first discussions began concerning Title IV, and in February 1969 we filed an application for a Title IV loan guarantee. In February 1970 we received the preliminary commitment, and on 8 October 1970 we completed the first project agreement made under Title IV. At that time we sold $8 million in debentures, and since then we have been on our way.

We plan to build about five villages for populations of 5,000 to 8,000, each with full income mix. We are skipping the neighborhood commercial element because, at least in our market, we could not support the small neighborhood center. Ours will be a basic village smaller than a Columbia or a Reston village, but larger than a Columbia neighborhood. Each village will have a convenience center. With the town center in the middle, serving also as a regional center, we plan to have access both from regional arteries and from our own internal loop.

In five years at most, Village One will be finished. We will start Village Two about the fourth year. We plan to go village by village, although we are now considering some innovative alternatives, such as one wilderness village of about 700 acres to be developed up near the University of Minnesota Arboretum. People will live in clusters on about 30 percent of the land. We will locate facilities so that arterial feeding will preclude any vehicular traffic in the center of this village. With close to 70 percent of the land in its natural state, this should be a lovely setting. Village One is about a mile and a half in diameter, with no more than a ten-minute walk from any part of it to any facility. Many people walk or ride bicycles to the village center, driving only when they have grocery shopping to do. Rental leases in the village center include an escalated percentage of the gross sales clause. We thereby help subsidize the merchant early in the game, while we stand to make a profit toward the end. The new town allows the spreading of both cost and revenue over a broad base so that certain kinds of operations impossible for small-scale developers can be encouraged. It is working fairly well, but the accounting system is amazingly complex. To take full advantage of the opportunity to spread the cost of revenue, every unit should bear this cost. However, since all the units will not be in place for twenty years, planning funding for such amenities as the greenways is difficult. Even if the money is available, twenty years of greenways should not be built at once, because people change their attitudes about these things. The difficulty comes in allowing flexibility for action, yet not unfairly burdening the first residents. For this reason, the accounting probability exercise is very sophisticated.

The geographical setting of Jonathan is sharply defined. The Minnesota River Valley to the south is very broad. The type of soil here makes it expensive to build bridges across the river. Lake Minnetonka to the north is a very large lake which is difficult to cross. The river, the lake, and Route 494, the beltway, all sharply delineate the region. Since we are near both the Mississippi and Minnesota rivers, with a strong pattern of very steep ravines, the watershed is delineated by the trees. Many glaciated pockets have been gouged out, and most bottomland has organic soils. The tree-covered lands are too steep to be farmed. The watershed is, therefore, a strong defining element of the land, and we do not want to prepare and impose a detailed twenty-year physical plan diagram on the site. Rather, we prefer to work toward a matrix or framework concept that would permit us to keep our options open as long as possible. The watershed, then, has become the obvious physical form for our framework. For example, a large wooded ravine is one of the main features giving form to the eastern end of the development. The physical planning in terms of form for Jonathan has been relatively simple; the land is so strongly delineated that it actually changes and directs thinking about it, rather than remaining the passive object for a developer's designs. We have designed the lake to serve also as a flood control device. Water is unloaded before spring flood time, and the lake is also used as a storage device. That is the only man-made lake on the site, but we also have three very large natural lakes.

Our goal of duplicating the Minneapolis-St. Paul metropolitan income profile presents us with a problem of strategy. How are we to develop housing over the full income range? Many people would say that putting in low-income housing in the beginning will discour-

age the upper-income people from moving in, and vice versa. Therefore, we have tried to bring them along together. The neighborhoods are small, with a maximum of ninety-nine dwellings each. Dwellings in each neighborhood will be in about the same price range. Right across the street or across the greenway there will be another small neighborhood with a different price range. As we began planning the communications system, we also discovered that, in order to have a unique address for each dwelling unit, it was better to plan for ninety-nine or fewer homes. This also facilitates the clustered mailbox assemblies and the machine-assisted sorting system toward which the post office department is moving. We think it makes sense to recognize the advantages of using computer storage and processing systems.

Quite recently, the Federal Housing Administration (FHA) put a floor of about $6,000 on the income for 236 low-income housing. This was a surprise. After setting up a program to take care of people whose incomes are low, they have said that if people make below a certain amount, they cannot use the 236 program. This will disqualify the bottom half of the lowest quartile, as I understand it. FHA is a deterrent to quality housing in this country today. Solutions for the fifties do not work in the seventies. Another problem is that most existing housing in Chaska is within reach of people down in the bottom quartile. Therefore, we must carefully stage what happens in Jonathan, and also look at what happens around us. We will take our share of this bottom half, but at the same time we are not going to go so fast that we destroy the existing market in our area, because we do have a very strong economic impact. Now we are faced with how to work at the local level, as well as how to handle this new FHA floor. We do not think Jonathan will be able to house many people in the bottom half of that first quartile in the immediate future. We have couples living

Rental townhouses, Jonathan. Illustrations courtesy of Jonathan Development Corporation.

there now with incomes as low as $4,600 per year; but, as I understand this new FHA directive, we cannot have those people any more. We find this terribly disappointing and irritating.

We do have 236 low-income housing, although the city fathers said we could not bring all those people in here to ruin the community's image. We really did not think that would happen, and it has not. We have some mothers on Aid to Dependent Children (ADC), some retired people on social security, some janitors and filling station attendants, and also quite a few graduate students. We have young people whose values are not necessarily oriented toward income and who qualify for the 236 program. They live in what is probably our most interesting neighborhood and are very proud of what they have. Furthermore, there are not any cars out there on concrete blocks being stripped.

We are trying to create some innovative housing. In fact, the Jonathan Housing Corporation was born out of the need for innovative housing. Our "tree loft" project is an example. We wanted a moderately priced apartment project, meaning rents between $150 and $200, but we did not want a center hallway with everybody's name card on the door. We wanted to have some fun with it, and we did. Every unit is a little bit different, and each has been occupied most of the time. We decorated one apartment completely with Montgomery Ward furniture to prove that housing does not have to be expensive to be fun. We think we have proved that these apartments can be marketed, and that they do not have to be what sold last year.

On the new town scale, there can be some innovative as well as conventional designs. We have conventional single-family homes. Our approach to single-family housing is to keep it plain; earth colors predominate, and the houses are comparatively unadorned.

We have a physical framework for things to happen within, and we have created and encouraged a "people framework" through providing social and recreational opportunities. We could have organized this in great detail all by ourselves. For example, we could have had the annual Jonathan cross-country touring race, planned by our own director. We could have put a lot of money into it, and probably had about forty or fifty entries. But instead we mentioned to the North Star Touring Club that there are some great places in Jonathan to cross-country ski; they came and skied. Then they mentioned to us that we had an old farm which could be used as a clubhouse out in an area that is not scheduled to be developed for a while. We offered to lease it to them for $5 per year if they would get out there, clean it up, and paint it. The next year they had the first Victoria-Jonathan-Chaska cross-country ski race, which they organized themselves. Jonathan did not do it; the people did it, and there were over a thousand entries. Creating the framework of opportunity is very important. We think future development efforts will probably be not so much in the physical area, but in the social and behavioral areas. Urban designers and technical people can be turned out by the dozen, but now we must learn how to let people "do their own thing."

Another framework for opportunity lay in a wonderful turn-of-the-century farmhouse made from brick manufactured right in Chaska. Although we did not know what it would be, we did know it was a building that should be saved. A group appeared who wanted an art center, a place where they could work. As if turned out, they were very aggressive; they managed to give classes in ceramics, painting, and all sorts of things. In the barn to the left of the house, the Jonathan Players presented *The Importance of Being Earnest* by Oscar Wilde. Jonathan did not do these things. When the local leadership appeared, we made available the physical framework we

Lake Grace beach and pavilion.

had created, and we assisted them financially. We put $1,200 into the art center budget for the first year to help them get started, and leased them the building for $1 per year. The people themselves provided the leadership and the creativity.

We rent skis at the recreation pavilion. People can go down there and rent a set of cross-country skis for about 50 cents an hour. We have bicycles, canoes, and sailboats to encourage all sorts of nonmotorized recreational pastimes. We try to offer many alternatives, and most of the people use them. Especially for the lower-income families, being able to have a canoe for practically nothing is nice. The road system and the greenway system are well underway and we have made a point of interspersing various activities throughout these areas, so that the school, village center, art center, and community theatre are not centralized. There was a great temptation earlier to put most of the human services together, and to really use this village center as a core. However, we use it only as a commercial and service center. We do have a community facility there, but other activities are dispersed. By mixing and spreading them throughout the automobile and greenway systems, more interaction occurs among the people. The idea seems to be working. For example, membership in the art center reflects a full population spectrum. People from all levels do have common interests. What we are promising, then, is that they can come together in the same activities. Maybe we will find later that some of these things should be done differently, but right now this approach appears to be working well.

In Jonathan we try to set a high standard for urban design. Certain restrictions and procedures are placed on all new construction. There is a design review no matter who is doing the building, and we go through the review process to see that it fits. The residents association also has an architectural review committee, and they operate in an advisory fashion. However, they do not have the power of veto, and once the neighborhood is complete, the residents will really run that neighborhood all by themselves. If we have a covenant in a neighborhood that does not permit street parking, for example, then that covenant holds for that neighborhood. If the residents association decides that parking is all right in their neighborhood for one reason or another, we will let them change it. We will let them govern their own neighborhood with regard to the modification of covenants. This is happening to some extent now, but we have not really been faced with any major problems. Neighborhood Three is complete, and a very vocal group of young professionals lives there. Since they are a strong group, it will be interesting to see what happens regarding covenants and design review control.

The Jonathan Association is based primarily on ownership. We have a lot of committees, and at present we outvote everybody and will continue to do so until about 75 percent of the village is complete. However, by that time the land use pattern, design quality, basic physical structure, and software and hardware directions will be set. We are listening to the people in an advisory way, but there is no way that we can give them the power to make decisions in the early stages of development. We are not worrying about the residents assuming control when the village is 75 percent complete, because this is what will happen through voting anyway, and we are not presumptuous enough to think that we are going to know all the answers. We do, however, have that experience which says that if too many people are involved in making early decisions, the development will never get started. We are attentive to the people's reactions to what we do. If, for example, all the residents of Jonathan came and said they did not want us to build any more of a certain kind of greenway or requested that we use incandescent lights

Lake Grace village center.

instead of gaslights, we would not try to out-vote them. But we will outvote them if they say the children from Neighborhood Five, which is a 235 program, or the children from 236 housing should not be permitted to use the recreation pavilion.

Two types of control affect Jonathan most directly: the formal government in the city of Chaska, because most of the development is in the city of Chaska; and our control, which is exercised through land ownership and through having our comprehensive plan adopted as local policy. We control the location of the major form-giving elements; greenway, transportation, sewer, and water plans. We have assumed control of these plans by selling our concepts and making them part of the city's comprehensive plan. In order for us to continue to exercise this broad control, we must do a good job. In the last election the people living within the Jonathan perimeter came within thirty votes of putting a man on the city council. They came within forty votes of putting a man on the school board. There are now 4,360 people living within the old part of Chaska, and by the third year we should have about the same number in Jonathan. The control of government structure will slowly shift as the political center of gravity moves toward Jonathan. We are not afraid of this kind of "check and balance," because we believe that what we are doing in terms of basic policies and community structure design is right, at least most of the time, and I think our policies will be supported at the polls. We see it as an acceptable risk.

We tried to assemble our land with respect to natural features. The 800-acre University of Minnesota Arboretum in the north and a ravine system in the south formed natural barriers, so we bought right up to them. We were selling our ideas all the time. The city of Chanhassen on the northeast quadrant recently adopted a ravine-oriented continuous park plan which tied right into the Jonathan plan.

Even though we did not have control over that boundary, we were successful in selling enough of our ideas so that they have adopted a similar plan. We are assisting the city of Chaska in obtaining a HUD open space grant to acquire all major ravine systems from Jonathan down to the Minnesota River. The question of how a developer controls his perimeter involves both obtaining physical features for boundaries, and, in those areas where he can penetrate the boundaries, selling his ideas to the surrounding communities.

Natural forces will largely determine the evolution of Jonathan's governmental structure. Most of the watershed is down the main ravine system, and most of the sewer trunk serves that area. The first step toward governmental structure will probably involve the creation of a joint sewer-water district in the northeastern quadrant, between the city of Chaska and the city of Chanhassen. The second step will be the alteration of political boundaries and the creation of a supercommunity including Jonathan, Chaska, Chanhassen, Victoria, and Laketown communities.

There is a need for broad and long-range planning for the direction of small communities in the United States today, because they simply cannot fund the kind of planning required to really direct their growth. The Twin Cities Metropolitan Council does broad planning for this area. Jonathan can afford a higher level of planning than any of the surrounding communities. However, there is a planning vacuum at the detail level in our region. Into that vacuum, we set our ideas; we talk to people about them, and we believe that, eventually, many of them will be implemented.

Jonathan may be a vital force in directing and channeling growth in the area through the use of the transit system as a form-giving element. Minnesota is no different from any other state. The highway department does not seriously communicate with the metropolitan transit commission and they do not always talk to

Neighborhood of single-family homes, Jonathan.

the state planning agency, so everybody operates independently. However, now the metropolitan council is beginning to exercise A95 Review for all federally funded programs. In our Standard Metropolitan Statistical Area (SMSA) the review authority is the metropolitan council. We are trying to sell the concept that transit systems should be used as form-givers and not merely as remedial agents. We are funding studies that show why the use of transit as a form-giver is important, and why it is important to put transit into areas that are not heavily populated. We think that, if we can sell the fifteen municipalities involved, we could have some kind of transit running into our region. The corridor between Jonathan and the Cedar-Riverside new town intown has great potential for realizing this concept. Jonathan has been named a diversified center within the definition of the metropolitan council development guide. The corridor has a small community, Chanhassen, with a well-defined core; it has Eden Prairie, with very low density and no core at all; it has Hopkins, which has a well-defined core, high employment, and high residential level; it has St. Louis Park, high in employment, high in residential level, yet with no well-defined core; and it has the center city of Minneapolis and the Cedar-Riverside terminus. Thus, if there is any place to study transit as a form-giver, and the cost effectiveness of it, we think it is in this southwestern corridor.

Our three principal kinds of circulation or communication are the automobile system, the pedestrian system, and the communication system (which is the electronic transportation of information). All three are redundant in some areas, yet there are certain things we can obviously do much faster with the electronics system than without it. One of the first things we hope to do with this system is to install a link with Cedar-Riverside. We also believe that the communications system should be considered a basic utility, although at first this

idea was not widely accepted. We wanted it installed early, however, because we thought it would be very difficult to introduce people to new ideas once the village was complete. We felt that the two-way communications system should be built in at the beginning, along with the sewer and water systems, so the town could grow with it. We have not yet been able to get the full system in, but, through HUD assistance, a demonstration center is underway in the village center. Next year we will begin to wire houses, and in about four years we should have the first village in operation with the whole duplex communication system. At that point the population should be about 3,500 or 4,000. In the system, individual houses on the network can interrogate other stations on the network.

A communications system such as this will open up new opportunities, particularly in education, health delivery systems, security, or almost any area involving the sharing of information. Our Independent School District 112 has discovered this system this year, with our help. Our communications specialists from Community Information Systems (CIS) and Independent School District 112 are now carrying out a joint research and educational demonstration program. At the same time, the five doctors in our clinic wanted to get involved with the communications system in an attempt to improve health delivery systems. They and CIS have responded successfully to a Department of Health, Education and Welfare (HEW) proposal for health delivery systems. Here again, we did not do it; we created the framework, and they responded. Links will be established connecting the Jonathan Clinic and the Waconia Hospital and another clinic in Waconia. The demonstration will involve the use of paramedical personnel, as well as quick diagnosis and referral procedures, particularly from the emergency room to the clinics where the doctors are. Although this is a small beginning, it is significant that the developer is not doing it; the people are doing it themselves. Again, all we had to do was create the framework.

The Jonathan site is readily accessible to and from the metropolitan area. A main line of the Chicago-Milwaukee Railroad runs through the center of the town and forms an assembled right-of-way running from Jonathan into Minneapolis and Cedar-Riverside. As indicated, we see possibilities for the acceleration of the transit pace. However, since the land is not flat, we must be very sensitive to the way it will be affected. Concerning roads, we have an interstate road, an expressway, and two trunk feeders. We have access into an internal loop with an internal arterial, from which there is direct access to the villages. In most cases we will also have a secondary access. There are usually two ways out of the village into the loop; however, neighborhood access is arranged so that people will not enter a neighborhood unless they need to. The industrial centers, which serve regional as well as town needs, are located in positions where both internal and external access is possible.

Solid waste disposal is handled in the city of Chaska by franchises issued to private collectors who put the waste into sanitary landfills. The system operates under control of the state pollution control agency. We are operating within their plan. We would prefer, for example, to simply require everybody to install a waste compacter. Then we could replace four $45,000 garbage trucks with a couple of pick-up trucks. The operation would be neater and more sanitary. We believe an opportunity exists here to view the town as a system, but we cannot control everything. Through the residents association we have a community recycling program. Three boxes for waste collection have been placed in back of the art center, since it is centrally located. People voluntarily separate their glass, paper, and metal and bring them here. The results to date are mixed, and we should do better.

We are confident that there will be improvements in community spirit as long as we continue to provide the framework and opportunities for participation. We believe in our idea of helping citizen leadership by letting the ideas develop to the point where problems are identified, and only stepping in to help if requested.

Everything is not running smoothly in Jonathan. We do have some problems, but we are learning from our mistakes and replanning certain items. We are not particularly happy, for example, about maintenance problems on our greenways. We designed the wrong kind of greenway in certain places. In order to get these places finished early for selling the houses nearby, we put in too much sod that now has to be mowed. We were far more successful in the areas where we kept things very natural, almost rough-looking. There we left natural ground cover wherever we had natural features. In areas where housing was being developed and the ground was torn up, we sodded it. It looks beautiful, but it is costly to maintain. Here is where experience has helped us design. Second, we have not been effective enough in scheduling the available community facilities. Although we have many activities, people often do not know about them. I think we can do better in communicating ideas and informing people of opportunities. The communications system should help out there. We have also had some trouble with motorized vehicles and snowmobiles. This problem lasted for about two weeks. We arranged to have Jonathan cleared as a wildlife sanctuary; this automatically eliminated snowmobiles and minibikes.

Progress is definitely being made in Jonathan. We think HUD's new community program is an ideal marriage between the developer and the government. This cooperation between the public and private sector is reasonable because it does not use the tax dollar; it uses only the full faith and credit of the

Jonathan industrial center.

federal government. It gives the strong developer the financial credibility he needs to go with large-scale development. However, the federal government should encourage, create, and implement a national urban growth policy. The closest thing we have to it now is the Title VII program, about half of which is not funded and which is centered around four types of new communities. This is simply inadequate; we need a strong national urban growth policy. The federal government could transfer this mandate to the states, requiring them to have a state urban growth policy before there is any assistance. This would preclude the necessity for federal involvement in small details. Inventories should be made of each states' natural features, problems, and planning needs. Minnesota, for example, still has a chance: the state is relatively underdeveloped; it is not highly populated; it has great natural beauty and fine resources. If we are not careful, we could ruin this potential quickly. We definitely need state urban growth policies. HUD is now processing about twelve good new community applications. They have about sixty applications waiting for processing, of which maybe half will be guaranteed. If there are 300 new towns in this country in the next ten years, it will be surprising. Yet that is just a drop in the bucket. Management is lacking. There simply are not enough people willing or able to put together the organization, and there are not enough resources to begin.

We hope the new communities now underway will stimulate others to try. We should not expect complete success; however, we need to begin moving so that we can properly understand this complicated process and learn from our failures as well as our successes. If we could turn Jonathan's clock back to the time of the initial "go–no go" decision, it is quite likely that all involved would vote go. We hope that others elsewhere will do the same so that the new communities movement in the United States will continue and grow.

READING LIST

Bryan, Jack. "New Town/In Town; New Town/Out of Town: Twin Cities of Minneapolis-St. Paul Have Produced a New Set of Twins." *Journal of Housing* 29 (31 March 1972): 119–131.

Cunningham, Benjamin H. "Designing the Environment for a Balanced Community: Jonathan, Minnesota." Seminar, Center for Urban and Regional Studies, University of North Carolina, 1970.

Einsweiler, Robert C., and Julius Smith. "New Town Locates in a Municipality: Jonathan Saves Money and Chaska Increases Tax Base." *American Institute of Planners Notebook* 1 (June/July 1971).

"Jonathan, Minnesota: First Private New Town Backed by a HUD-Guaranteed Loan." *House and Home* 37 (May 1970): 36.

"Jonathan New Town." *Planning* 36 (May 1970): 60.

Jonathan New Town: Design and Development. Chaska, Minn.: Jonathan Development Corporation, 1971.

Jonathan's Progress. Vol. 1, no. 2. Chaska, Minn.: Jonathan Development Corporation, n.d.

"The New Town: A Proving Ground for Bold New Ideas." *Better Homes and Gardens* 47 (September 1969): 70–73.

"New Town in Minnesota to Receive Federal Aid." *Wall Street Journal,* 16 February 1970.

"Taking the Debt Sweat out of New Towns: 'Jonathan' Opens Doors with HUD Guarantees." *Professional Builder,* April 1970, p. 55.

United States, Department of Commerce, New Communities Development Program Documents. *Project Agreement between the United States of America and Jonathan Development Corporation.* Springfield, Va.: 1972.

United States, Department of Housing and Urban Development. "HUD Issues Commitment for First New Community." *HUD News,* 13 February 1970.

St. Charles, Maryland

Charles E. Stuart

St. Charles is located on a site which seems intended for a new community, and which indeed has titillated urban planners and developers for a long time. The new community movement in Charles County began approximately fifty or sixty years ago, when the government planned to purchase what is now our site. They wished to develop a recuperation area called Panama City for workers who had been stricken with malaria during the construction of the Panama Canal, but this was never done. The next attempt to develop a city there was in the early sixties. A developer with many ideas, very little cash, and a beautiful wife named Linda decided to build a new town for his wife and call it Linda City. He produced a twenty-four-sheet billboard depicting an exotic girl gesturing suggestively toward the woods and saying that Linda City would

be right there. Only a few lots were developed before he failed.

The founder of the existing St. Charles was a developer who tried to disprove all the basic laws of economics. In the business world there is an axiom: "One must sell something for more than one pays for it in order to make a profit." This second developer proceeded to build lots and sell them for less than they had cost him. Consequently, he went out of business quickly. The only people who benefited from this experience were the two builders who were then constructing single-family residences on the site.

Enter, in 1968, the third developer, our parent corporation, Interstate General Corporation, a large Puerto Rico-based real estate and construction company. We felt very sanguine about our possibilities for success, because, statistically, it was time for a developer to win! Interstate General Corporation's management had commissioned surveys in the United States to determine where population growth would take place in the next decade. One of the areas with predicted dramatic growth was Washington, D.C. Surveys showed that the Washington market growth would occur in two directions: northwest toward Loudoun County in Virginia, and southeast toward Charles County in Maryland. Fortunately, just as Interstate began looking for suitable property, the last developer was going through the throes of insolvency with 8,000 acres hanging as a millstone around his neck. That was four years ago, but since we have yet to begin residential construction, the land has done nothing but cost us interest and development money; from time to time it seems like a millstone around our necks, too.

At the time of our purchase, the Title IV program of the 1968 New Communities Act was becoming operational at HUD; we became the second new community to receive a federal guarantee under this act. Jonathan, Minnesota, was the first to qualify for the program. We spent $416,000 on planning and engineering, $120,000 in legal fees, $61,000 in printing fees, and $865,000 in underwriting costs, to name only a few initial expenditures in preparation of the application. However, perhaps only with government backing could a developer of our size have borrowed $24 million (which is the amount of our guarantee). While we are paying 7.75 percent interest on our money, we would probably pay 10 to 12 percent without federal backing. Clearly, then, federal participation in this program has helped make St. Charles and other new communities possible.

Until St. Charles, Charles County had not experienced major urban growth. People moved there because they liked the outdoor life. There were large lots, farms, miles of waterfront along the Potomac, Port Tobacco,

and Wicomico rivers, and plentiful hunting and fishing. These residents were loath to see people coming down from Washington to live. However, the previous developer had convinced the zoning board that he would build a beautiful city with many of the features of Columbia and Reston. Although he had grandiose dreams, he just did not have the ability to produce. He lacked the necessary capital, and, while he was sure that land sales would carry him, his pricing was wrong and his dreams vanished quickly. When he failed, his promises were unfilled; no swimming pools, open spaces, parks, and amenities were provided. The people had been hoodwinked, in a sense, for although they had beautiful homes for their money, they did not receive everything they had paid for.

The earlier developers had not devoted much thought or attention to planning. The first section was basically a grid; some curvilinear streets were later designed. About 1,500 single-family detached homes have been built, each on an 8,000 foot lot, all in approximately the $25,000 price range. Of five models, three predominate so the visual effect is one of monotony. In spite of this sameness, the community does present a good appearance, because all of the homes are nicely maintained by young couples who are probably owning homes for the first time. Everything is green, the grass is always mowed, and the owners are doing their best to landscape. Nevertheless, when you see this shape, which is now virtually extinct in urban planning, it creates a sorry scene. Another design fault was lining the main access road to the community with the back yards of houses which faced parallel side streets. Since these yards are filled with doghouses, trash boxes, storage sheds, and all the flotsam and jetsam of backyard Americana, they do not present a very good first impression of St. Charles. While we have spent in excess of $25,000 on landscaping and improving this roadway, our planners determined that a new major entrance was necessary. Therefore we purchased land which gave us access to Maryland Route 5, and we began construction of St. Charles Parkway, which will be the main road through the new town.

Another problem with the existing neighborhood occurred because the homeowners' deeds contained no obligation to contribute to a neighborhood association. There is presently a St. Charles Citizens Association which is strictly voluntary and has attracted only several hundred families out of 1,500. This association hopes to carry out the dreams of the original developer and build swimming pools, parks, and playgrounds, but they have been hamstrung by lacks of interest and money. To aid them, Interstate General has donated some sixty acres of land, of which four acres can be rezoned commercial. With this property they will be able to develop commercial leases to generate income and thus finance improvements on other citizen-owned property. Although we had no obligation to help these people, as we were strictly the purchasers of the land adjacent to their community, we felt that they had pioneered and actually made our portion of St. Charles possible. For this reason, we have done what we can to aid the "old St. Charles."

What later became Charles County was discovered in 1608 by John Smith, when he sailed up the Potomac to the Port Tobacco River. By the 1770's the county was a bustling place and Port Tobacco was a major shipping port. In 1790, when the first U.S. census was taken, Charles County had a population of 20,613. The same number (and some think "the same people") existed here as recently as 1950; for 160 years the population of this small rural county remained completely static. Tobacco, oystering, crabbing, lumbering, and working for the U.S. government were and are the major occupations. Charles County is located just south of the District of Columbia, and 60 percent of its land is covered with

trees. Commercial lumbering is a major enterprise. Unlike New York City, where it seems as if you can drive a hundred miles and still be in town, a short drive from Washington brings you to very lovely country.

Our site is located approximately twenty-five miles from Washington, about the same distance as Columbia and Reston. Finding an 8,000-acre parcel is in itself a rare occurrence so close to a major city, and we were fortunate in avoiding the land assemblage process. The property was owned for many years by the Reynolds family of Richmond, Virginia; they used it as a hunting preserve. Some fifteen years ago they sold it to a man who had purchased it in an attempt to interest the government in building Andrews Air Force Base there. Unsuccessful in this venture, he was left with the 8,000 acres which he sold to us for nearly $13 million. Our attorney in La Plata recalls that when he was a child, the entire site was sold for $70,000.

Typical of the terrain in southern Maryland, most of the land is rolling and wooded. There are only four or five cleared areas on the entire project site, unlike Columbia, where a number of farms existed. The area was probably farmed a hundred years ago, but it was allowed to reforest and was last logged off during World War II by Nazi prisoners of war. There are now many good second-growth trees, both hardwood and coniferous. These are at once an asset and a liability. Certainly they add to the desirability of a residential area, but the additional cost involved in clearing substantially increases the sale price of a lot. We are currently spending nearly $900 for clearing an acre which originally cost us only $1,500. Most important, however, we are attempting to save every tree we can, so that we can be successful in preserving the wooded image of St. Charles.

The most valuable inheritance from the earlier developers was a sewage treatment plant consisting of a lagoon and a spray field irrigation system. This method of sewage treatment was developed at Pennsylvania State University and is probably one of the most outstanding means of sewage processing in use today. Primary treatment, which is a sedimentation and bacteriological treatment of sewage, is very common and takes place in lagoons which are from four to six feet deep. There "good guy" bacteria attack "bad guy" bacteria, breaking down and digesting the solid matter. In traditional systems there are secondary and tertiary treatments of one kind or another (filtering, adding chemicals, etc.), but in our system we spray the effluent directly from the lagoons into wooded areas and irrigate the foliage, which then grows at about twice its normal rate.

We presently have twenty acres of ponds, called lagoons, to which raw sewage is pumped, held for approximately forty days, and then discharged into the surrounding woods through a large sprinkler system. The method is completely pollution and odor free. There is neither runoff nor any of the problems inherent with other sewage disposal systems, such as phosphate and nitrate removal. When raw sewage or even most treated sewage is dumped into a river or other watercourse, the phosphates and nitrates cause eutrophication and the algae grow rapidly, choking out marine life. Phosphates and nitrates are, of course, natural fertilizers, so that the spraying of sewage into the woods simply fertilizes the trees. The chemical balance of the ponds is very critical. If we dumped industrial effluent into them, contaminants would most likely kill the active bacteria; therefore we can treat only human sewage. In the winter ducks and geese live happily on the ponds, and they look in every sense like natural lakes.

The only difficulty with this approach to sewage treatment is that it requires about one acre for every fifty homes. If New York City were to have this kind of system, it would require all of New Jersey as a spray field! We

are now processing in excess of 600,000 gallons of sewage a day, and it seems to be working very well. This system is temporary, however, since the county ultimately intends to install a central sewage system. When this happens, we will abandon the lagoon and spray fields, and use the land for other purposes. We feel this entire treatment facility is an excellent example of problem-solving and advantageous use of what is available, which in our case is land.

When Interstate General purchased the property in 1968, there was no zoning in Charles County which would permit the construction of a new community. Therefore we had to convince the county fathers of the desirability of a planned unit development (PUD) zoning ordinance; this was a long process. We were successful, and in the spring of 1971 the county passed a very flexible new town zoning ordinance with a maximum density limitation of 3.6 units per acre. This zoning ordinance permits the construction of townhouses, apartments, condominiums, and industrial and commercial centers throughout the new town, with administrative review only at the planning commission level before building permits are issued. In July 1971 we applied for PUD zoning, and we received it in July 1972. Accordingly, we passed the last major hurdle which always confronts large-scale development.

The basic exhibit required in the PUD zoning application was a master plan showing major roadways and principal land use allocations. An inspection of our twenty-year plan depicts a series of fifteen neighborhoods clustered into five separate villages. Our studies have shown that most Americans want to return to living on a less complex scale—to rural, semi-rural, small town, or suburban living. Few wish to live within a major metropolitan area. St. Charles has been designed from the beginning to meet their goals.

Neighborhoods will be the basic units of St.

Aerators in a lagoon which is part of the St. Charles sewage recycling system. Illustrations courtesy of Earle Palmer Brown & Associates.

Spray nozzle shooting effluent from the lagoon over a wooded area.

Charles, each accommodating approximately 1,500 families. All neighborhoods will be oriented toward family life, with the elementary school, its playgrounds, and open space as the focal points. Interstate General is dedicating to the county board of education, free of charge, twenty acres for each elementary school; this acreage will become the principal recreation area for the neighborhood. Incidentally, the current typical acreage for elementary school construction in the United States is approximately ten to twelve acres. The school occupies the center of the enclosure made by the neighborhood loop street, and most of the cul-de-sacs projecting from the loop street are internal so that children will be able to walk to school along footpaths without having to cross a road. Throughout the neighborhood, neither busing nor chauffeuring will be necessary to deliver even the smallest child to school.

Next to the school site will be the neighborhood center, a five-acre parcel with some commercial activity, including a gas station, convenience store, and coin-operated laundry, as well as the community center and the recreational complex. Each recreational complex will consist of a clubhouse of substantial size (approximately 4,000 feet), a swimming pool, locker rooms, tennis courts, and picnic areas. This neighborhood center will be built by Interstate General and will be installed before the first neighborhood residents arrive.

One of the unique qualities of St. Charles is the neighborhood association. There will be no hierarchical or layered form of government in St. Charles. Every neighborhood will be an independent entity with its own citizens association. This is in keeping with our goal of facilitating the return to small-town life. The neighborhood associations will have complete responsibility for the maintenance of their open space and buildings, as well as the management of neighborhood problems. We will require every neighborhood to employ at least

one full-time manager, and there will necessarily be a number of assistants. We envision the manager as the type of person who is typically found in a YM/YWCA—one who loves children, has a whistle around his neck, and can be found on Saturday mornings directing volleyball at the playgrounds. Obviously, his will not be an office job.

Financial independence is guaranteed to each neighborhood association by covenants on the land which require the homeowners and tenants to join the association and pay an annual assessment. This fee will be based upon the assessed valuation of their property, and the funds derived will be used strictly for the annual operating budget of the neighborhood association. In a typical neighborhood with 1,500 housing units, the average annual assessment may be $50 per unit, resulting in an annual budget of some $75,000, which is more than adequate.

Other new communities have elected to have the neighborhood association responsible for the construction of amenities such as the clubhouse and pools; hence the annual assessments are substantially higher, since the costs of the improvements must be amortized. We have included the cost of these improvements in our lot sales price, with the result that the home buyer is paying for the clubhouse and swimming pool in his mortgage over twenty-five to thirty years instead of over five or ten years. Since the net monthly payment is the principal concern to the prospective home buyer, and since the lengthening of debt has the effect of reducing such installments, we feel we can give the homeowner more for his money with this approach.

Another feature of the separate neighborhood association is that citizen participation will be increased because of an individual's stronger opportunity to influence the direction of the organization. For example, if several hundred families with little girls wish to hire a ballet instructor to teach at the neighborhood

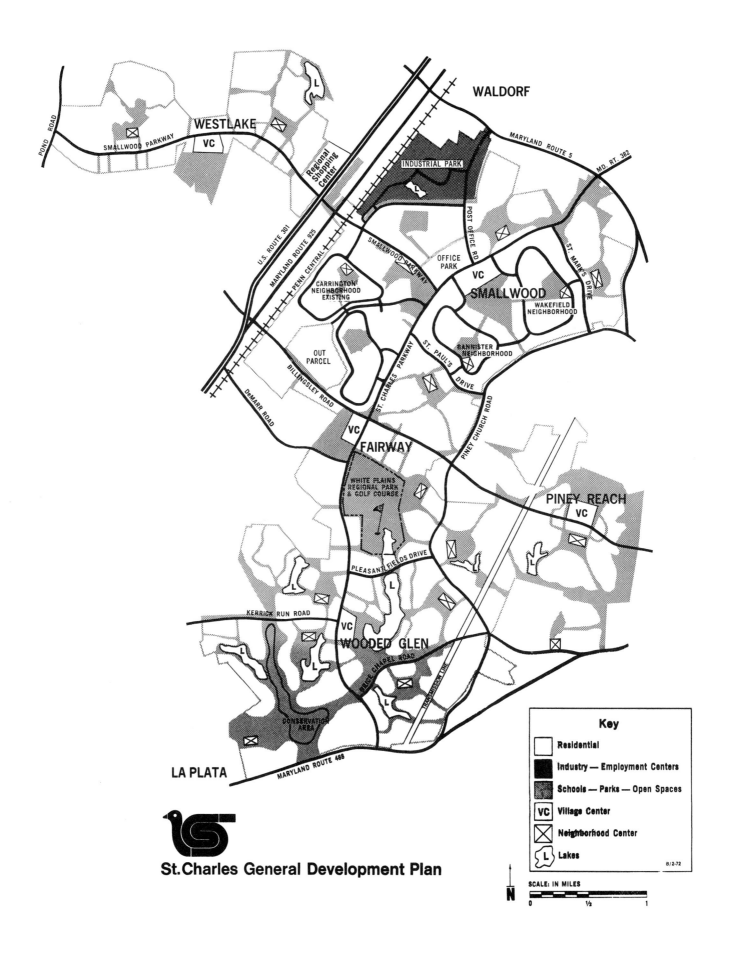

St. Charles General Development Plan

Key

- ☐ Residential
- ■ Industry — Employment Centers
- ▨ Schools — Parks — Open Spaces
- VC Village Center
- ⊠ Neighborhood Center
- Ⓛ Lakes

B/2-72

SCALE: IN MILES

0 ½ 1

N

center on Tuesdays and Thursdays, they could do so if they could convince the majority of the neighborhood association that this is how the funds should be used. The association can do whatever it wants with its money after the required maintenance, insurance, and other operating expenses have been met. Interstate General will in no way impose its judgment on the neighborhood associations.

The individual neighborhoods will be loosely clustered to form an entity called the village. There will be five villages in St. Charles; we consider these subdivisions as the principal centers for recreational, educational, cultural, commercial, and social activities. The village center has been designed as a revival of the old Spanish plaza or New England town square concept. In a typical New England square, the town hall is on one side, commercial stores on another, the church on the third, and the school on the fourth. With a slight adjustment for good urban planning, including traffic flow, this will be achieved in the St. Charles village centers. They will be places where social interaction takes place and will serve as the small town center for some 15,000 people. We have presently planned approximately 150,000 feet of pure commercial space, a joint middle school and high school on seventy-five acres of ground (elementary school, high school, middle school sites are more than twice the average size), a day care center, churches, restaurants, a library, a medical service building or doctors' offices, and all of the other requirements of such a small town. When these are all designed to interact harmoniously, with attention to the architecture of every building and its place in the overall site plan, we believe we can produce the finest small town centers in the country.

In the event that there is a demand for community facilities which could not be supported by an individual neighborhood, each of the neighborhood associations will be required to contribute some portion of its operating bud-

get to the village to fund these amenities. As an illustration, if three neighborhoods decide that they wish to create an indoor ice-skating rink, they may do so at the village level, and each neighborhood will contribute to it if the majority of its citizens vote for participation.

Most planners, architects, and developers think of new communities in terms of exciting urban design possibilities, and indeed they are that. Nonetheless, the essential objective is to provide housing at a price which the market can afford, and this is where many new towns experience their first difficulties. The cost of village centers, neighborhood centers, expanded open space, oversized school sites, and superior road and drainage construction could drive lot prices to the very top of the market scale. Therefore, the greatest challenge the new community developer faces is to achieve desirable design objectives and, at the same time, to produce housing at a reasonable cost.

In return for the $24 million guarantee, the federal government has exacted from Interstate General certain requirements and performance goals. Among these is the achievement of a "balanced" community. We are required to match housing availability and production to the family income profile as defined by the Washington Metropolitan Statistical Area Index. Simply stated, we must match low-income housing to the low-income requirement, high-income housing to the high-income requirement, and keep the balance graduated in between. This is a severe test.

We will provide in each neighborhood, to the greatest degree possible, a broad range of housing types and prices. There will be single-family housing on 6,000, 8,000, 10,000, and 15,000 square foot lots, as well as townhouses, triplexes, rental apartments, and other types of housing. The traditional American dream has been an individual family dwelling complete with picket fence and ivy, but that dream is fast becoming impractical with today's construction costs. Last year approximately 50 percent of the housing starts in the United States were multi-family dwellings, because such construction greatly reduces the unit cost. Accordingly, we believe that St. Charles will be able to provide low and moderate income housing, but that it will, by necessity, be in the forms of townhouses, apartments, condominiums, or other multi-family structures. Single-family housing, particularly in new communities, will be affordable only for those families with substantial incomes. The average price of the single-family lots sold to date has been $10,000. Builders typically plan on homes with a selling price of four or five times lot cost, and certainly a minimum multiple of three, so single-family housing in St. Charles will probably be above $35,000 per unit.

Using the old rule of thumb of housing investment being 2.5 times the annual income, it is readily apparent that the minimum requirement will be $14,000 a year in earnings in order to purchase a single-family detached dwelling. The lower and moderate income families thus will have to be housed in multi-family dwellings. This should not be objectionable, however, for such multi-family dwellings in new communities will have better design and greater proximity to recreation areas and other amenities, and they will be in every way superior to multi-family residences in urban centers. The lesson to be learned from this illustration is that there cannot be superior planning, engineering, construction, amenities, and other such new town qualities without some adjustment in the housing mix, unless the new towns are to become merely high-priced suburbs for well-to-do families.

The achievement of this mix by type and range of housing severely tested our planners, although we feel that in our first neighborhood we have provided a workable balance. While we have not placed $45,000 homes next to $22,000 townhouses, we have integrated and distributed the various styles and prices throughout the entire neighborhood, so that

there will be no "wrong side of the tracks" or "instant ghettos."

Another requirement of our project agreement with the government is the institution of a design review committee, which will be charged with the maintenance of high architectural and construction standards by the builders operating in St. Charles. We are not trying to achieve exotic designs in themselves, but to insure the compatibility and harmony of various buildings throughout the community. Each builder is required to submit front elevations, exterior color schemes, site plans, roofing material samples, and other construction documents to the design review committee for approval. The committee has the absolute authority to reject any proposed building. As the developers, our instructions to this group were to evaluate each submission with an eye toward the preservation of neighborhood unity, rather than toward winning awards for architectural pioneering. It is sad but true that, in construction, the more simple the design, the less the cost. Every deviation from the rectangular box with a shed roof constitutes an additional increment, and the builder's job is to gauge the market and determine how much people are willing to pay for additional design. The design review committee will not override the judgments of the builders, but it will be primarily responsible for the maintenance of compatibility.

Perhaps the greatest distinction between new towns and large residential subdivisions is the provision for commercial and industrial improvement. We believe it is madness to live in the suburbs an hour away from your work and spend two or more hours a day fighting traffic. New towns mark a return to the old custom of living where you work. We have allocated 25 percent of our land for industrial and commercial use, and we hope most residents will be able to find employment within the confines of St. Charles if they so desire. This in itself presents the planners with the

Building in the first St. Charles industrial park.

added problem of achieving compatibility between residential and industrial areas. Certainly this has not been achieved in most cities and towns across the country, since their industrial areas are not usually as attractive as their residential locations. We have designed our industrial parks with broad buffer zones of trees surrounding them, and we will require heavy landscaping of all structures built within. Furthermore, a stringent set of restrictive covenants will control noise, vibrations, smoke, odors, and objectionable outdoor storage.

We have scattered our industrial and office parks throughout the entire community, and we believe that one of our most exciting challenges is the successful establishment of industry within walking distance of employee housing. In fact, the inclusion of the paved pathways and walkways to encourage pedestrian movement is one of the key concepts of St. Charles and an inherent part of the open space program. From the beginning, one of the planning requirements has been to have virtually every kind of activity available within walking distance of any neighborhood, including industrial and commercial employment areas.

A significant difference between Interstate General Corporation and some of the other developers of new communities is our conviction that the developer should not become overly involved in either community governance or the operation of the social systems within his community. As explained earlier, each neighborhood association in St. Charles will be a totally independent entity; after the neighborhood center has been turned over to the citizens, Interstate General will not even have a seat on the board of directors. We believe that the developer's prime responsibility is to provide the best physical planning and the highest quality of construction in order to obtain a new community environment. The social needs of the citizens must be considered as part of the physical planning process; in

fact, the injection of social considerations into the planning process is one of the principal distinctions of a new town. Moreover, even after the developer has included long-range social objectives in his physical planning process, he must take steps to insure, and in some cases sponsor, the development of the necessary social systems. An example of this kind of action might be the seeking out and bringing together of a group of doctors in order to create a community clinic. However, at this point we feel the developer has fulfilled his obligation to fertilize the establishment of social mechanisms, and we have no intention of going beyond this level of involvement. Interstate General Corporation will not own and operate day care centers, clinics, or libraries. We will not force the citizenry of different faiths to band together and build an ecumenical church, nor will we push any of the residents or citizens associations in directions in which they do not wish to go—or in any direction at all, for that matter. Our job is planning and developing the new town of St. Charles, and our expertise lies in those fields. We will do our job, and we will encourage the community organizations to do theirs. The result will surely be that St. Charles will be a better place to live—which, after all, is the objective.

Several years ago I attended a new communities seminar and spent two days with urban planners, developers, architects, engineers, economists, and students discussing what I shall broadly term the "state of the art." At the conclusion of this conference, an architecture student took the floor and asked: "Why are they called 'new towns'? What we have been discussing here for two days isn't new, or exciting, or innovative at all, but rather a reapplication of the skills which already exist in urban planning, land development, architecture, and construction. There is nothing new about 'new towns' but their name."

Indeed, the student was right. There are no

dramatic breakthroughs, no mind-boggling achievements, and no great technological advances to come out of new towns. Men have been building cities for thousands of years, and the potential for pure innovation does not exist. What is happening, however, is nonetheless exciting. We are building, in relatively short periods of time, by revolution, if you will, cities of a size comparable to those which grew by evolution in this country over the last 100 or 150 years. Never before has it been possible for a small group of planners to site every building, road, park, fireplug, and other appurtenance of community living, nor have such concentrated, coordinated construction efforts ever been attempted. The endeavor in the new town movement today is to take the knowledge which exists in all of the contributing disciplines, and coordinate it to produce planned communities efficiently and economically. That is the real challenge, and one which we feel we are meeting effectively at St. Charles.

READING LIST

Commonwealth of Pennsylvania, General Assembly. *Senate Bill No. 939; Pennsylvania Land Development Agency Act.* Harrisburg: Printer's no. 1071, 19 July 1971.

Interstate General Corporation. *St. Charles.* Brochure. St. Charles, Md.: Interstate General Corporation, n.d.

————. *St. Charles Communities: Report to HUD.* St. Charles, Md.: Interstate General Corporation, November 1971.

————. *St. Charles Industrial Park.* St. Charles, Md.: Interstate General Corporation, n.d.

Maumelle, Arkansas

Edward Echeverria

Maumelle is a planned new town, located twelve miles northwest of Little Rock on the Arkansas River. Still in the early stages of its development, this new community will be a testing ground for innovative concepts in education, for a multi-purpose community-wide communications network, for new types of low-income housing, and for a comprehensive health care system. Maumelle's primary purpose is to show that Little Rock, as well as other urban centers, can achieve balanced and humane expansion through the development of satellite new communities. Here mixed-income housing, jobs, recreation and open space, and education, as well as all urban services, will be provided on an integrated basis. Maumelle is planned for the full range of income groups, including the lower and middle income family fed up with the grim life of the average industrial worker in urban centers such as Chicago, Cleveland, and Detroit.

Maumelle is the brainchild of Jesse Odom, former president of the National Investors Life Insurance Company, and Edwin Cromwell, a Little Rock architect, who saw the opportunity to build a new town when 5,300 acres of land on the east bank of the Arkansas River became available for purchase. In 1967 the National Investors Life Insurance Company retained the interdisciplinary team headed by Albert Mayer, Edward Echeverria, and Edwin Cromwell to work out a development concept for Maumelle.

The first obstacle was the lack of investment guarantees for the two major anticipated expenditures—the infrastructure and education. Development of the water supply, sewage treatment facilities, and preservation of the natural environment were to cost an estimated $6.5 million. The Department of Health, Education and Welfare (HEW) and the Pulaski County Board of Education approved the plans for the innovative Maumelle school system and agreed to run it if the development corporation would build it. However, the success of the education system, which was designed as the key factor structuring the residential community, required a substantial planning grant to solve complex problems involving the multipurpose educational structures and communications network. At the time, there was no New Communities Act, and therefore no possibility of massive governmental participation in financing the infrastructure. When the enormity of the undertaking became clear to the National Investors Life Insurance Company, it decided that it had exceeded its scope, and subsequently sold the project to Jesse Odom for private development. Since the entire building program including housing, commerce, and industry was to cost about $450 million, Odom waited for the passing of the New Communities Act so that the necessary investment guarantees would be provided for the essential elements of the infrastructure.

The pattern of urban expansion in Little Rock and other metropolitan areas today is characterized by an undifferentiated spread of suburban development over the countryside. This wastes land and results in the loss of open space for conservation purposes and recreational use. This pattern overextends communication and utility systems, adding to the cost of development and housing. It results in the uneven intake and distribution of city and suburban tax revenues. Most important, this endless, repetitively sprawling pattern results in the loss of a sense of community for families who may identify both with their immediate neighborhood and with Little Rock as a whole, but who cannot relate to a community level between these two extremes. The present pattern is marked by the haphazard and unrelated location of community facilities such as shopping centers, schools, and recreation facilities. Work centers unrelated to residential areas frequently cause long, costly, and time-consuming commuter trips to work. Where concentration points of shopping and work places do exist, they are often overcongested. Street systems are generally unorganized and poorly designed so that heavy traffic frequently uses local residential streets. No separate pedestrian ways are provided, and play areas, where they do exist, can only be reached via the street. Maumelle offers an alternative to the prevailing pattern of urban sprawl, in a concept which seeks to combine maximum efficiency of urban concentration with a pleasant, healthy environment.

DESIGN AND LAND USE

The form-giving concept behind the plan for Maumelle represents an attempt to break the pattern of urban sprawl by leaping beyond the suburban fringe to create a new center for urban expansion in an area largely rural and endowed with attractive natural features. The Maumelle site, although located somewhat beyond the present boundary of suburban development, is nevertheless clearly part of metropolitan Little Rock and easily accessible. The north entrance to the town is located less than half a mile from the Morgan interchange of Interstate Highway 40 with Route 65. A new access will be created by construction of I-430, which will cross the river two miles below the town. Maumelle, which will be closely interrelated with the larger metropolitan community of Little Rock, is not intended to be a totally self-sufficient new town. Instead, it will be a satellite community. Although theoretically all Maumelle residents may find employment within minutes of their homes, it is anticipated that many will commute to other parts of the region to work and, in turn, people from other parts of the region will commute to Maumelle to work.

An integral part of the regional concept of Maumelle is the creation of a surrounding greenbelt. The Arkansas River forms part of this protective belt for three miles on the south side of town. A large state park, to be located in the White Oak Bayou area located off highway I-40, has been proposed to satisfy the present and future needs of the metropolitan area. The park would provide a wilderness and recreation area for Little Rock residents while effectively creating a barrier against the tide of urban sprawl. Although some development will occur west and north of the new town, growth can be limited by setting aside greenbelt areas in these locations as well, particularly along the Arkansas River, which itself offers extensive recreational opportunities.

Ultimately, Maumelle will accommodate 60,000 people. The marked contrast between the Maumelle concept and the present pattern of suburban sprawl is illustrated by the following figures. In Maumelle, an estimated 20,000 families, with an average of five families per acre, will be accommodated on approximately 4,000 acres. With normal suburban development at two families per acre, these same 20,000 families would require 10,000 acres. The Maumelle plan saves 6,000 acres which can be utilized for greenbelts, thus benefiting all residents of metropolitan Little Rock.

The urban character of Maumelle is achieved without permitting congestion. The town will, in fact, seem very open. Approximately 40 percent of its total area is planned for open space and recreation, 36 percent for residential purposes, and 15 percent for industry. As a result of careful planning, less than 10 percent will be used for major roads, transportation, and utility purposes, including the sewage disposal plant and water supply facilities. Even within the development areas an intensive pattern will be permitted only within the village and town centers. The build-

ing coverage will not exceed 20 percent in most residential areas, and 30 percent in the industrial areas. Maumelle will be green and will have large open areas for recreation. It will not have the piecemeal quality of most suburban areas, where the open space is decimated and lost to any use other than for private families.

Considerable unplanned commercial strip and spot industry development is occurring outside the Maumelle limits. The area has no zoning or other land use controls to insure rational planning. Therefore, other vehicles must be sought. A recommended new approach is the introduction of development rights.

Between Maumelle and Little Rock there is the potential for a parkway along the river. In order to preserve a large part of this land for parks and open space by concentrating the commercial areas around the housing configuration and avoiding strip or corridor development, a plan is being devised which will encourage landowners along the river to forego development of their own properties in return for a share of the economic benefits of development in the planned commercial areas. Along the six-mile stretch of riverfront between Maumelle and the expressway interchange, each landowner will be granted development rights proportionate to the frontage and depth of his holdings. The dollar value of the total development rights will be directly proportional to the total construction permitted in the area according to general plan. The development rights will not give a person the right to build, but only the right to trade—that is, to buy and sell rights in sufficient quantities to implement an approved plan. For example, the developer who wants to locate a gas station at a strategic point must buy up the rights of other landowners who have no planned development on their land. If he is unwilling or unable to do so, he cannot build. The principle of this system is that only so many gas stations and other facilities are needed along the river, and that to preserve the riverfront only a necessary, limited number are desirable. The system not only serves to control development, but also allows its economic benefits to accrue equally to all land-owners on the basis of their holdings. Since this is an obviously radical approach to dealing with land speculation and development, a number of hurdles must be overcome before development rights find their place in the legal system.

The initial planning was done at a 1":500' scale. Urban forms, functions, and densities were established to test the feasibility of a town center to be built along the dam of the main lake on the downstream side. During the initial planning stage of four months, a diagnostic survey was made of the slopes, soils, subsoils, drainage, and vegetation. Also included were geological and climatological analyses. These elements were composed in a series of overlays from which the specific urban form and development plan then emerged. The result was a series of villages located along a semicircular loop road around a town center facing the industrial area.

The Maumelle land use plan provides for the creation of five villages or neighborhood areas. Each village will comprise 2,500 to 3,000 dwelling units and accommodate about 8,500 to 10,000 people, as well as a village center and middle school. Each village center will be a minor urban concentration providing the basic facilities and services most frequently utilized and required for home life. The middle school will form an integral part of the village center, along with churches, libraries, social centers, local retail shops, consumer services, and some professional and other offices. Because a village is more than a collection of services, and needs a social fabric of its own, multi-family housing has been designed within the center. Beneficial social interactions will be generated by integrating these various activities at one location, thereby achieving a good balance between choice and convenience.

The town center will be the focus of town activity and will have the greatest concentration of social, educational, governmental, economic, and cultural functions. Town government offices, the central post office, fire and police department headquarters, the central library, and the community college will lie in or adjacent to the town center. These public facilities, in combination with major retail shopping facilities, consumer services, and offices, will create the greatest concentration of people and vehicles in the town. To best manage this combined concentration of people, vehicles, and activities, and to create an urban environment of the highest quality, all development will be in accord with a detailed urban design plan. This plan will provide for a mixture of public, commercial, and office activities at higher densities than permitted elsewhere. It will achieve a balanced urban environment by defining the scale of urban bulk and open space for pedestrian movement, relaxation, and recreation within the framework of land use, circulation, and vehicular parking systems. In many cases, mixtures of uses will be permitted and encouraged within buildings. The town center will probably become a commercial focal point in the metropolitan area's western growth corridor.

The area designated for the town center is located on the main boulevard access system. Approximately seventy acres have been set aside for the center, including a substantial amount of landscaped open space around the lake for use by shoppers, workers, and residents, as shown in Table 1. Approximately thirty-five acres of the town will be used for office, commercial, and retail development. Entertainment facilities will include restaurants, bowling alleys, cinemas, and other day and nighttime activities. Major town center commercial buildings will be designed to sup-

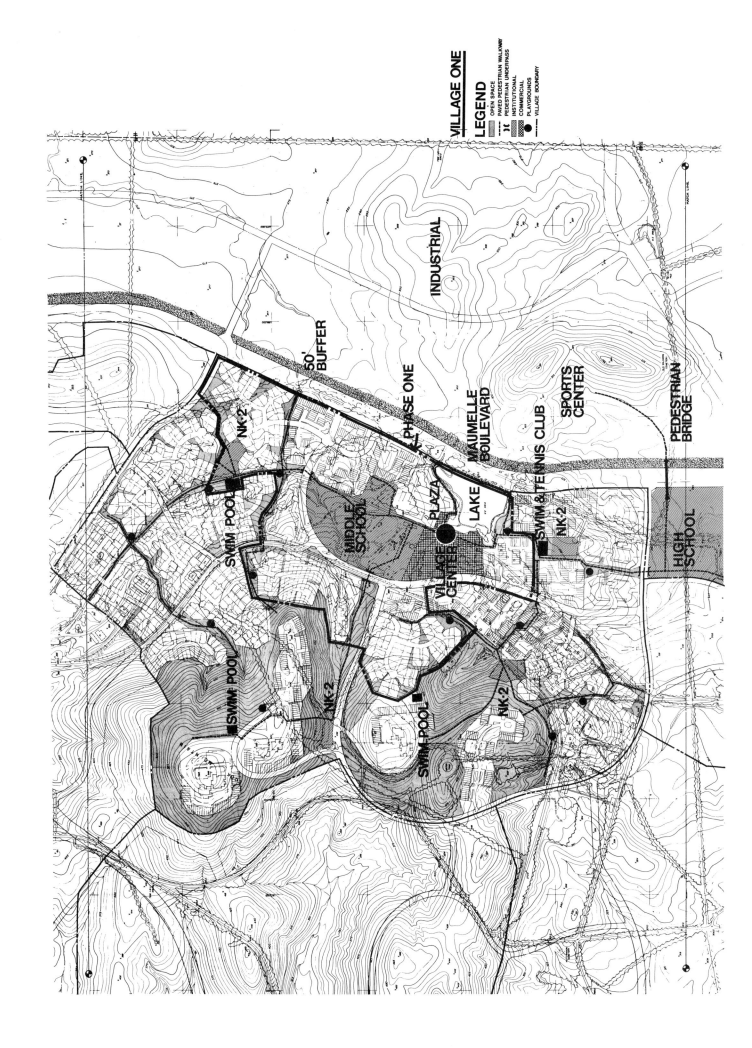

VILLAGE ONE

LEGEND

OPEN SPACE
PAVED PEDESTRIAN WALKWAY
PEDESTRIAN UNDERPASS
INSTITUTIONAL
COMMERCIAL
PLAYGROUNDS
VILLAGE BOUNDARY

INDUSTRIAL

50' BUFFER

PHASE ONE

MAUMELLE BOULEVARD

PLAZA

LAKE

VILLAGE CENTER

MIDDLE SCHOOL

NK-2

SWIM POOL

SWIM POOL

NK-2

SWIM POOL

NK-2

SWIM & TENNIS CLUB

NK-2

SPORTS CENTER

HIGH SCHOOL

PEDESTRIAN BRIDGE

Scale model of Village One, Maumelle. Illustrations courtesy of Cromwell, Neyland, Truemper, Millett & Gatchell/architect engineer, and Planners Incorporated.

Table 1. Land Use Distribution

Inventory of Land Use (June 28, 1972)

Townwide	Use		Area	
Residential	SFD	(single-family detached)	341	
	SFC.1	(single-family cluster)	355	
	SFC.2	(single-family cluster)	176	
	TH	(townhouse)	466	
	MF.1	(multi-family)	0	
	MF.2	(multi-family)	208	
	MF.3	(multi-family)	177	
				1723
Commercial	C.1	(commercial)	43	
	C.2	(commercial)	39	
	TC	(town center)	69	
				151
Industrial	I.1	(industrial)	789	
				789
Public	Cemetery		10	
	Community college		95	
	High school		40	
	Middle school		105	
	N-K.2 (nursery school-kindergarten up to 2nd grade)		32	
	Lakes		136	
	Undeveloped open space		945	
	Parks		166	
	Pedestrian walks		94	
	Sports center		47	
	Airfield		30	
	Sewer plant		80	
	Water plant		10	
	Utility stations		10	
	Type 1 roads		159	
	Type 2 roads		57	
	Type 3 roads		44	
	Type 4 roads		66	
	Type 5 roads		144	
	Railroad		5	
				2275
Total				4938 Acres

port both office-hour and after-work restaurant and entertainment activities. Day care centers, nurseries, kindergartens, and related multi-use facilities necessary for the residents of the town will be provided in these areas as private commercial ventures, established either as residents association projects or by the developer through other appropriate means.

The five village areas surrounding the town center will themselves be divided into housing clusters. Each housing cluster will consist of forty to fifty dwellings fronting on short access streets. The local street will usually have a cul-de-sac or loop configuration with access to a neighborhood collector street.

Maximum use will be made of the neighborhood concept as the smallest unit with clusters of homes and apartments. The neighborhoods will be designed to stimulate both inter- and intragroup communications and participation, and they will be integrally linked with the individual village centers and with the town center. Each village will provide as broad a spectrum of housing types, prices, and features as possible, including single-family detached residences, cluster housing of different types, townhouses, and low-density garden apartments. In strategic locations, these will be supplemented by medium and high density multi-family units in medium-rise and high-rise structures. The housing mix within each village will vary not only by type, but also by cost, to insure a mixture of income groups and types of families by size and age. A variety of financing methods will expand opportunities for the purchase of single-family detached homes and the purchase and leasing of apartments. Other financial plans such as condominiums, cooperatives, homeowners associations, and public interest housing organizations will be provided. Substantial provision for low and moderate income families housing will account for approximately 46 percent of the community housing supply, and thus directly reflect the housing needs in the Little Rock area. This means that all persons who work in Maumelle will have the opportunity to live there if they choose.

By the end of 1972, the infrastructure for the first 600 dwellings to be built in 1973 will be under construction. Projections for the first five-year program call for 2,000 to 2,500 dwellings, with an absorption rate of 400 units per year. The maximum share of the Little Rock market which could be counted on is 10 percent. However, a higher percentage could be captured by concentrating on consumers at the lower ranges of the market—for example, the production worker who averages $150 per week. One of the developer's goals is to build a three-bedroom townhouse, including land and improvements, for $15,000. The average house of the same quality in Little Rock costs from $20,000 to $22,000. Instead of houses on sixty-foot frontages, with individual lawns, extensive roads, and utility networks, Maumelle will have townhouses on twenty- to twenty-two-foot frontages, cutting site development costs by half. By means of modular construction instead of stick building at $14 per square foot, a three-bedroom house that can compete in Little Rock's housing market can be created.

The Foundation for Cooperative Housing is testing the feasibility of building clusters of 120 to 200 dwellings for sale as co-ops, on fifteen- to thirty-acre tracts using modular units. Strong leadership on the part of the Maumelle Development Corporation will be required to realize the production of these $15,000 houses.

The Maumelle income profile could conceivably be skewed even lower to include the $125 to $130 per week worker. This could be achieved by introducing the mobile home in a modular design. A framework has been designed to fit over and around the trailer for the support of module add-ons, such as bedroom nuclei or bathroom modules. Such development, properly designed and screened, could provide low-cost dwellings for families of modest means. A family could move into the community with its trailer and pay a minimum $250 down to move onto the land. The concrete pad, lot, and amenities, including laundry and community center, can be provided for as little as $3,000 per mobile unit. The clusters would be limited to 120 to 150 dwelling units in any one tract, to fit the same village community as the townhouses and single-family houses. It is hoped that by producing modified mobile homes and controlling their concentration, it will be possible to successfully integrate lower-income families with the rest of the community.

If Maumelle can provide the basic house, along with the mobile home and modular dwelling unit, it will be able to meet the needs of low and moderate income groups as no other new town has yet been able to do. Furthermore, giving people four or five housing choices will optimize opportunities for creating social, racial, and economic variety within the town.

Around the golf course, which is located on the stabilized flood plain of the Arkansas River, single-family detached houses on one side have been matched by cluster housing along the fairway. The 110 prestige lots now being marketed will be the first houses visitors and residents will see as they enter the recreation areas of the town.

A hierarchy of homeowners associations will perform many of the functions of local government. The family cluster association will govern the maintenance of common roadways and driveways. The second level of homeowners associations will oversee the activities of the cluster associations. They will comprise the 450 to 750 family associations which manage common swimming and tennis clubs. The second-level associations will be, in turn, part of the 3,000 family community-wide association.

The land use plan provides for a network of open space to be developed in phases along with residential development. Visual and physical enjoyment will be provided for the residents of the town through scenic walks, trails, lakes, and leisure activities in centers, as well as by the woods and valleys. Particular emphasis will be placed on water-oriented recreation through maximum utilization of the four lakes and the marina canal on the Arkansas River. Each resident will have a number of recreational options available to him, including nearby open space areas where he can relax and enjoy the natural environment, activity areas where he can play tennis, golf, or swim, and pleasant natural settings where he can hike, fish, or boat. Many small parks will be scattered throughout the town to take advantage of wooded lots and stream valleys. The village centers will be fully developed with recreation areas, paths, tables, benches, chil-

dren's play equipment, and barbecue stands. Paths through parks and along lake shores will also serve as recreation and nature walks. The Maumelle residents association will be responsible for the adequate maintenance of public open spaces and recreational areas throughout the site. Maintenance of smaller open spaces within each development area will be the responsibility of the residents of each neighborhood or cluster.

When ultimately developed, Maumelle will provide approximately 17,500 jobs; 12,000 persons will find employment in the 970 acre industrial park, 3,000 in commercial enterprises, shopping areas, and offices in the town center, and 1,500 in education, engineering, road maintenance, and other town services. Some 6,000 persons from the Little Rock metropolitan area are expected to come to work in Maumelle's industries, while approximately the same number of Maumelle's working population will go elsewhere for employment.

Of the 970 acres of Maumelle's industrial park, 789 along the eastern boundary of the site are designated for sale. The convenient rail and highway access in this area, as well as the service areas and the wide choice of locations, will attract a variety of industries to Maumelle. These will provide employment for residents with various skills and different income levels, creating the economic base necessary for a balanced community. The area was chosen for its flat topography and prevailing wind characteristics as well as for its vehicular and rail access. Access from Maumelle Boulevard at four strategic locations provides prestige sites visible from the boulevard along the entire length of the industrial area. The plan provides for the full range of industrial plots from small incubator plants to large industrial plants requiring fifty or even one hundred acres with a full range of services. There are four basic groupings of plot size: three to five acres, six to ten acres, ten to twenty acres, and twenty acres or more. In

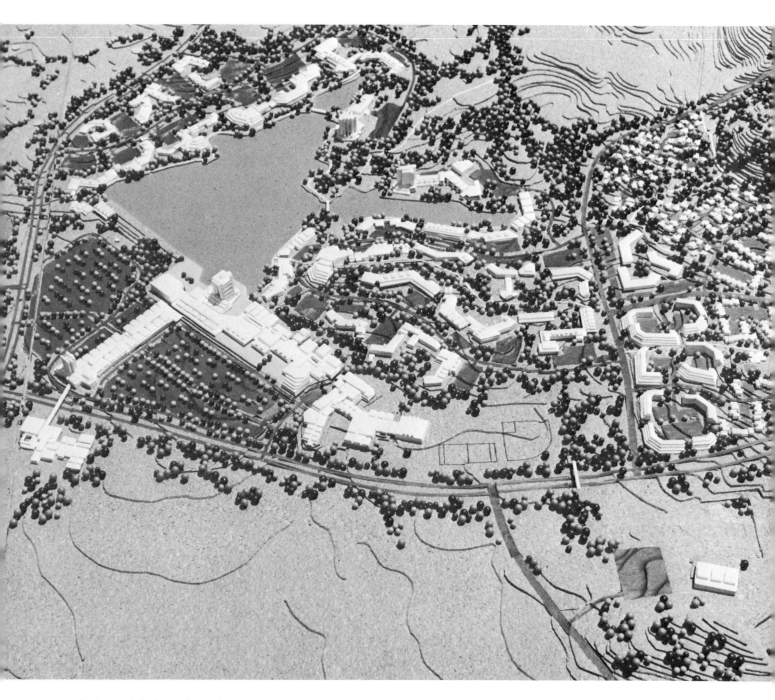

Scale model of another village, Maumelle.

general, those industrial plots situated closer to the service center will be smaller to allow them to take full advantage of food, banking, and automotive services located within the center. Rail service will be provided to all industrial plots north of the town center or the Marche entrance road. Central spine service to both sides of the railroad line can be provided without affecting highway traffic.

The industrial park is designed to provide a park-like development for industry with controls based upon industry type and performance. The various guidelines contemplated will provide an efficient operating environment for industries and will protect them from the encroachment of commercial or residential uses as well as from other industries adverse to their operation and expansion. The guidelines will also reduce the impact of industries on the surrounding community.

Two service centers are proposed within the industrial park area, one at the northern entrance and the second at the Marche Road crossing near the town center. These centers will provide locations for service functions which are excluded from the village and town centers, as well as for services to the industrial park. Since these essential activities might involve some disturbance to adjacent uses in other locations, they will be concentrated in the service centers at points well removed from residences, schools, and recreational areas. The centers will accommodate heavy commercial uses including automotive services, building supply yards, machinery repair and servicing, laundry and dry cleaning plants, printing and publishing warehouses.

THE SYSTEM OF SERVICES

Education, health systems, and traffic and transportation systems all function as integral parts of the communication system, which is in itself one of the most significantly formative features of the Maumelle development. Each Maumelle school is designed to meet the spe-

cific needs of its age group in a suitably individualized environment. Each neighborhood will include an NK-2 (nursery-kindergarten to second grade) campus. Children at age five or six will be able to walk to school alone, and will therefore achieve some degree of independence. Furthermore, the school will put children in small groups within intimately familiar surroundings.

The village campus will represent a pooling of more extensive educational facilities, providing children in the eight-to-fourteen age bracket with a wider range of experience, broader age group contact, and more sophisticated educational tools just a little farther from home. The school will be subdivided into smaller administrative units to dispel the sense of alienation often perpetrated by larger institutions.

The high school campus, or community school, will serve to integrate the learning activities of the older students with the activities of the community as a whole. While the educational center will permit the use of sophisticated equipment and facilities by many people, it could also be broken down into smaller administrative units in order to better respond to individual students' needs. A recognized pioneer in this approach is the Flint, Michigan, community school system. The plan has since been adopted by a number of cities. Over the last few years New Haven has carried through a version of the community school. The physical facilities for the high school will be in office and commercial retail space in multipurpose structures within the town center.

The purpose of locating the combination high school and community center in the town center is to provide and encourage as many activities as possible. The increasing sophistication and high cost of facilities demand that their use be maximized, not limited to a small sector of the population for a limited number of hours and months. The community center should encourage as many people as possible

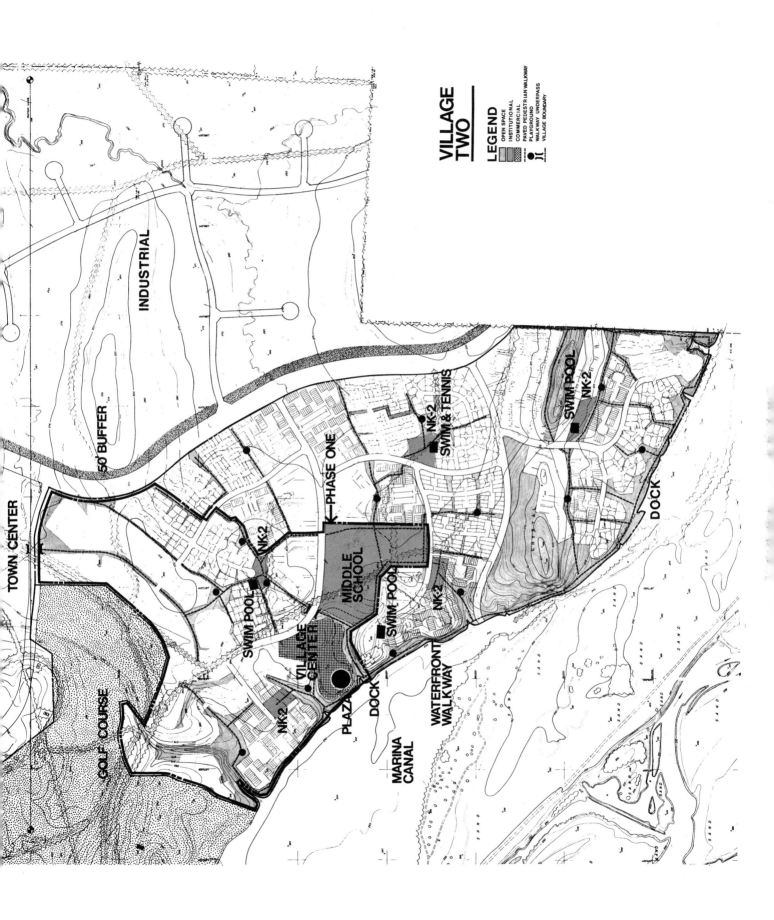

VILLAGE
TWO

LEGEND

OPEN SPACE
INSTITUTIONAL
COMMERCIAL
PAVED PEDESTRIAN WALKWAY
PLAYGROUND
WALKWAY UNDERPASS
VILLAGE BOUNDARY

TOWN CENTER

INDUSTRIAL

50' BUFFER

GOLF COURSE

SWIM POOL

NK-2

VILLAGE CENTER

PLAZA

DOCK

MARINA CANAL

WATERFRONT WALKWAY

MIDDLE SCHOOL

SWIM POOL

NK-2

PHASE ONE

NK-2

SWIM & TENNIS

SWIM POOL

NK-2

NK-2

DOCK

to participate actively in various community activities, whether recreational or educational, in order to foster a sense of community.

The Maumelle school system will be incorporated into the Pulaski County School District. School district funds will not be required, as the system has been designed to be self-financing. It is hoped that federal monies will also be available for operation through the state education program. Thus the entire district will find the Maumelle system a benefit, rather than a burden.

A community college which will focus on training and retraining geared to the requirements of Maumelle's industries is also planned. It will be located on the east side of the main city road, adjacent to the industrial area, and across from the town center and the high school. This location was selected because of its proximity to the industrial area, and because it would take too much land from the core residential area if located there.

Maumelle, with a projected population of 60,000, is not expected to require a hospital of its own; the Little Rock hospital, fifteen miles away, will be adequate to meet the new town's needs. Yet in the face of rapidly rising medical costs, a new way must be found to provide a quality health care program which will maximize efficiency and reduce cost to the individual. The new town offers a unique opportunity to implement and test innovative methods for providing and financing quality health care. New towns are particularly suitable for testing new health care systems, since the size and makeup of their population, with consequent medical needs, can be accurately projected.

The health care system proposed for Maumelle is a "triage" or three-level system; it will be able to handle a large number of people with minimum investment in equipment and highly trained personnel. The elements of this triage are: a central core of doctors, specialists in the basic fields; an inner screen of a limited number of doctors and trained para-

medicals; an outer screen of trained paramedicals. The screen is a telecommunications system which may be connected with medical institutions in the metropolitan area providing diagnostic services for facilities at Maumelle. An outer screen is located in each village, possibly at the middle school, and is charged with screening out normal cases and providing simple treatment. The inner screen receives patients referred by the outer screen for more complex diagnosis and treatment. The central core of doctors receives those patients who cannot be diagnosed and/or treated by the inner screen. However, doctors would be instantly available for consultation with any of the paramedical personnel through Maumelle's closed circuit communications system. This system will also make possible a central medical records facility with "print-out" devices, as well as the placement of monitoring capabilities at local subcenters or individual homes.

The system was developed in collaboration with specialists in health working in the Little Rock area. Among them were Dr. Bettye Caldwell, director of the Child Development Center; and Dr. Robert Merrill and Dr. Neil Sims of the University of Arkansas Medical Center. It is anticipated that one to two doctors will be needed per 10,000 population at Maumelle. This is half the number generally required, due to the pooling of facilities and equipment, and the more efficient treatment of patients made possible by screening. Moreover, it is recommended that the planning function continue as an integral part of the health care system's implementation to keep it flexible and responsive to the changing needs of the growing new town.

Preventive medicine, including that for mental health, is gaining importance in the United States today. A program must be worked out whereby preventive medicine can be efficiently and inexpensively administered on a regular basis. The public health facilities located at the middle school and high school campuses appear to be ideal for drawing large numbers of people into preventive medicine programs.

Due to Maumelle's potential for efficient pooling of health care facilities and equipment, prepaid group health insurance is regarded as most economical. The combination of a carefully worked out health care system having widespread appeal, with an accurate projection of health care needs, will help keep costs at a minimum while maintaining quality service.

In the last twenty years innovations in technology, particularly in electronics and communications, have found application in many areas. Almost every hospital, large business, and industry, as well as the government, makes use of sophisticated (although often limited) communications systems and equipment. The key factor is size. The continuous research necessary for constant improvement is costly, and the finished product reflects this. To make the installation of sophisticated electronic equipment economically feasible, it must usually be done on a large scale. For this reason most private individuals have not benefited directly from such technological innovation as broadband cable telecommunications systems. Because there are only a few persons in any established community who can be approached for cable television, the costs for installation have been excessively high, creating a deterrent to wider participation. Programs and services offered by communications systems have also been extremely limited, and the risks to the entrepreneur excessive. Consequently, nowhere in the United States has the potential of an advanced community telecommunications system, serving a large number of people in a wide spectrum of ways, been fully realized.

Many kinds of services could be made available through a complete telecommunications system; most important, they would be relevant to all segments of the population. The new town offers significant opportunities for innovative applications of modern telecommunications technology. The capital costs of telecommunications systems can be included within publicly guaranteed costs of land development, decreasing the burden of debt service, which in turn would introduce an important element of flexibility into operating economics. Furthermore, planners of new communities can build telecommunication into the provision of community services, such as education and medical care, from the beginning, rather than adding them afterward to an already developed service infrastructure. In addition, it is possible in a new community to plan for 100 percent penetration of residences and, indeed, for virtually total saturation of the community with telecommunications capabilities, in contrast to the constraint of the partial, voluntary penetration prevalent in older communities. The feasibility of attempting innovative uses may be considerably greater in new communities, where costs could be better controlled and where there is no need for allocating resources for the traditional service to major segments of the population, while testing innovations for other smaller segments. For example, while remote medical diagnosis of patients by television has been demonstrated successfully at Boston's Logan Airport, it is quite expensive. On the other hand, telediagnosis from outpatient centers in a new community would be feasible if links between these centers and a hospital were installed as part of the overall communications network.

A telecommunications system for Maumelle could make important contributions to the achievement of community objectives for residential, industrial, and municipal development. By contrast, commitment to a telecommunications system in isolation from community objectives (or, indeed, as the determinant of those objectives) should be strictly avoided. Specific community services which could be considered as objectives for Maumelle include: child care and preschool education, elementary and secondary education, external degree programs, vocational and adult education, medical care, physical security and law enforcement, traffic control, environmental monitoring, community and municipal information, participation in local governance, and shopping and other commercial services. A carefully planned, community-wide broadband telecommunications system could make substantial contributions to the Maumelle new town. In this respect Maumelle is the ideal testing ground and could serve as model for other new towns. It has therefore been strongly recommended that provision be made to develop a communications program tailored to Maumelle's specific needs, and that the economic feasibility of such an operation be determined.

The Maumelle plan strives for maximum separation of pedestrian and vehicular traffic, for safety and for service. These goals can be achieved by a complementary series of networks: arterial streets, collective streets, neighborhood loop streets, and pedestrian walkway systems. A local bus system with connections to a metropolitan transit system at the town center would provide public transportation within the site, as well as connections to Little Rock. The major street is Maumelle Boulevard, which runs north and south through the town providing access from Route 40 on the north to the new Route 340 on the south. A major loop street interconnecting with Maumelle Boulevard at two points links each village center with the town center. Within this large loop, a system of collector streets serves the hilly areas in the center of the site. The industrial area has its own separate service street system connecting to Maumelle Boulevard on the north, Marche Road in the center, and again to Maumelle Boulevard at the south end of the site. Each neighborhood is served by local loop streets with access to service streets leading directly to homes. The local service streets are cul-de-sacs and loops to provide maximum safety. All roads and interchanges will be designed and constructed to provide generally accepted levels of internal transportation, speed, and convenience; adequate linkages to existing transportation systems; high standards of vehicular and pedestrian safety; and attractiveness and concern for impact on residential and other development.

A system of pedestrian circulation comprising greenways and walkways interconnecting schools, parks, and homes has been designed for the entire site, making it possible to walk from a home to a village center and even on to the town center. The pedestrian circulation system will also be designed to accommodate bicycles and wheelchairs. Where needed and feasible, pedestrian underpasses and overpasses will be provided to allow safe and convenient passage of pedestrians across roads with significant traffic.

Vehicular traffic volumes projected by the Maumelle development plan vary from ten trips for each single-family detached unit in the low density areas to four vehicular trips per dwelling in the town center.

The following procedure used in determining the evening peak traffic assignment for Maumelle used certain basic assumptions in order to determine the number of trips for various purposes. The basic assumptions for this study were:

6000 residents of Little Rock will work at Maumelle industries.

6000 residents of Maumelle will work at Maumelle industries.

4000 residents of Maumelle will work at Maumelle services (in town center and village centers).

10,000 residents of Maumelle will work in Little Rock.

80 percent of local residents will go to local jobs by automobile, with average auto occupancy of 1.3.

Four commuter buses per hour to Little Rock will transport 160 workers. (This, being a negligible part of the total traffic picture, was ignored in the analysis.)

10 percent of the employees will be absent on an average day.

70 percent of evening exodus from industry will occur in the peak hour.

10 percent of peak hour trips will be in the off-peak direction.

The town center will generate trips at a daily (weekday) rate of twenty inbound and twenty outbound per 1,000 square feet of leasable floor space (1,200,000 square feet was assumed).

Village centers will generate trips at a daily (weekday) rate of thirty inbound and thirty outbound per 1,000 square feet (80,000 square feet each was assumed).

During the evening peak hour, 7 percent of the daily trips in each direction will occur at the town center.

During the evening peak hour, 8 percent of the daily trips in each direction will occur at each village center.

Trips to and from residential areas will be distributed in proportion to the number of residents in each.

Industrial employment will be equally distributed between the two areas.

With these assumptions, the trips generated were determined:

Industry to Maumelle residences
$$\frac{16,000 \times 0.9\,(\text{attendance}) \times 0.8\,(\text{autos}) \times 0.7\,(\text{peak hour})}{1.3} = 2320.$$

Industry to Little Rock
$$\frac{6,000 \times 0.9 \times 0.7}{1.3} = 2900.$$

Town center
$$20(\text{trips}/1000\,\text{sq}') \times 1,200(1000\,\text{sq}') \times 0.07 = 1680.$$

Village centers
$$30 \times 80 \times 0.08 \times 5(\text{centers}) = 960.$$

Little Rock to Maumelle
$$\frac{10,000 \times 0.9 \times 0.7}{1.3} = 4850.$$

Off-peak (residential to industry)
$$0.1 \times (2320 + 2900) = 522\ (\text{say } 520).$$

These trip generations are shown in matrix form; no consideration was given to trips among residential areas, or to trips between schools and residential areas. These should constitute a very small percentage of evening peak hour traffic.

The various kinds of trips were distributed, using a simplified gravity model technique and ignoring the time factor. It was assumed that trips between residential areas and village centers would be made according to least distance. Matrices were set up to record the trips among each residential area, each village center, the town center, each industrial area, and Little Rock. The road network was then coded, with a number assigned to each intersection.

The trips displayed in each box in the coded road network next were routed by the shortest path from origin to destination. A table was

Table 2. Trip Generations

Destination / Origin	Residential	Town center	Village centers	Industrial	Little Rock	Total
Residential		1680	960	230		2870
Town center	1680					1680
Village centers	960					960
Industrial	2320				2900	5220
Little Rock	4850			290		5140
Total	9810	1680	960	520	2900	15870

set up to record these routings, with column headings by intersection numbers and subcolumn headings to indicate turning movements. When all trip routings had been accomplished, each subcolumn was added and the appropriate turning movement was displayed on a map.

Checks for errors were made by comparing adjacent intersections for correlation of traffic volumes. When errors were discovered, checks were made with the assignment tables and trip matrices for appropriate corrections. Average daily trips on Maumelle Boulevard were computed at ten times evening peak hour. This calculation on other roads would require different factors, depending on local conditions. The traffic and transportation systems in the Maumelle plan have been carefully and thoughtfully designed with an eye to maximum efficiency, more than adequate capability, and the ultimate in convenient service.

Maumelle is planned as a new community with a distinctive character. Primarily a satellite settlement related to the existing metropolitan center of Little Rock, it will function integrally within the region as an orderly alternative to the present pattern of haphazard, unoriented urban sprawl. The town itself will be green, with many open spaces and numerous settings for water-oriented recreational activities. Variety is a keynote in Maumelle planning. A wide range of housing types and costs will insure a socially and economically diverse population, thus going far toward encouraging interaction and integration among people of different economic levels. However, special emphasis is being placed on providing interesting and exciting housing for low and moderate income families. The innovations in the educational system reflect the neighborhood and village concept and are based on the belief that children are a major portion of the civic community. As these children grow older and move from nursery school to high school, their settings for learning are situated nearer the town center. Thus they move out

into the heart of community activities as they become more and more able to participate in these activities. The plan for the communications networks also reflects the desire for the participatory living so essential to the neighborhood ideal. Broadband telecommunications systems will integrate and support the educational health care, traffic and security, and environmental monitoring systems. While serving regional needs as a satellite community for Little Rock, Maumelle itself will provide many job opportunities and will be a community where amenities are obvious, where recreation is accessible, where education and occupations within the town are a visible component of the fabric of life, and where communication is instantaneous and perhaps as complete as it can be in any living situation today.

READING LIST

Echeverria, Edward, and Edwin Cromwell. *Final Report Maumelle Newtown.* Little Rock: Cromwell, Neyland, Truemper, Millet and Gatchell, 1972.

Mayer, Albert, Edward Echeverria, and Edwin Cromwell. *Design Concept for Maumelle New Town: Supplement to the Stage 1 Report, March 1967 through August 1969.* Washington, D.C.: Planners, Inc., n.d.

————. *Maumelle New Town, Pulaski County, Arkansas: Stage 1 Report.* Washington, D.C.: Planners, Inc., March 1967.

Odom Development Corporation. *Maumelle: New Town in "New" Region.* Little Rock: Jess Odom Development Corp., n.d.

United States, Department of Commerce, New Communities Development Program Documents. *Final Environmental Statement: Maumelle New Town, Arkansas.* Springfield, Va.: National Technical Information Service, 1972.

————. *Indenture of Mortgage and Deed of Trust: Maumelle Land Development, Inc., to the First National Bank of Little Rock, Trustee.* Springfield, Va.: National Technical Information Service, 1972.

————. *Project Agreement between the United States of America and Maumelle Land Development, Inc.* Springfield, Va.: National Technical Information Service, 1972.